Culture and Human

Culture and Human Thought

The Core of Who We Are

GARY EDSON

McFarland & Company, Inc., Publishers
Jefferson, North Carolina

ISBN (print) 978-1-4766-9074-2
ISBN (ebook) 978-1-4766-4832-3

LIBRARY OF CONGRESS AND BRITISH LIBRARY
CATALOGUING DATA ARE AVAILABLE

Library of Congress Control Number 2022045204

Front cover images © 2022 Shutterstock

Printed in the United States of America

*McFarland & Company, Inc., Publishers
Box 611, Jefferson, North Carolina 28640
www.mcfarlandpub.com*

Table of Contents

Preface

THIS BOOK IS ABOUT THINKING. It includes some other things, but it is basically about thinking. Thinking about thinking is nothing new. I have been thinking about writing this book since I wrote my first book 42 years ago. Each time I entered the classroom or lecture hall, I thought about the importance of thinking and how to impress upon people that importance. However, like others, I allowed that thinking to come to nothing perhaps because I also realized that it is impossible to induce people to think about anything. Nevertheless, thinking and culture have continued to be a meaningful part of my life, thus, I decided to put my thinking on paper.

So, this book is an introduction to thinking and culture and is far from the complete story of either. I have tried to write about things from the perspective of the this-or-that principle. Chuang-Tzu (4th century BCE) said, "Everything is 'that' (another thing's other): everything is 'this' (its own self). Things do not know that they are another's 'that,' they only know that they are 'this.' The 'that' and the 'this' produce each other."[1] (Like "tall" needs "short" to have meaning.) Fortunately, neither this nor that can be said to be completely right or wrong. The difference between things is not absolute. Knowledge, a part of the culture idea, besides being "this" and "that" is probably an accrual of information devoid of knowing how, why, or when it will be applied. In fact, it may be that knowing how or why something is important and more than just thinking; it is also feeling and perception. Facts often tell little about a subject; unlike cultural elements that express the ideas and concerns of most people (myself included). These elements recognize the character and temperament of people, and that recognition is basically psychological. Thus, this book is about reality.

In my writing I have tried to stay with the nature of reality (when possible) as well as amending the ideas that incorrectly interpret thinking as defined by preconceived concepts and words inconsistent with the nature of things and people. In other words, I have tried to avoid

1

stereotypes and misguided language. The tradition to which things are attached, is the belief by which people will act in response to conditions (negative or positive). This thinking is a perspective of reason based on knowledge.

No book can adequately define and explain the importance of thinking and culture to human beings. However, this book is arranged to give importance to some of the issues and although the idea of thinking and culture is very simple to understand but difficult for some people to realize. To assist in realization, I use various examples to illustrate the ideas. Where possible I have used tangible examples to signify the sublime.

This book is also about belief (mine included) and the processes that involve people in thinking and culture as they celebrate their identity and the meaningful events of their lives. It is about the activities associated with humanity. This book is not about one person or one people but all people emotionally, culturally, and physiologically engaged in their communal environment. It is also about intellectual knowledge because knowledge is thinking and culture and neither is theory nor technique.

There can be no clear starting point to thinking or culture. Both are as old as humanity, consequently neither has a true beginning. The methods of determining the relationship between humanity and culture are varied and include art, theater, music, poetry, and philosophy, plus many other correctly and incorrectly identified activities. Culture and thinking are about reassurance, and people want and need reassurance and approval of those beliefs they endorse and practice. In this writing it is not my intention to criticize or commend any belief; rather, it is to think about similarities, differences, and conditions that are their foundation.

A part of comprehending any book is seeing and understanding the relationships between different ideas expressed in the work. The connection between culture and thinking is, as stated, knowledge and knowledge may lead us to queries about the truth of our own beliefs. When this action is achieved the book is worth the writing.

Changing the subject from this book to people, I want to acknowledge *"the most beautiful person in the world"*—my wife, Wan-Chen—for her assistance with this project. Without her help it would not have been written.

Gary Edson
Winter 2022
Liujia, Tainan City,
Taiwan

Introduction
to Thinking and Culture

WHY IS IT THAT NO ONE thinks any more; rather, they react? People are apparently unable to remember any form of thinking. Thinking appears to be a forgotten idea deleted from the memory of society. People believe in their own world, but that does not make it fundamentally more correct than any others. An honest attitude does not come from simply thinking but from respectable behavior; whereas most people prefer a blind existence that does not include thinking or culture. The corruption of human nature refers to this attribute. Attitude is a way of acting and talking that people have, and currently it is completely detached from the influence of culture. Why it is—how engrained is it—what causes the non-thinking among us is a question for philosophers and psychiatrists. This question has important consequences in social values.

Attitude is a conceptual part of a person's thinking practice. The notion of attitude does not denote any one act of a person but is an appraisal of many associated activities. When a person has a negative attitude about the community from which they come, then the person's words and deeds are always less appreciative of that community than another person's. The belief is that an individual with a poor attitude is not inclined to act in a positive community-oriented nature.

Thinking is a simple act that influences people's ideas about life and the activities of that life. It is a way in which people make sense of the world they experience. Thinking is one of humanity's most unique qualities. It is instrumental in the development of many achievements and is of existential benefit to people, but there is no agreement as to how it is defined. This writing is an example of thinking not exactly the writing but the printing. It was thinking that inspired Johannes Gutenberg to develop the printing process (about 1439), and before that Bi Sheng invented movable type during the Sung Dynasty (960–1279). In China they had ideas that translated into creative thinking. The ancient

Chinese believed civilization began when signs of writing on the back of the Divine Tortoise from the Luo River and as drawings on the body of the Celestial Dragon appeared. These marks were the first signs revealed to the Sage Kings of antiquity. Or, think about the Cyrus Cylinder a ceramic barrel-shaped form, created between 539 and 538 BC. The Iranian piece is a record the defeat of Babylon by Cyrus the Great.

Thinking is connected to the first important element of humanity—speaking. The vocal ability to articulate ideas, wants, needs, and expressions does not belong to one people or one culture; it is of world importance in its truest form. Speaking, like writing required thinking as well as intellectual and physical capabilities. Thinking, even at the most basic level, is necessary before activation of the muscular to form words orally or in writing. Oaths, curses, and blessings (spoken or written) are activities composed of words, and their meaning and effectiveness is ensured by tradition. Thinking that defines the imposition of such forms of expression gives important power to the people and imposes harm or goodwill upon those hearing the words.

The concept of thinking consists of various psychosomatic happenings. It is more than being cognizant of idea when pondered from a specialized point of view. Thinking is usually considered an intellectual practice that involves logic, and it is valuable in how people make choices. It is also important and distinctive because it can contemplate only one concept at a time because the procedure of thinking deliberates both the motivation and the expected reaction. The direct response to any circumstance is founded on inclinations that are comprehended but do not produce the anticipated consequences.

Ethical thinking, in contrast, involves calculation to initiate the correct reaction to the situation. (Some form of social ethics [morals] is a part of human condition. Social ethics is basic to people everywhere.)

A review of thinking is often divided into two areas. One part of thinking looks at pragmatic issues, where items originate, exactly how they are constructed, and in what ways they relate. The review of these issues tries to arrange elements corresponding to their distinguishing characteristics. (Unfortunately, people try to change the character of things. Their meaning may be virtuous, but what they believe is good may not be the same for others.) This assessment devises conventional statutes that describe the association of things. For example, in the Islamic Republic of Iran and in the country of Azerbaijan there is the thinking that goes into the making and playing of the Kamantcheh/Kamancha, a string instrument that has existed for over 1,000 years.[1] This kind of thinking involves the production (making) of the string instrument and the physical effort involved in playing.

An additional topic of thinking considers the quest for wisdom. Examples are the thinking of the secret society of the Kôrêdugaw and the rite of wisdom crucial to the cultural uniqueness of the Bambara, Malinké, Senufo and Samogo peoples of Mali,[2] or the False Face Society of the Iroquois in the United States.[3] These social activities are based on wisdom as an element of thinking. This part of the thinking process is for the review of ideas. It is in this location of the brain that ethics is considered.

Countless conjectures are made regarding cultural interests. The ideas expressed are not so dissimilar from those experiences by people every day. This idea is exemplified by symbols, and the symbols often have special powers. In this time of worldwide exchange people rely on symbols as elements for reference. Identifiable symbols are used to generate remembrances, unite thoughts, promote reactions, and to replace unknown languages. Sometimes, these cultural representations (symbols) are creators of contemplation and deliberation. Often, the mnemonic components are representations of the communal history of the people.

Identifying and confirming cultural elements is often considered as simply "putting exceptional things in order." Thinking about bringing the past into the present or identifying the present with the past is idealizing culture. The substantiation of culture is perhaps best when viewed from the human perspective; it is a thinking similar to the idea in ancient China where the heart was considered the center of both feeling and thinking. The heart is the essential organ of perception, and it is viewed as unifying with the happenings of the outer world. Thinking is every person's concern, and the scope of philosophical belief and practice are of an inclusive and humanistic value.

Thinking involves truth and reason. It is also about knowledge and knowing. Thinking is about the things people imagine to be important to them and their present and future life. It is about values and choices people make every day. (Right and wrong are judgments and have no validity yet people pass on these invalid judgments as fact. Judgments are opinion.) Every occurrence in life is defined by the choices, and every choice should be the result of thinking. It is a direct, true, and focused relationship; however that connection is often disregarded or overlooked. Behind the concept of thinking about culture is the larger notion of humanity. Because culture reveals the genius of a people; it is a way of discovery and a way of positioning the past in present-day thinking. The past can be a magic mirror that permits people to see into a former time that can revivify history.

Reviewing culture as a way of thinking requires a sense of humanism that goes beyond subjective assessment.

It is a fact that the world's culture is diminishing in scope and diversity. Culture (as an idea) is being homogenized due to the blending action of cross-cultural exchange, telecommunication, multi-national commerce, and a variety of other social and linguistic activities. The positive aspect of inter-dependence is awareness of the commonly shared values and the importance of all people. The negative impact is the loss of identity and in the worst situation, loss of pride of a people or nation. The identification of culture is a method for giving humanity a presence in contemporary society.

Culture may be viewed differently in different areas of the globe, but each place includes inherent values that are elements of world humanity. The humanism of China and India, as well as other areas of the "East," is equal or exceeds that of Europe and North America, as do humanistic events of South America, Africa, the Middle East, and Australia. The Eurocentric assumption of primacy in the humanist arena is unfounded conjecture. Culture is the carapace of humanism—the outer shell that contains the logic, reason, and the essence of individuals and nations.

Culture has been described as partly material, partly human, and partly spiritual. It exists in the same way that beliefs, values, and customs exist. Culture can mean "(1) a body of artistic and intellectual work; (2) a process of spiritual and intellectual development; (3) the values, customs, beliefs and symbolic practices by which men and women live; or (4) a whole way of life."[4] Culture is the values, customs, beliefs and symbolic practices by which men and women live. As a way of life, it seems to be inclusive of "things." (The concept of "culture as value" was first published in 1977 and restated by Peter Winch in 1998. The idea of culture as value is challenged today.) Culture is the physical and emotional heart of humanity.

Culture is viewed in different ways. Some persons see it as exciting journeys of the mind, the spiritually uplifting of learning or an interesting object. Cultural activities are often considered unique events for people at the center of humanism; however, other people are far less enthusiastic about such activities. The cultural event should be a time for initiating these resources as expressions of value for a community and a people. The cultural activity safeguards humanity and its allied history, natural surroundings, and sociological and creative endeavors from a reduction to mindlessness or destruction.

Viewing culture as a philosophical issue and not just as a social concern can offer new or different perspectives on the responsibilities associated with the identification, protection, and use of cultural elements. Humanity requires a viewpoint of the relationship of culture and society that conveys the essential nature of the individual as a measure of social consciousness. Culture is the human dimension that verifies the social scale and defines the relationship of the individual to society. The cultural object often has distinctive status in the related social environment. Culture defines humanity. It identifies the values and explains society, acknowledges our present and projects our future. It is who people are as human beings—the good or the bad.

As people try to reinforce their role of protecting and promoting social values, the issue of preservation becomes more apparent. The ultimate question is undoubtedly one of protection as the cultural space defines its role within the host community. Every society is involved in the development of cultural values of some form. Consistent with this process of social development, people in most locations are seeking guidance in ways to better communicate the culture that is the character of its people. This process of cultural identification and protection is ongoing and constantly evolving as a means of self-awareness. Consequently, preservation challenges institutional integrity because it is a form of social consciousness identified by understanding, in the sense that it is a way for defining the importance of humanity.

There are few challenges that culture face as critical as identifying and defining values. The questions are fundamental. Consideration must be given to the role of culture in contemporary society and what must be done to successfully contend with an expanding array of competing activities. The challenge is to anticipate the requirements of the community as the technological, entrepreneurial, and expediential nature of society changes. It is reasonable to assume the community will continue to follow these patterns of change. These tenets appear to be gaining in importance worldwide so no nation or people, regardless of social or economic status is exempt from their influences. All people are seeking cultural understanding as a form of recognition.

Cultural understanding is a process that involves the heart and mind, and for many societies is an interactive procedure. Culture in the communal setting is linked with a specific activity and by that connection an idea develops. The connection between culture and the idea confirms simple recollection within the community. In the observation of a specific cultural idea the observer sees the essential elements that give the culture distinctiveness. Nevertheless, rarely does the object (culture) correspond precisely to the form by which it is identified. When a form agrees with an archetypal image (idea) in the observer's mind, it is possible to be identified and appreciated. Connection with the object-generating community supports the recognition activity. Once the idea as a cultural element is isolated from change, it is a transformed and disconnected element. External to a set of symbols, the cultural object is common and no longer has a communal meaning.

When looking at cultural elements, the information observed is often combined with information from the past as retained in the person's memory. The resulting impression is a combination that is particular to the individual, but with significant additions of conventions coming from the person's history and social background. The impression of the cultural element includes both social and historical references and these factors influence the importance of the element. Although these qualifying conditions occur subconsciously, the effect is often significant.

Cultural elements do not have the distinctiveness they once had. The unknown is no longer unaccustomed to most people based on the amount of material available. (The knowledge of people in the past was good although limited by current standards. They did not know that they were using things that would later be determined to be patrimony history.) For them a model A Ford was just a car, and a carpet beater was a carpet beater. They took the products for what they were meant for and were pleased for the convenience. Older cultural elements may stimulate a sense of sameness, that is, they stimulate the remembrance of like items, and that thinking promotes a feeling of informality. The cultural element may evoke a sentiment that is personal; a feeling that summons a part of a person's history as a nostalgic encounter. It is a unifying event that can lead to a greater feeling of individuality and communal merit. Culture is a look into human experience as well as the idea of patrimony.

"Objects that lack any familiar elements or configurations remain incomprehensible."[5] Odd things are confusing to the person's mind and imagination. Human perspective reaffirms the arbitrary character of the principle of continuity by forming an acceptable visual image of the object. Many things resemble something else. The object is almost like something that is common and understandable to the viewer. Social patrimony identifies objects; however, seemingly dissimilar elements often represent social or cultural continuity that is acknowledged by different people and locations.

The relationship between the "things" associated with patrimony is abstract but can become more essential than the element itself. For example, Timbuktu in Mali is the location of mosques and holy places that played an essential role in the spread of Islam in Africa at an earlier time[6]; however, for many people Timbuktu is simply an exotic idea of a distant place. They envision Timbuktu as a movie setting, not an actual place. The idea (pseudo-culture) holds greater meaning than reality. An idea is subjective, that is, it is manifest in the minds of the individual, whereas truth as a shared value is by nature objective.

The socially disconnected object often looks usual and unrefined. This impression displays societal partiality based on style and shape that is confounded by visual recollection. In visual knowledge transferal, identification is improved by differences in form, design, and hue. As an example, Ak-kalpak craftsmanship of a traditional male hat made with white felt in Kyrgyzstan has a deep sacral meaning.[7] More than eighty varieties of Ak-kalpak can be identified by the different designs showing sacred significance. These traditional hats are constructed on past practices that are saved in both the communal and personal memory. Visual information allocated to an article (hat in this case) in the scheme of items are associated with a cultural perception of the world.

People are the catalyst for awareness of past practices. The past is used as a measure of the continuity of people, a common time. This identification with past elements reflects the characteristic of unity. Similarity and difference in past considerations are judged as the basis for human understanding. They are also the source of remembrances that unite and divide communities. It identifies in its most basic form the defined of relationships based on shared memories.

The concept of the subjective ideal defines a person not the situation. The population of any given location is a collective abstraction that attempts to define itself by referencing selected elements. Fundamental determinations may remain abstract even when history is detached from the selective realities that support humanity and the patrimony to be modified. The two elements, the past and present, react upon each other to cause a level of social perplexity to which the individual usually responds indifferently. Ambivalence is protection, but this attitude questions the relevance of history. In the book *The Law of Cultural Property and Natural Heritage* the term "cultural materials" referred to ceremonial and ritual bronze vessels associated with rites. Emperors, members of the dynastic families, scholars, merchant-gentlemen, and the wealthy, privileged gentry of Chinese society collected cultural materials, or relics, for two thousand years. "Cultural relics and materials were ... enjoyed and appreciated by the ... stratified Chinese society."[8] The concept of cultural preservation and protection developed out of acknowledgment of such materials as symbols of social status and economic wealth.

Understanding is a potential that identifies with the responsibility of humanity. Understanding as meaningful is resident in the mentality of individuals and is the principle for acknowledging and validating information. This understanding is not simple cognition but a true reflection of the ideal of knowledge as a meaning that exceeds normal comprehension. It goes beyond the object, act, or event to the unlimited potential of information. Understanding is a projection of values that extend beyond the measures of immediate perception to include other possibilities. Understanding invokes visual thinking.

In the agenda of human existence, many elements falling under the notion of culture evade direct understanding. Culture is a declaration of identity as well as a measure of time that began with a society's earliest recollections and extending beyond the present and into the future. The things of daily existence, material and immaterial, are a combined of elements that can be altered, refined, or rejected. A person may believe that it is more important to visit the Taj Mahal in India than the historic Mosque City of Bagerhat in the southwest part of Bangladesh.[9] The decision is personal and unpredictable; however, it is fair to say that aspect of culture verify the significance of both the Taj Mahal and Mosque City of Bagerhat. To be certain, belief is often the primary factor in deciding the balance between thinking (as idea forming activity) and action. There is in most circumstances no clear division of the physical and mental, or mental and emotional. An energy (force) is often required to avoid recessive thinking, that is, returning to a state of emotional decline, and to explain the unknown elements that influence human thinking about existence and culture.

Culture activities are a certain sort of reality. It is essential in the way things are made, what is made, the special conditions relating to those things and their relationship to human ideas and recollections. Culture as a human endorsed element falls within the realm of the reality of conscious. It defines the essence of humanity. A human being's thinking is composed of all kinds of elements; but a cultural importance defined quality is the core of knowledge and understanding.

The culture of every person is the product of language, habit, nuance, gesture, and beliefs, the total of which identifies people as members of a specific nation or culture and the environment in which a person lives and works. That totality is described as "culture." Objects, places, and other physical and ideological manifestations reinforce that identity, but may not in themselves constitute true elements of patrimony or social validation. Culture is a manifestation of human life, and it is in the interest of humanity to trace the processes and practices of people to their basic forms. The "origins" of humanistic activities are fundamental to recognizing and analyzing the stages of human and social development. This knowledge is, in turn, central to interpreting the cultural practices for the public.

Culture influences the quality of life of individuals and communities as a positive connection between everyday life and intellectual and spiritual growth. "The past from which we are removed is the human past. In addition to temporal distance, therefore, there is that specific distance which stems from the fact that the other [the human in the past] is a different man [human being]."[10]

Culture is more than customs, ideas, and tradition. It often includes belief that is not necessarily limited to sacred considerations. Therefore, patrimony is most often a set of conditions adopted by a cultural grouping to meet the basic requirements of that group. However, due to the scattered nature of contemporary society, primary group identity has been replaced by the general assimilation of social conditions that reflect the need for individual validation. These routines are transmitted by means of imitation, social conditioning, and teaching. The use of these secondary practices is reinforced as they are transmitted from one generation to the next. This integration of non-tradition-based activities alters the coherent whole of the group and challenges the validity of uncorroborated practices (patrimony) allegedly based on cultural history.

The significance of culture is profound. Its value often exists beyond the concept of culture itself and is identified as primary for humanity. The form and nature of cultural spaces include museums as well as cultural centers, parks, science centers, arboretums, aquaria, and historic buildings and other sites. There are varieties of each of these classifications that have a critical responsibility for gathering, protecting, and presenting different aspects of culture (artifacts, art, dance, music, literature, etc.).

The concept of cultural pluralism identifies an important ideology for humanity as cultural inclusiveness identifies, preservers, and defines tradition, as well as informing humanity. Cultural spaces exemplify true and meaningful cultural pluralism while maintaining local responsibilities and integrity. They (cultural spaces) should endorse the concept of cultural and social democratization to ensure the honest and unbiased representation of humanity without limiting the specialness of individuals and communities.

Culture must define its social responsibilities. This orientation may result in different levels of service to people but does not change social or cultural commitment. (The idea of cultural pluralism is important but must be considered carefully. Loss of identity promoted by an inclusive attitude can be harmful to individuals and communities. Cultural heterogeneity should not mean cultural homogenization—the sameness. Every culture has an identity that should remain intact.)

The concept of cultural heterogeneity identifies an important ideology for humanity as cultural inclusiveness identifies, preservers, and defines patrimony, as well as apprising humanity. Cultural spaces are an example of true and meaningful cultural heterogeneity while maintaining local responsibilities and integrity. Cultural spaces should endorse the concept of cultural and social democratization to ensure the honest and unbiased representation of humanity without limiting the specialness of individuals and communities.

According to Giorgio Agamben (contemporary Italian philosopher), "Culture exists only in the act of its transmission, that is, in the living act of its tradition."[11] He states: "There is no discontinuity between past and present, between old and new, because every object transmits at every moment, without residue, the system of beliefs and notions that has found expression in it."[12] This may be true because the transmission of nothing results in a nullified culture. For example, it may be assumed that blind people have nothing to do with art and beauty, or the deaf with music. These are not just physical disabilities; there is also intellectual. All people can make the decision to turn away from art, beauty, music, and other cultural elements because of lack of understanding. The value of the how and the why may be lost (or misplaced). Although it is impossible to talk of culture separate of its diffusion, and it may be there are no ideas whose reality is worthy of sharing. If there is a relationship between the process of dissemination and that being dispersed, then there is undoubtedly little merit in the act beyond the transmission.

This idea is the simple issues of thinking and culture: not as science but as human everyday considerations. It is an inclusive look at thinking as a cultural activity. The mind is concerned with the understanding, awareness, and attitudinal ways of thinking about the cultural traditions of a nation/state, a people, and a person. The people think according to a convenient cycle instead of planning for the future that is unknown by the current time and generation. That thinking limits both the people and their attitude, but it minimizes the importance of culture.

Communities and groups constantly create and recreate cultural traditions as transmitted from generation to generation in response to their environment, their interaction with nature, and their history. Culture provides people with a sense of identity and continuity, thus promoting respect for human diversity and creativity. Consideration is given to such practices as is compatible with existing international human rights instruments, as well as with the requirements of mutual respect among communities, groups, and individuals, and of sustainable development. People usually treat others with respect because they are humans, and because it is the right thing to do.

A person does not think in discrete ideas, but in groups of thoughts. Undoubtedly, different people think in different groups of ideas, but in the context of idea-groups, minimal variances and explanations produce an idea of divergences of view which seem more serious than they are. Groups of thoughts (ideas) are the result of many influences. To think a person must first remove himself or herself from the maze of conventional thought groups and consider other less traditional options. To illustrate, thinking and talking about culture as an idea is multifaceted and may not be the same for everyone because the meaning of the word "culture" is not self-evident. It may be used to express the social idea of superior or elite or relating to intellectual and artistic activity. Culture in the reality of human existence includes a variety of meanings with reference to the sense of propagate "something." Culture of social behavior is often a confusing concept with an array of implied meanings.

Although people are constantly looking for means to deal with the ambiguities of their life, they are depending on intuition or group studies to understand forthcoming achievement or failure. Premonitions (gut-feelings) impact the welfare of the person and the society. Important determinations reached without sufficient material about the future could end in misfortune. Judgments (opinions) by individuals may affect the existence of one person or a family whereas the decisions of governments can influence the lives of many people. Consequently, people often seek experienced prognosticators, but the judgment remains an opinion.

Much of the world has substituted material gain for cultural and intellectual values. Culture, in real time and real understanding, is a vital element that makes people human beings and a part of the social community. Without culture and tradition people have no sense of humanity. The humanist character should never lose its cultural, expressive, and moral elements; however, the essence of humanistic principles requires clarity, and this can only be achieved if the ideal is as true to fact as it is meaningful to sentiment.

Culture is a person's birthright just as property and thinking that is passed from one generation to the next—patrimony. These hereditary values may be described as culture just as communities and nation/states claim special events or times in history. These aspects of culture reflect communities concerned for survival. Each aspect of culture has its own purpose, meaning, and value, and each is derived from communal revivification. Cultural patrimony is thought of as the material objects and immaterial features of a group that are passed from previous generations, preserved in the present and conveyed to forthcoming generations.

Things to think about:

1. What is culture?
2. Why is culture important to humanity?
3. Who is Bi Sheng?
4. Why is it that, without culture and tradition, people have no sense of humanity?
5. Why has the world substituted material gain for cultural and intellectual values?
6. Do premonitions impact the welfare of a person?

ONE

Thinking About Culture

"ONE OF OUR MOST AMAZING QUALITIES as human beings is our ability to think. Humans think in all sorts of ways and about all sorts of things. Sometimes our thinking is complex and awe-inspiring. At other times it is simple and practical."[1] Dagobert Runes wrote in 1961 "People think alike."[2] The exceptions to his statement are due to ego and desire. That is why people who think alike think so differently. He said about people: "their egos are different, and their affections are different. All man's [people's] thinking is motivated by these two great passions."[3] In the same publication Professor Runes writes in support of his original statement: "Man's [people's] principles of logic, the fundamental categories of this thinking process are universal and identical.... The structure of civilized man's [people's] thinking apparatus of the past and of tomorrow, as far as we can analyze documents and actions, is the same."[4] Difficulties occur because people have natural requirements, and because the people exist in an ecosystem that offers the resources of their endeavors.

To think, people must separate themselves from the wrong ideas that govern the practice of thinking. It is true, these erroneous thinking changes from country to country, and from time to time, but people are trained from childhood to think in groups of ideas. This ideology influences people's ability to think clearly and independently. The idea of thinking involves several diverse psychological activities. It is beyond being aware of something when contemplated from a particular standpoint. Thinking is a conceptual procedure that involves deduction about both the impetus and the expected reaction.

Thinking is a pursuit of special importance for humanity, but there is no agreement on how it is properly identified or known. Thinking permits people to understand the world they encounter, and to form computations about it. Thinking is about finding answers to questions or finding solutions to problems. It is beneficial to a people and community with wants and goals because it creates strategies to achieve those

15

objectives. Right thinking is not found in what is normally described as the mind but in a creative and active attitude.

Although thinking about culture is of existential value for people, there is no agreement about how it is understood. Thinking, the process, is inclusive of imagining, recalling, solving problem, daydreaming, concept formation, and a variety of other procedures including magic. It is the other procedures that people often overlook. For example, people regularly re-evaluate their cultural history as new elements are remembered and given prominence. This kind of thinking is not unique considering the vagueness of the definition of culture. Things from the past are located and re-located to better respond to present needs and expectation. The relationship between "now" and "then" changes as ideas, reason, and memories intervene into the remembering process. The idea of "social" thinking is not to be confused with our efforts to make sense of our own or others' efforts. Past events have little impact on the present unless they are remembered and communicated socially and recognized as tradition.

The importance of culture as an influence on current and projected action is not an element included in the "typical" definition of humanity; yet it is a constant reference for normal activities. The past is a recurring reminder of right and wrong. "...[H]istory ought to have some meaning for the pursuit of truth."[5] The "matters" of human existence relate to patrimony. "...[W]e always bases our particular experiences on a prior context in order to ensure that they are intelligible...."[6]

Cultural elements should be identified with truth, but the idea of culture cannot be considered as true except as a thought. Cultural elements may have been "ordinary" in their original context, not ordinary in the sense of crude or meaningless, but ordinary as a part of the originating society. They fulfilled a purpose in an acceptable manner and complied with the idea and nature of their time and place. The idea of culture is an inclusive in manifestation; the cultural element should have significance that identifies with the time and place it represents.

Culture is a tribute to life—a perspective of humanism in the form of purpose. "This [culture] is easily recognized in the monumental remains of antiquity ... in the Upper Nile and in Attica, at Zimbabwe or Stonehenge, [it] is the physical evidence of an old way of life, the testament of a collective mind that has recognized itself and moved on."[7] Unfortunately, the ideal of cultural patrimony is a part of the past selected in the present for current purposes, whether they are economic, political, or social. The worth attributed to these objects and places resides less in their inherent importance than in the current expectations and demands.

"History and heritage [patrimony] are core elements of all cultures—the ideas, materials, and habits passed through time—so cultural values are, like historical value, a part of the very notion of patrimony. There is no heritage [patrimony] without cultural value."[8] Culture and patrimony in this sequence may be considered synonymous; however, the idea of culture has greater symbolic meaning than the historical reference. Stonehenge for instance can be viewed as unique because it happened only once (as far as we know at this time) in one location, and it has remained the same during a process of world change. This attitude is caused by an element that expresses itself in certainty and through the reality that it exists.

Identifying these emotional and physical requirements of people is basic in developing cultural practices. The information to be conveyed by each interaction is critical to effective exchange. All exchanges are normally in one of two ways: one that thinks of a material want and the other that addresses an emotive need. The concept of the event is verified externally by the purpose in which it is to be used and inwardly by the intent behind that use. Culture activities should stress the relationship of the essential happenings of life and the way of thinking a of group (person or community). The forms of conduct that people pursue have an influence upon the diverse stages of their lives including their social and cultural activities.

If culture is viewed as the most inclusive context of human behavior and consists of all forms of knowledge, belief, morals, laws, and customs, then it must include learning by members of society. Culture shapes the thinking and behavior of people, and cultural progression is the ongoing process of people pursuing those aspects of life they have reason to appreciate and that reflect the prospect of economic as well as social progress. Culture is seen as addressing the two psychogenic aspects of humans—people are afraid of the exotic and they have an unlimited capacity for belief. The differing elements of culture embody the concept for surviving as used by human beings, and regardless of how curious some of the activities may be, they have a specific importance to the community's survival. These activities provide adequate ways of dealing with conditions that are a part of normal life. Accordingly, a community (a group of people) who have a system of values by which to live cannot without great inefficiency sustain a part of their lives where they are to think and act according to a different set of values.

People at various cultural phases divide their activities into sections and organize those events into arrangements by priority. In that arrangement, sentiment and enthusiasm are usually moderated by knowledge and wisdom to generate the essence of permanence. Perhaps the stability of people is nullified when challenged by happenings that are heretofore unfamiliar. People become anxious when confronted by what they do not comprehend and are especially troubled by those events that change one occurrence or situation to another. "...[T]he more rationalistic we are in our conscious minds, the more alive becomes the spectral world of the unconscious."[9]

People are a representation of the world in which they live. Consequently, they are continuously inspecting and evaluating that world, as they know it. They are the alike but unlike within the world because the force that motivates their biological and rational quintessence and defines them as who they are is gained from their surroundings. Neither a person nor their psyche can be labeled as whole and inclusive devoid of the other. Regardless of race, gender, age, and ethnicity, and discounting social categorizes (rich, poor, etc.), it is easy to learn the nature of a person by their way of behaving about the area in which they live. People in disagreement with the template of their existence are often considered as abnormalities.

People have different thought about most matters but that does not alter the commonality of humanity. There are experiences that individuals and communities should forget and there are those that should be remembered. Culture includes both the appropriate and inappropriate. Cultural and its related activities should be elements of social narration where related stories are preserved and communicated. These activities can inspire people, help them to see the possibilities of their lives, and change the way they view the world by sharing this communal practice.

An example of social inclusion is thinking about life and death, and the realize that belief in renewal as a commonly held concept in many places of the world. The earth verifies the renewal practice as it conveys new life after utilizing the remains of the depleted. Death is described as the definitive change from a life of action to one of inaction. Nevertheless, it is also a method of corporal modification that connects with other activities that are a part of the life cycle. The symbolic portrayal of death and the relating act of rebirth (renewal) are important facets of the physiological change of a person. This practice is "represented in the nativity and belief is bathing in the Ganges to free the individual from sins and liberation from the cycle of birth and death"[10] or the resurrection of Jesus Christ. Other cultures advocate the idea of renewal in which the psyche of a person is conveyed to another human being. This belief sanctions a divine experience for the dead that gives up an earthly presence for a continuous presence in a state of unending bliss—a paradise.

"Such places [paradise] had to exist because they were key elements in complex systems of belief. To discard the idea of a terrestrial paradise would have threatened a whole way of looking at the world."[11] People live in an iconoclastic state that is made understandable by a paradigmatic and sacred condition. It is a situation where reality is contextually defined, and where people may change the conditions that blocked the way when accomplishing a specific goal become too difficult. Often the process of avoidance includes deciding that the relationship between the objective and achievement of that objective is not directed by reality but by belief. Therefore, different beliefs or convictions are contrived to deal with complex situations, and to address the irregularities of life. It is a way of belief.

Thinking about culture and cultural patrimony (the objects and history that is inherited from past generations) often exist outside of chronological time of history and may be defined by its special activity in its location as a memento of a particular past. Such culture is highly meaningful to the incumbent group (or person) but may be meaningless to others. These activities are concerned with a particular narrative of the past, more than their agenda for the present. The concept of culture often exaggerates circumstances to support a social idea, belief, or fantasy. This culture acknowledges human contact and identifies a pattern of activities that corresponds with group thinking. The social contact draw locations and activities together and gives them a sense of importance. This arrangement gives objects and events a place in sequential time and connects them with human activities.

Thinking gives a broad expression (understanding, awareness, and view) of culture within the context of contemporary society. The concept is to unify the ideas relating to culture and draw attention away from commercial endeavors that impinge upon cultural integrity. People in contemporary society are endeavoring to realize themselves personally, financially, and geologically through their own history. The gathering of documents, photographs, data, and other information about people, places, activities, etc., reinforce personal and communal stability. Fraternal patrimony serves much the same purpose except (usually) on a personal level. People seek information about academic, military, professional, social friends and colleagues, and various organizations based on historical connections. These fragmented concessions have authorized the externalization of culture (the separation of culture and humanity). Social awareness is also about moving away from materialistic ideology and back to the humanization of people and their cultural thinking.

The culture of thinking is usually considered as including a variety of elements that are conveyed by means of learning in a social environment. Culture in almost all societies includes art, music, rituals, as well as food and clothing. The idea of material culture denotes the tangible manifestation of culture, such as architecture and art, while intangible includes those such as literature and philosophy.

In fact, culture is neither material nor immaterial in the common sense of the idea. Culture is cerebral but may be ascribed to a collection of articles, objects, or symbols, but the reality is thinking. This method permits the idea of culture to change and to take diverse constructs without rejecting former expressions. Accepted ideas may be distorted, re-formed, or abolished and in all instances, it is the idea that is the culture, and the sentiment assigned to that activity. Thus, culture is described as the emotions recognized by the senses that accumulate ideas entrenched in the person's consciousness. For example, Suri Jagek, translated as "observing the sun," is the traditional Kalasha, Pakistan meteorological and astronomical knowledge system and practice. This practice is traditional and based on the observation of the sun, moon, stars, and shadows with respect to the local topography.[12] It is transferred by personal exchange.

Culture is based on human intellectual and physical actions that represent the activities of individuals of a cultural group both personally and collectively in connection with their setting and themselves. Things that are admired by one people can be disregarded by others. Culture influences sensitivity and is influenced by sensitivity. Nonetheless particular items continue as important over time, surviving the support of specific civilization the Temple of Angkor Wat in Cambodia,[13] or the Petäjävesi Old Church in Finland[14] are examples of lasting importance.

The concept of universality may be a distinguishing factor shared by culture and civilization. (Cultural universals are traits that have global commonality.) Cultural elements have a nature that goes beyond personal value whereas, abstract or intangible elements represent an individualized aspect of social culture. The personal element has the flexibility of social evolution, in contrast, the true elements maintain a permanence of form and identity.

Culture is an understanding of humanity as the individual relates to their surroundings. Their explanation of the world is in terms of human reasoning rather than myth and tradition and is an amplification of humanism that offers a special view of life. Like all social activities, culture is about respect and respect is a basic human value. (Not everyone understands the significance of culture or respect.) The importance of culture, no matter how it is defined, lies in its meaningfulness.

Humanism emphasizes the significance of the human element, and culture as a reference may be recognized as a human value based on purpose and understanding. If culture is who people are, and why they are, the experiences they have, the places they live, the knowledge they have or do not have, then it is humanist history, and it is human values. Every consideration assigns a personal importance to each aspect of the historical process.

Because people are practical to address cultural issues they often create a secondary environment—an ancillary existence or a duplicate life style. This duplication results in a standard of living that is influenced by the cultural quality of the associated people and the competency of the individuals. A new standard of living imposes new needs and new requirements on human conduct. This alternative environment is as complicated as the normal conditions. Consequently, these so-called "cultural identities" must be transferred from generation to generation. In every generation there is a need for the planning of practices and principles to meet the needs of this cultural identity. The foundation of the duplicate culture must be renewed and sustained. A culture owes its longevity and sustainability to fulfilling a series of fundamental needs.

Ways of Thinking, Feeling and Acting

The concept of humanism refers to the special attributes—ways of thinking, feeling, and acting—that people have usually separated from the influence of culture. What these attributes (characteristics) are, how entrenched they are, and "what causes them are amongst the oldest and most important questions in philosophy and science. These questions have particularly important implications in ethics, politics, and theology."[15] Logically the joining of culture and humanism confirms the veracity of both elements and magnifies the relationship of one by the other; the combining of two parts of the social and international essence. The culture and tradition are not defined by the identification of objects and locations, but by the reinstatement of humanity into associated values. It is, therefore, true that tradition has meaning for humanity.

Culture is a world portrait, a composition of vivid ideas and valid elements that illustrate an inclusive panorama of humanity and vital elements that become more meaningful when they are understood and believed. Belief is a part of all societies, and it is demonstrated in different ways; for instance, in Algeria there is the annual pilgrimage to the mausoleum of Sidi 'Abd el-Qader Ben Mohammed (Sidi Cheikh),[16] and in Serbia, the Slava, where they celebrate Patron Saint Day. Belief is creativity, and creativity is represented in literature as with Zajal in Lebanon or recited Sung Dynasty poetry, and the arts as flamenco in Spain and petrykivka decorative painting in Ukraine. The creative processes embodied in cultural elements are essential parts of humanity.

Creativity is the exploration of the psyche. It has to do with the person's ability to tolerate the barrage of opinions, figures, and every other concept rising from the subconscious. Creativity is the faculty to imagine the impossible and visualize the incredible and at the same time keeping these issues from public attention. Creativity is derived from the human past to illuminate that part of the mind that requires an expression of "culture." Creativity is many things but until it is expressed it is not real.

Accessing culture is a composite issue that relates to many aspects of humanity; however, associating cultural elements with the past often establishes a false relationship. Discussion of culture that is not about design and technology is usually directed to placing the activity within the milieu of other human activities and their experiences. Culture is those elements originating in the past that have survived periods of modification and have been themselves frequently subject to change.

A tradition relates to values with special significance originating in the past and passed from generation to generation within a group. The picking of iva grass on Ozren mountain in Bosnia and Herzegovina or preserving the traditional knowledge of the jaguar shamans of Yuraparic in Colombia are examples of cultural traditions that merit preserving. If social thought is purely traditional, it has a logical basis, and will accept only that which is usable in the current circumstance. Tradition may displace recollections that impede the activities of a community and permit its members to be a part of the society. Traditions are specific and strongly binding social practices, whereas invented (new) traditions are "unspecific and vague as to the nature of the values, rights and obligation of the group membership...."[17]

Culture communicates far beyond the minds or locations in which it is generated. It influences the appreciation of elements of everyday life, and the level of respect and understanding of the person and the activities of a people. If culture is the physical object that a people (group) inherited from past generations, preserved in the present, and passed on to future generations; then that cultural expression must be something of value. The concern is that the object, a manifestation of tradition, is confused with the true concept of culture. The objects should not become the ends instead of the means of defining culture.

Culture is made of discrete but unifying elements. Social arrangements can be very difficult with many differences, but the culture should unify the distinctiveness to a particular people. The components are in a constant process of transformation as new stimuli are merged into the cultural schema. The flexibility of socio-cultural components relies on the competence of the community to assimilate the modifications into the cultural agenda.

The values associated with culture change according to the requirements of the individual as well as the society in which a person lives. Such needs are associated with the true world (as it is known). They are liable to be related to the innermost nature of things (objects and events) instead of their outward appearance. This idea of cognizance is considered basic in pursuit of survival whether economic, ritual, or emotional. Modern needs (true and imagined) have not altered appreciably those concepts of early people though defined differently. Although, various matters inspired by delusion and supernatural ideas have supplanted procedures intended to make the subconscious conform to the ideas of society.

Considering culture to be a real view of life or at least some aspect of life is appealing but may not be true. Culture does, however, provide a label for the sites, locations, or events form the basic information about the (so-called) view of life, but such a view may not be important other than a general reference to history. The emphasis may be on the object and not on the humanism. The humanistic viewpoint goes beyond the idea of preserving the history of a certain people at a certain time.

Being mindful of the humanistic standpoint may offer new or different perspectives to the responsibilities associated with the identification, protection, and use of cultural elements. Humanity presumably wants a viewpoint of the relationship of culture and society that conveys the essential nature of the individual as a measure of social consciousness. Culture should identify the human dimension that verifies the social scale and defines the relationship of people to society.

The idea of culture is not simply a hypothetical issue but a perspective of practicality. The idea of human advocacy—the notion that people have the right and responsibility to give meaning and purpose to their lives and the endorsement of the concept that patrimony as culture is representative of the traditions—has unique value not just as "preserved objects" and signifiers of history, but emphatic measures of the genius of humanity. Cultural objects are as people have conceived and made them, and they will be admired and preserved, as humans have them. This preservation is in accordance with the concept of differentiated care. (Differentiated care is based on the idea that people care for the things that are theirs and care little for the things of others. For this special attention to be validated, there must be specific differences between entities [objects or events] that is not simply subjective.)

Endorsing the idea of culture is a way of preserving the social values for humanity; reality is often found beyond the objects recognized by the senses. Despite good intentions, the people who believe they are faithful spokespersons for their cultural predecessors transform the thoughts they try to repeat. They over-emphasize imagination and understate facts. There is little wonder that the activities of these people are often nothing more than impressions but are viewed as representing actuality.

"Social culture" is a concept consisting of various objects of special importance to different communal groups. Whether this value is viewed as representing developing or developed locations is irrelevant. The culture is a collection of elements and practices that are material and spiritual with which people can deal with the problems and issues encountered with life. Consistent with the idea of culture, patrimony may be transmitted, wholly or in part, from one generation to the next.

This opinion applies to activities or objects that are often other than humanistic in essence, but instead historically quixotic or socially bleak. The challenges encountered between the activities of the past and the expectations of the present often cause individuals to lose sight of their objective of truth and reason. Social culture as history is often aligned with the "consensus" view of past events and tends to focus on commonly recognized communal values. Often such assessments are subjective and founded on supposition that are distant from actual events.

Objects and events relating to culture have both essential and accidental qualities, given the tentative nature of historical resources. These resources that remain unchanged are defined by the object's essential properties. The accidental qualities of trivial cultural elements, in contrast, are those characteristics that change in various ways—time, space, circumstance, and condition. These ideas have applicability to those inconsequential things that are assigned cultural importance. The importance undoubtedly must be more than how a "thing" presents itself to the observer in the immediate surroundings.

The sharing of personal or communal cultural-related information is as unintended as a conversation, discussion, and photograph, or as direct as an actual observation. The originating culture and the retention of social and cultural importance of that society defines the personal elements. "The absence of the object and the codes by which we make sense of that absence are produced by the process of technical inscription."[18] Truth and logic are not purposeful considerations when defining personal practices.

Although culture is an ambiguous term in most instances, it is in most communities simply viewed as the fundamental nature of human beings and the world in which those persons live. It is a broad and deceptive term that becomes personal as defined by individual preference. Culture can be used to define everything from a building and monuments to songs, festivals, and languages. Though used to describe a range of objects and activities, culture is more than the customs and traditions of people. It often incorrectly identifies conditions adopted by a community to meet the requirements of that group. There is implicit in the idea of culture something of value: something that many people believe is good, perhaps even honest.

When confronted with artificial patrimony, the person generates their own understanding of that experience. The conveyed character of the object or event depends on the way the person perceives it and their prior knowledge and experience. For example, a ceremonial mask from the Torres Strait Islands may be identified as African. There is no universal quality. A genuine element of patrimony can influence other emotions when it has a universal value. When it is authentic, it becomes an interaction occurring at a more inclusive level. "Meaning-laden objects reflect and recount experiences and emotional connections; they reveal the life world. The intellectual and emotional potential for learning from objects creates a broad base for meaning making to occur."[19]

Each cultural event has the potential of being "more" than a part of history and a part of a time and from a place that was before the current time, a reflection of the thinking, beliefs, and practices of people. Such understanding can separate itself from the possibility of being of this world. This understanding is the separation of self from the process of thinking. It is a detachment from the inbuilt or natural standards and requirements that redefine purpose and practice.

When a shape, form, or image is viewed for the first time it is analyzed by comparison to the familiar. In this way, the visual perception of an object is defined by the intellectual or aesthetic sophistication of the viewer. However, the viewer may fail to acknowledge one's visual parameters of the object because appearance does not depend on the retinal valuation alone. The true image is decided by the amount of visual experiences with such elements. Consequently, the impression of the object or event is more than emotional: it is the honest perception of things. The wholeness of the visual understanding is not decided by the idea but the principle. When an object and activity is viewed against its socio-cultural background and in relation to other elements, then it is understood in its completeness.

Undoubtedly, one aspect of culture is material, and another is ethereal, and perhaps the ethereal part is more important. Without the ethereal the uniqueness of culture would be diminished and only an idealistic concept distorted by personal bias remains. The connection of culture with identifiable value must be achieved through reconciliation of creditability. This position connects cultural unity with human recognition and elevates culture as a whole. Although culture has roots in the activities of humans, it is the specialized social activities identified as culture that may have existed for generations. The cultural idea has survived and that endurance has made it important to humanity.

Culture is a lot of things. It is a reference to a past and a model for reactivating or recreating ideas about how things were done. Authentic culture as patrimony may not follow a continuous line through time. Alternative practices such as the traditional weaving of the Ecuadorian toquilla straw hat may not be authentic culture patrimony (the hats are recognized for their traditional pattern at the same time as they have gained commercial value). They have changed. The tradition does not prohibit innovation although the resulting experience is compatible with the example. The revised activity or practice thereby has the authority of social continuity.

The Festival of Folklore in Koprivshtitsa in Bulgaria is an example of patrimonial practice that relies on the past, but has changed for contemporary lifestyle. Thousands of Bulgarians of all ages meet in August to present and share their cultural experiences. This event began when local musicians realized a need to safeguard traditions imperiled by development. The festival increases appreciation of a living patrimony and records it for future permanency.[20] Although based on personal practice (the musicians), this event recognizes the belief and practice of the people.

People assume that culture evolved to a higher level of meaning adds new possibilities of achievement as people progress through social time. Authentic cultural elements have value in themselves and attempting to assign greater and lesser importance is inconsequential. Higher value cannot be assigned to elements that are more satisfying or involve a greater degree of meaning. The assignment of arbitrary importance to cultural elements is contrary to rational and reason. The intangible aspect of all culture is important, an importance that includes truth, respect, and socio-cultural acknowledgment. The preservation of meaning is a necessary responsibility of all cultural activities.

Cultural resources often have extraordinary emotional and

intellectual influence since they evoke a feeling of prestige and, therefore, a sense of pride. Cultural elements help to generate an environment where the people acquire an awareness of the continuity that exists in human creation, glimpse a past that they can endorse with gratitude, and project the future to which they will transmit the results of their own efforts.

Cultural ideas may pass from generation to succeeding generations to give a sense of continuity and community. Often communities shared myths and ritual practices to verify and endorse the group's identity. Myths, legends, and rituals explained the history of the people. (In this way the ritual is a way to express emotions and not a ceremonial routine.) In time these cultural elements changed to become more inclusive although persons from outside the group (or community) might not understand the meaning and significance of the event. For example, the Kachina dance of the Pueblo (southwestern United States) is a ceremony where members of the ethnic group dress in costumes and perform a traditional ritual. Although visual understanding for many cultures is a relational process, understanding in all cultures is based in an awareness of the symbolic connection between content and form elements satisfying the relationship of a socially defined beliefs. Culture reinforces perspectives of life and spirituality and expands social reality beyond human limitations. The cultural life for many persons is a reflection of the history from which they emerged, but as the world becomes more complex culturally and boundaries between cultures become more fluid, societies are losing their cohesion and isolation.

The concept of culture theoretically connects a proceeding social practice to the following one continuing from the earliest time to the present. Each society in theory continues the activities of its predecessor and each establishes the basis for its succession. The past is the foundation to the present and the future will build on that base. Time, as people understand it, is a dimension of reality, and an influencing factor for true patrimony.

Patrimonial elements may not rely on the host culture for their identity and existence as a manifestation of the environment that produced them, although the elements are aspects of humanity. The cultural element may have no intrinsic value in and of itself. (Intrinsic in this use indicates a "stand alone" or "in itself" value.) Human beings assign importance to cultural elements based on human values. David Lowenthal wrote in 1985: "The surviving past's most essential and pervasive benefit is to render the present familiar. Its traces on the ground and in our minds let us make sense of the present."[21] People may not recognize the importance of cultural elements. The idea of culture is a psychological concept made real because people can make it real and relevant.

The search for the meaning of all kinds of things is a primary part of human life, and culture is an essential part of the investigative process regardless of the form that search takes. Philosophy and belief are two ambiguous but linked terms. Philosophy and belief often have entirely different connotations for different people. When people speak about philosophy or belief, they have very different opinions about them. Many identified beliefs with religion or myths. The Procession of the Holy Blood in Belgium dating to the Middle Ages and Dancing Devils of Corpus Christi in Venezuela are examples of cultural elements based on belief. When thinking about philosophy people assume an academic concept, a separation of ideas.

People know little about the world outside their immediate surroundings despite the availability of technology. Thinking about culture is an essential part of recognizing the world and discovering its significance is paramount. However, people spend minimal time thinking—although most humans are concerned about some form of value most of the time. Thinking about past issues allows objectivity, but culture endorsement requires an increase in inclusive understanding and the ability to accept emotional and intellectual growth at both quantitative and qualitative levels.

Objects or events are not identified as culture patrimony at their inception. Regardless of any presumed value (monetary, aesthetic, social, or scientific), the assumption of cultural legacy is not randomly assigned. It is a value extrinsically applied, that is, people assign the notion of culture. "Objects are not static entities whose meaning is projected on to them from cognitive functions of the brain or from abstract conceptual systems of culture. They themselves are signs, objectified forms of psychic energy."[22]

Inescapable Community Stories

Comprehension of the developmental attributes of a community is not possible without mention of the circumstances that came before and the diffusion of powers of the people. One way of knowing the boundaries of those powers, and a way for judging cultural conventions, is with myths. Through myths, people justify the world and the powers that influence their lives in methods gratifying to themselves. Myths are a mixture of the wishes and anxieties that comprise the beliefs of human beings.

Rituals as a cultural experience frequently portray the happenings of myths, even though the connection is not plainly described. Occasionally myths are the precise message for the ritual action, whereas in other situations the myth is merely a resource that promotes a ritualistic state of association. It is also possible that myths and rituals motivate each other, and that correlation fosters the enhancement of both. This connection is evident when both myth and ritual are modified or transformed to suggest changing communal conditions. "Rituals remind us of how we are connected to and dependent upon other humans. Consequently, rituals can help humans form and maintain genuine communities."[23]

Myth is not a conviction that can be easily substantiated. Myths thrive on the lack of exact information. Mythological thinking is a cerebral conception. It is most often a reaction of emotion and fancy of basic human requirements. Mythical thinking contrasts with rational thinking in that it dispenses with the idea of rejection and disagreement. In rational thinking a concept has only one focus, whereas in make-believe thought it can have many focal points. Rationally an idea is composed of parts, each with a particular function, and each part is essential for expressing the concept of the whole. In mythical thinking the parts can denote the totality thus identifying its complete effectiveness.

Myths as communal stories are inescapable. They confirm instead of clarify, and they impact peoples' lives both deliberately and subliminally. They are life-stimulating and encouraging forces that can influence the activities of the people. Myths are an element of the rudimentary biological makeup of humans because they validate the idea that the abilities of life are developed from simple but consuming beliefs. In practice, myths demonstrate that humanity and life have a simple (often supernatural as with religion) source. They corroborate the importance of people and their surroundings.

People do not always consider stories about the past as imaginative narratives; they may regard them as actual truth, and narratives relating to the reality of their community and personal lives. Stories and actuality are often so intertwined that they are impossible to unravel. The culture of a people or community is often a personal part in everyday life. Personal practices are then a means for experiencing the past rather than ends unto themselves, and this information identifies the objects' relation to daily reality.

The human cultural experience including the concept of creation is an essential resource of myths. Those mythical happenings (true or false) add to the thematic arrangement of communal happenings and accomplishments. Some myths, though founded on and backed by emotional justification of incorrect beliefs, are taken as realities, and embraced as communal beliefs. (Japan's Shintō belief that the siblings Izanagi and Izanami create land on earth[24] is an example of a myth believed by many thousands of people.) Usually, myths do not depend on truth, only the facade of truth. Nevertheless, myths can be a good source of information about the thinking of a community and its residents. Often the myths are based on "real" or believed people or events. Myths may explain apocalyptic incidents about a significant segment of the history of the community. Myths in various cultures are believed to give a true or realistic history of what happened at the beginning of time and where people and natural elements originated. People fabricate myths to justify their world when there are unanswered concerns about their life and the location in which they reside. They generate myths to find impermanent or permanent answers to everyday questions.

Myths are necessary for focusing on the difficulties of social change. For instance, to deal with the extremes of human nature and to give stability to the communal organization, the idea of conflicting elements (paradise and purgatory, life and death) are often integrated into an origination myth. People moving into the so-called paradisial status are described as immortal. They are believed to have admission to paradise. (In Tibetan mythology the Sun and Moon came out of cosmic dust and travelled through the sky as one, until they were torn apart.) The myth reiterates the message of paradise (heaven) lost due to human carelessness and the significance of recovering a state of social unity.

Myths in all places affect the awareness of the people by exemplifying cultural morals or by providing a means for venting their feelings. When a community has inconsequential historical documents to corroborate their authentication, there are many myths to be utilized. Conversely, when there is an inclusive historical record to confirm communal verification, the myths are limited and less impressive. Myths such as those concerning individuals, are symbolic accounts, generally of unspecified original that supposedly narrate genuine events and that are connected to an identifiable belief scheme. Such traditions (myths) are unambiguous versions of divinities or human beings that are often bizarre and at a point in time that is vague but that are believed as occurring separately from regular human events. The loss of validation for endeavors that are believed to be indifference for a certain tradition (myth) can have an adverse effect on people.

The past is being redefined as the symbols and myths of people are recovered. As people investigate the past, it is not just the myths that are fascinating and meaningful; the artifacts and events also reveal unknown beliefs and ideas. These activities show that the same symbolic ideas can be found in the rituals or myths and on the objects of people currently living.

The myth is not entirely psychosomatic. At all times, myths contain an element of truth. Numerous locations given importance by specific persons and groups have major significance. They may be known intuitively, and not by the discerning eye, but known. Mythological places may have once been real (in the mind of those conveying the information) because they are central parts in a complex scheme of ideas. To disregard the idea of heaven or an earthly utopia (Shangri-La) would jeopardize an entire way of seeing humanity. A humanitarian view of a world that is trying to understand itself. All humanity needs a sense of stability, but not all seek it in their domain.

Sacred belief existing separately from the material realm is a significant component in the advancement of the human intellect. Early societies incorporated several kinds of concepts devoted to belief and sacred issues. Cultural confirmation of faith (sacred belief) as a psychologically gratifying ideal has an essential function in the beliefs of humanity from the commencement of identified history. Belief also permits those periods when people require release from a condition that is too undeveloped, or too inflexible. Hence, they relate to a person's freedom from any restrictive mode of life as the individual progresses to a more developed state of being. Belief in all forms of religion allows a person to escape from the mundane way of life to a sanctified life that is more refined. For example, in late April, the twin villages of Saloor-Dungra in the state of Uttarakhand (northern India) are marked by Ramman and hold a religious festival to honor of the tutelary god, Bhumiyal Devta.[25] It is a particularly sacred time based on religious belief.

People in all areas of the world have rituals to praise or give thanks to a selected deity or other entities. The Holy Week processions in Popayán, Colombia; the Feast of the Holy Forty Martyrs celebrated in the Republic of Macedonia, the Makishi masquerade in Zambia, and the Gióng Festival at Phù Dông in Viet Nam[26] are examples of ritual activities with a commonality of purpose. Rituals are performed in different times and places, but all have the commonality of purpose to provide sanctuary for practices and that meaning is understood by humanity.

People achieve an improved understanding of the past by taking part in ritual undertakings involving tradition and by creating from that happening an appreciation that has a sound instructional, as well as emotive elements. Ritual events stabilize the people's awareness of who they are. Established activities give a stable form to the culture of the people that otherwise is lost in the instability of indifference. Belief is affected by the socio-culture situation around it because it promotes its own apprehension, as well as the presentation of guiding missives and their application. Such beliefs function in a location that compels a verifiable understanding of group tradition to advocate group involvement.

Contrary to myths, neither culture nor thinking is separated from the ordinary world; they are real in a sense in which the ordinary world is not. Ordinary knowledge cannot penetrate beyond appearances, but with authentic culture, the element is as it is, and more than it appears to be—a truth in intention. The meaning of cultural requires the protection of this valuable aspect of the world. The focus may be on the material but just as with all culture, importance lies in the meaning not just the substance.

Things to think about:

1. What is culture?

2. Why can neither person nor psyche be labeled as whole and inclusive devoid of the other?

3. If culture is neither material nor immaterial in the common sense of the idea, what is it?

4. Why do cultural activities endure?

5. How does ideology influence people's ability to think clearly and independently?

6. Is creativity the exploration of the psyche?

7. Are different beliefs or convictions contrived to deal with complex situations and to address the irregularities of life?

8. Do the objects relating to culture have both essential and accidental qualities reinforces by the tentative nature of historical resources?

9. Does culture endorsement require an increase in inclusive understanding and the ability to accept emotional and intellectual growth at both quantitative and qualitative levels?

10. How do myths affect the awareness of the people by exemplifying cultural morals?

11. Why do people achieve an improved understanding of the past by taking part in ritual undertakings involving tradition?

Two

Creativity
as Cultural Expression

"MEMORY, LANGUAGE, IMAGINATION, and reasoning are leading participants in cultural processes, but require image making. As for the creative intelligence responsible for the actual practices and artifacts of cultures, it cannot operate without affect and consciousness."[1] Because feelings are the arbiters of cultural practices, the values of artistic creations are considered from a feeling (emotional) point of view. Either feelings or reason can sanction the idea, but the outcome includes both.

Art was identified by philosophy as one of the ways to eliminate the inconsistencies between the idea of an abstraction and actuality, and the qualities representing the senses and bringing them back into unity. The psychological relationship between the idea and thinking about culture (as art) is only as salutatory abstractness standing for ambulatory concreteness. The relationship between the ideas associated with the thinking process is abstract but may become more essential than the cultural ideology itself. The idea may hold greater meaning than reality. An idea is subjective; that is, it is manifest in the thinking of the individual whereas, truth as a shared value is by nature objective.

Art can be explained (if it requires explaining) as a human endeavor by which an individual intentionally and by way of symbols, presents to others reactions to life so they are affected by those feelings and likewise understand them. It is the philosopher's brain and the poet's heart that is to accomplish this objective. The artist generates something that is to matures in the intellect, beliefs, and sentiment of the viewer.

Art as a creative human action has to do with the creation of visual art, poetry, philosophy, and writing among others. These works of art communicate the maker's creativity and ideas meant to be valued for their expressive ability. The activity of making art is demanding if done honestly.

Because of a desire to express their inner vision, the artist has often represented the lifeforce of the time. Consequently, the artists as creative persons may appear to have forgotten not only aesthetic conventions but those of humanity as well. What remains is the creativity and the work, and the things that identify the effort as art. It may be challenging for the viewer to know if the artist's objectives are honest and meaningful or their efforts are intended only for appearance. Frequently the viewers need to familiarize themselves with a different genre of line, form, and thinking before judging the quality or merits of art (in all its forms).

Art and culture in the Western World are usually considered in a linear way. Beginning (in relatively recent times) with the religious influence and proceeding through a variety of "isms" to the present. The art "world" is a mixture of all styles and forms. None of these isms can be said to mark the end or the beginning of a new time or art form, but each is thought of as a demarcation of change. In contrast, much Eastern art and culture is circular like a rolling drum—a helix that constantly renews itself. It keeps moving, ever-changing and ever remaining the same. With a few exceptions, the influences of the West are obvious and exaggerated but absorbed.

Art like culture refers to a few human activities involving the creation of visual, auditory, performance activities, as well as philosophy and poetry that express the artist's imagination or ideas, intended to be meaningful because of their expressive capacity. Art considered in this way is expressing and communicating the creator's inner vision and ideas. In art, beliefs are important for the development of new forms of artistic expression. For the true arts practitioner there is often no difference between reality and appearance or truth and falsehood at least not where social intent is involved. (This is not the case for the dilettante.)

The artist/creator may not know they rely on imagination to visualize their work. It is common for the work of art to be seen in the mind's eye prior to initiation. Imagination is a mental activity used in combination with psychological imaginings. It is a "principle in human life underlying every reason, for the rational functions, according to our definitions, can lead to understanding—can participate in the constituting of reality."[2] Imagination is an extension of the intellect. It is the person's ability to acknowledge the ideas and images that exist in the cognizant mind, and in the case of the artist—to express them. The importance of the creation is not that it shows the thing observed, but that it interprets the creator's idea based on their interaction with reality. To think is to portray things without intending to represent them as they are conceived. One can use creativity to signify options other than the real, to stand for occasions other than the present, and to denote other viewpoints. Different from sensing and supposing, visualizing something does not require a person to think of it as real.

A reason for art is to give importance to personal viewpoints, but neither art nor point of view are the result of skill alone. Skill without passion (the passion to create) is insignificant, and the creator is the maker of desolate art. The reality that skill is abundant but passion (intensity or commitment) is deficient seems to be a basic hindrance of originality in various disciplines. This way of dealing with creativity by avoiding the encounter with passion plays into this trend. Just as technique is a method of avoiding a direct confrontation with passion. When the elements in an artwork are able to influence others, it is because an encounter is happening on an unassuming level. For example, consider Willem de Kooning, an American abstract expressionist painter; Yukio Mishima, Japanese writer; or Jean-Paul Sartre, a French writer and philosopher: these are people who combine skill, ability, and passion.

For the past five hundred years civilization has stressed skills. Hence, the success of skill and practice (as technology) are a menace to its own being as well as the creative process. Because if people as creators are not exposed to the illogical and transitional aspects of inventiveness, then technology (skill and practice) is denying the creation process. Creativity supports the pleasure and the enlargement of human lives. The creativity of human life may be threatened by the technological assumptions of a modern society. Skill (technology) is valid but is not a replacement for creativity (or culture). Creativity is essential for all aspects of human life.

Technology in its various forms (good and bad) has guided humanity from earliest time, and although the form of technology changed from rudimentary to sophisticated, people both profited and lost from the introduction of technological processes. In 1937, the American sociologist Read Bain wrote that "technology includes all tools, machines, utensils, weapons, instruments, housing, clothing, communicating and transporting devices and the skills by which we produce and use them."[3] Humanism pays the larger price as politics and technology contend for idealistic values. The objectives of politics and technology are clearly identified as domination (technological, political, and financial), whereas the objectives of humanism are subtle, poorly defined, and diverse.

Technology is a tool that must be given socialized dimensions if it is to be effectively used. Undoubtedly, the contrast of the two elements, technology and humanity, has different implication in different locations and for various applications. The growth of the society, the inclusive attitude, and a greater sense of social identity and responsibility are guideposts for technology use.

Culture as an inclusive way of thinking provides a distinctive kind of reality. In contrast to technology, culture fulfills the need for a philosophy of the ways things were made, when they were made, and their relation to human ideas. Culture as authentic patrimony helps to define humanity. Words, theories, and activities are elements of the composite human beings, but humanism is based on knowledge. "Humanism appears to involve at least two related notions: respect for human values, notably those of dignity and individuality, and a concern with the aesthetic side of life...."[4] Respect for human values is paramount in defining both humanism and patrimony. Every community generates its own culture, through beliefs, customs, values, and usage, which are continually created and re-created.

As culture is transformed and assimilated into different practices, the advocates of that culture may have to adjust themselves to the unaccustomed circumstances. Such changes may require modification in individuality that will ultimately result in additional adjustments to social order. Many artists are involved with the idea of culture, especially in the struggle for recognizing the importance of diversity. There is a growing liaison between artists (visual arts, poets, writers, and philosophers) and people in general as all strive for more inclusiveness and understanding. There is an effort by artists as well as communities and the public for cultural comprehension. Diversity and inclusion are elements of most discussion, consequently artists and communities who share these ideas have a feeling of mutual values that will have a meaningful influence on the artistic production of the world.

Discourse about art that is not just technology (skill) is primarily dedicated to locating it with other idioms of human expression. The failure to realize this causes people to think that non–Western art is made by people who lack the abilities of Western artists. What they are saying is they do not understand the art and therefore believe the artists lack ability. Unquestionably artists in all parts of the world are dealing with the same abilities, skills, ideas, and passions. Some are superior and some are less developed, just as in the West.

Art exists on the one hand by the view of the observer, and on the other hand, as considered by the artist—differentiated perspective. It is a matter of importance as well as meaning and design. The view is absolutely the same but totally different. This is not to say that one view is correct, and the other is wrong, but they are different. Each has a reason for their likes and disliked. The observer is more or less critical of merit and more critical of the "look" of the art, than the artist; and the artist views the merit (creativity) of the work and places less meaning on superficial appearance. (This evaluation is based on aesthetically meaningful art, not non-art.)

Creativity is the idea of bringing something new into existence. Artistic creativity implies a high degree of understanding and is the manifestation of the individual in the process of realizing himself or herself. There is a significant difference between art as an object and actual art. Art is not an ornament that is for looks. It is not for causing life to be more attractive but the formation of a newfound truth. True artists (regardless of method or media) and other ingenious individuals are the ones who communicate life itself. They speak of reality: for example, *Salvator Mundi*, a painting by the Italian Leonardo da Vinci, or Wang Wei, a revered poet of the Tang Dynasty, eight century China, or Wen Zheng-ming Chinese painter, calligrapher, and poet during the Ming dynasty. The many such artists are the ones who increase the spectator's awareness. Their resourcefulness is the expression of an individual satisfying his or her personal motive in the world—a world of self.

Humanity is often asked to consider what art is. It is doubtful that people inquire about aesthetics each time they confront a work of art, instead they must consider whether it is art or non-art. ("...aesthetic experiences are experiences that are complete, unified, intense experiences of the way things appear to us, and are, moreover, experiences which are controlled by the things experienced."[5]) Often when assessing the merits of a work of art the idea of "beauty" is considered. "Is it pretty?" Beauty in this instance is inevitably a determination based on opinion. The opinions of beauty may be question of liking and not a judgment of intellect. The beauty of the art is often based on personal satisfaction (a pretty object or event). When aesthetic opinion tries to decide what the beautiful is, it looks not at the beautiful but the ideal. It is as though the real object is not what art is but what it is not.

To decide what distinguished art from non-art, non-art must be considered in the same way as art. It is only at this level that it is possible to discover its reality. The non-art may have the physical components of a work of art the colors, words, and movements with the exclusion of that undefinable "something" critical to the merit of genuine art. The work of art must be identified by the viewer as real or true, such as the paintings of Magdalena Carmen Frida Kahlo y Calderón, a Mexican painter, or Sue Ferguson Gussow, American artist, educator, and writer. Nevertheless, when encountering a work of art, people often act like novices who studied art in the classroom and must refer to the lesson to orient themselves. The truth must exist within the believer because peo-ple in the contemporary world have lost all appreciation for aesthetics.

Aesthetics cannot explain why one work is considered art and meaningful and another object or event is not. Moreover, an individual may admire a work of art (visual arts, music, poem, or literature) that does not have stability, unity, and other traits; on the other hand, a per-son may find a work of art unsatisfactory when its assets are the same stability, unity, etc. Although aesthetics is often employed to deal with the nature of beauty and the philosophy of art, it is based on a subjec-tive feeling. Aesthetic values are often expressed as judgments of taste.

Beyond its vagueness of conformity, the reason for not giving aes-thetics more attention is its development as an aligned part of many activities, and there is no reason to consider it alone. Since aesthetic expression is based, at least in part, on personal judgment and people depend on noncognitive information to assign cultural values, there is no reason to determine between aesthetic expression and another means of elucidation. The human mind promulgates the presumptions of psychological models of tangible objects and events. Judgment shapes the thinking process, and that activity guides the transmission of infor-mation and images. In this action, the physical and mental worlds coin-cide and may appear to be identical at those times aesthetic expression appears to be real.

Inventiveness should be considered in the efforts of the philosopher as well as in the person seeking beauty because beauty is a meaningful component of our being. As is ugliness. It should be of no astonishment that intellectuals since early times have been interested in the individ-ual's feelings about beauty and ugliness. (Ugliness is a crude term.) Seemingly, creativeness and uniqueness are identified with individuals who do not always act in accordance with their culture. Beauty in art or at least the idea of beauty reaches a more superior level then true beauty. (The Uilleann pipes, the national bagpipe of Ireland, may not be a favorite of beautiful music, but it is for many people.) The spirit of art is not inconsistent with honesty and truthfulness when rightly stated. This model is also the essence of art, as completing an appreciation of its facilities. Physical beauty shows itself under the aspects of regular-ity and conformity of harmony and simplicity of matter. The awareness of beauty is not of beauty in general, instead it is the beauty of a certain subject or person.

The idea of beauty, whether in art or nature, is that of a beauti-ful object complete with parts that form a meaningful whole. Accord-ing to Georg Wilhelm Hegel (1770–1831), as stated in *Aesthetical and Philosophical Essays*, "beauty in art or the ideal of beauty in a higher degree of perfection that is real beauty. The ideal in art is not contrary to the real, but the real idealized, purified, and perfectly expressed."[6] A beautiful object can be called inspiring, because its parts are in balance (perfect harmony), they may be less defined, but stir a sense of the limitlessness within the viewer. Art may be considered truer than either history or nature because the forms in art include more reality than the physical world. Objects that produce this feeling for the beautiful can be categorized under a type called "physical beauty." Beyond physical beauty is the area of the mind that regulates intellectual beauty that includes the values that control the creative brain of the artist, poet, musician, and philosopher. This area of transcendental and meaningful beauty is the essence of beautiful.

Beauty appears to the viewer (or listener) as a measure of conventional pleasure without the consideration of a conceptual idea and without a reason to require an opinion. Belief in art is not in opposition to truth nor does it necessarily conform to the real. Art is meant to make people think about the truth and the vastness of ideas about beauty or the ideals of beauty. Beauty and its depiction in art leads to perception of what philosophy is to cognitive understanding. "Works of art [all art] are conscious expressions of belief, fictions composed of a vocabulary of line and color, light and texture, enriched by tropes and metaphors."[7]

Thinking about beauty as attractiveness and its opposite unattractiveness are procedures of sensual and expressive awareness. Essentially there is no such thing as "thinking" about beauty, rather it is the feelings about the impression of beauty. There may be no judgment (opinion) about beauty because beauty is only a response to the sensations created by a certain object or person. What is normally called aesthetics is simply a conversation of circumstantial and emotional elements and useless intrusions into personal thinking. To appreciate aesthetics is to sense the sensual power of beauty. Contrary to some thinking, aesthetic beauty cannot be compared to "cute." However, the identity of an object as beautiful is not a given. It is possible this way of thinking is too complicated to be considered beyond challenge. Assuming there is a creator who imagines, purposes, or produces the work of art or event and then combines it with the essence of the object or event already present. The meaning of the object exists before the actual object itself. If there is no creator to conceive the object embodiment, then the object must come into existence first, and then create its own meaning out of interaction with its surroundings and humanity.

People believe that art and beauty are connected, even the same. That idea is dubious, for there can be no reliance on either because they change, nor is it realistic to believe that the identical criteria can or should be used when deciding the essentials of either art or beauty. If the assumption is that art is described as that which is aesthetically pleasant, then the idea of "pleasant" is based on the opinion of the observer, and that the equivalent can be stated as "beauty," then art and beauty can be linked. These restrictions disallow the utilization of this hypothesis. Art is not a display of a capricious element identified as beauty, nor is it a manifestation of human passion or amusement, but it may incorporate all these characteristics. The worth (monetary or importance) of a work of art (regardless of media) is established by human interest. No work of art has inherent beauty, and no object (true art or not) has inherent value as culture.

Gottlob Frege (1848–1925, German philosopher) claimed that "the word 'true' determines the subject matter of logic in the same way as the word 'beautiful' does for aesthetics and the word 'good' for ethics."[8] It is that beautiful (for aesthetics) and good (for ethics) are values of reference and have only relational meaning that can be explained by using negative examples. "Beautiful" is easily defined by referencing to unattractiveness. True is the opposite to false, and good to bad. Trying to explain or instruct a person on how to think about these answers is a difficult undertaking. Even the idea of thinking is elusive. Even though thinking is a pursuit of pragmatic usefulness for people, there is no concurrence as to how it is explained. The difficulty of explanation involves the correlation between word and its reference.

The understanding of beauty or unattractiveness involves procedures of sensual and emotional judgment. The study of art (all forms) is usually presented as a series of events separate from the societies in which those activities occurred, and the images or events are introduced. In fact, all art is affixed within the social framework of its creation. A "history" painting, for example, may come from religion, mythology, literature, and historical events, or it may be allegorical. History painting is defined by its subject matter, not the artistic style. *Diana and Actaeon* painted by Titian in 1556–1559 is an important work in this genre due to both the aesthetic and historical nature of the art. The stories shared within a community are often more interesting, more real, and more related to life (local) activities than to actual history; consequently, the culture derived from these communal exchanges has minimal historic relevance.

Art is a way of making beauty. The desire to prettify is a curious trait of people. It is a psychological part of our lives that contributes to the self-actualization of an artistic connection between the individual and community. At issue is the discrimination between "art" as an individual preference and art as the marker used by historians and art historians when designating objects that have no obvious use. It is contrary to the creative act of producing something that is valid and that has aesthetic merit.

Unlike history painting, people have tried to describe the making of ancient images as magic or religion but rarely as simply art. The supposition can be that early image makers were hampered by limited intellectual and aesthetic understanding and that their work shows those constraints. It is just as plausible to believe the previous image makers were exceptionally proficient crafts persons considering the materials available. The images of Toulouse-Lautrec, nineteenth-century French artist, or the poems of eighth-century Chinese poet Tu Fu need no defense. These objects and people reflect the culture, the tradition of their craft, and the producer's personal principle and values. They make valid statements of their time and place regardless of where or when that may be.

Art is meaningful to those who create it, knowing "the power of art to be genuinely transformative, to modify irrevocably our habitual ways of thinking, feeling, and receiving."[9] If there is a unity in all the arts that validates counting them in one classification as art, it is that they correspond to some impression of beauty of feeling that may or may not exist (beauty of expression, beauty of feeling). That idea allows people to react to art with more than foolishness in a deficiency of understanding of what the arts are about or an awareness of the culture from which they originate. Two examples are the art of Chinese calligraphy as an element of art that is valued but often misunderstood.[10] The art of Chinese calligraphy is a creative process that requires observing, comparing, and study; and Mongolian calligraphy as written in classical Mongolian script consisting of ninety characters inscribed vertically to compose words.[11]

Real (true) art (calligraphy, drawing, painting, printmaking, sculpture, philosophy, poetry, etc.) is not to be confused with the concept of art appreciation or art history, just as poetry should not be compared to pulp fiction. These approaches to the subject of art have little meaning in the discussion of beauty or aesthetics. They denote the importance for those looking for contentment while knowing the unlikelihood of satisfaction and they elude the difficulties that are usually faced in the search of real artistic expression. There is little philosophy in the history of art to justify a pronouncement of learning. Participation can be deceptive and the prudent should avoid the temptation of hiding from reality.

Art is an energizer of life that initiates a unique existence for the real and the imagined. While art (all forms) may be a cultural curiosity it is of a comparatively recent time. As a creative motivation to human life it has instigated many philosophical influences on socio-cultural development. Some data suggest that art as a concept originated 26,000 to 32,000 years ago; a quite contemporary happening when balanced with the earliest stone tools from more than two million years ago. (Older "art" has been found that can be dated from 100,000 years ago. Markings in the Cueva de Ardales near the Spanish province of Málaga are thought to be 65,000 years old. The marks are not "art" in the truest sense of the word but representative symbols.)

That such markings have spiritual meaning seems evident, as they were considered as having a usefulness within the generating society though infrequently thought of as works of art. Objects, although often visually attractive, are not designed to symbolize a model of beauty or the manifestation of an emotional need. (Perhaps beautiful to the creator.) They are more likely to join two atypical worlds—one realm connects to the normal necessities of humanity, and the other is engrained in the traditions that influence daily life.

Early visual art was a form of social communication and in that expression developed into a measure of the cultural patrimony of humanity. The occurrence of art to be a form of image-making is present in all cultures. Whether something is believed as an art form or not depends on the cultural outlook of those making the decisions. People create theories about the meaning and function of the visual arts, and describe them as either an important symbol or a curiosity. They use historical reference as well as political and spiritual metaphors to describe the significance of art, and when all else is unsuccessful, people say it is traditional.

Art may have as its objective to disclose to the human conscious an idea when it is apparent that the subject of the depiction is not guided by a sensible imagination. Opinions pursued are not a creation of the mind, but the result of a collaboration of belief and mind. Opinions often interrupt the normal direction of thinking to advise the mind of the correct or incorrect ways of life activities. Some options are better than others, but none are certain. These images are not random, but not every method is designed to convey accurate or authentic ideas.

Undoubtedly there are changes in cultural practices just as there are changes in all social activities. These changes shift the lines of thinking and bring new energies to people, because they offer new visions and new insights. The creativity in cultural works is a challenge that requires courage to address. Peoples' thoughts are organized in ways that are based on philosophy, impressions, and values characteristic of their culture. The physical and mental worlds overlap, and in some instances, they seem to be equal. It is on these occasions that art, regardless of its form, is particularly applicable for adherents of culture.

Some persons claim that only individuals educated in the arts can gain the full and true importance of viewing a work of art, but such thinking is not honest or true. Like and dislike are not the same as perception or understanding. It is possible to think there is a measurable difference between experience and intellect. People may be more adept at one encounter than another; nonetheless, everyone has values that determine preferences. Identification of the essential nature of an object involves recognizing the truth of the intellectual process.

Art must be considered as a special type of human activity and a distinct category of endeavor. It is one of the most intriguing and unique attributes of people. Art is a form of ingenious expression developing from an intentionally regulated effort. One of the unique qualities of art is its symbolic attribute that is an endeavor unlike any other human activity. As the deliberate organization of colors, shapes, and other elements in ways that constitute a personal awareness of arrangement, it is a fundamental element of the acknowledgment of viewpoints and ideas that are vital to the lives of most people.

It is possible to draw a comparison between "visual art" and "science" (image making, and describing the imagery through the complexity of scientific exploration). There is no question that technology had a considerable role in visual expression. (Until the seventeenth century, art signified any skill or talent and was not distinguished from crafts or sciences.) Permutations such as processed pigments, metallic alloys, adhesives, and hundreds of other processes altered the form, shape, color, and design of the imagery and so did the nature of musical instruments. (There were no computers to influence writing.) Two factors remain consistent and must be recognized when discussing the similarity of science and visual expression: (1) all art is abstract and (2) all art is real regardless of what form that art takes. The image is abstract in that it is a depiction of a concept; it is not the item. The image is palpable in that it has proportion. Objects (images or events) can be touched, inspected and when required interpreted.

Economic and politic influences are becoming predominant factors often displacing the traditional responsibilities relating to cultural elements. Culture embraces a holistic approach to reveal understanding that includes the environment, the sciences, technology, and as well as the arts. Culture shares a sense of responsibility to act for the common good of people. The special importance of culture comes from the interaction between the elements and people in all their activities. The associated events acknowledge the special relationship and emphasize the symbolic reality of culture.

Culture fulfills the functions required by society. It is an activity where the past and present come together by agreement and for a purpose. Culture has a purpose and by fulfilling that purpose, it gains a value shared by the people involved in that activity. Cultural elements may be symbolic, that is, having emotive as well as inspirational values for the initiating people. Culture has the responsibility of maintaining these symbolic references to the world as a benefit to humanity. The symbolic elements in culture have unique meaning and are kept safe to ensure availability for present and future generations.

Almost every form of visual communication is based on symbols as a way of information transmission. (Everything is a symbol.) Traditional similes are essential as they continue the symbolism of the community with which they are related. Therefore, it is logical to believe that early in the development of the human consciousness there was an understanding that symbols disclosed a characteristic of truth.

Symbols Disclose a Characteristic of Truth

A symbol is a mark, sign, or special word, and is understood as meaning an idea or object. Symbols let people go outside what is recognized by establishing connections between different ideas and events. All interaction is accomplished by means of symbols. Traditional symbols convey the connection between a person's current reality and the past, such as the animal painting in Leang Tedongnge cave in Indonesia—a wild pig—believed to have been executed 45,500 years ago.[12] A component of elation is an element of each authentic symbol and tradition; for if we honestly endorse the symbol or tradition, we are for that time removed from ourselves.

Early symbols, often called "art" by contemporary viewers, had a magico-religious purpose. Those marks were viewed as having a unique value within the generating culture but not as works of art. Aesthetically pleasing objects were not intended to show an ideal of beauty or make a statement of ardent need. They often attempted to unite two very diverse realms—one realm assigned to the collective unconscious and the other based on legends and beliefs that determined daily survival. Those symbols were special images for explicit objectives that were placed in the collective memory and passed in direct transfer from generation to generation.

Visual understanding for many cultures is a comparative process.

Symbols are identified with a specific event and through that connection the symbolic model evolves. The relationship between the symbol and its purpose assures easy recognition within the social bounds. Symbols transfer information and augment understanding. The symbolic message is an active part of communication that is implicit in all modes of information transfer. Symbols often convey ideas that are beyond human understanding, and they are beneficial for reinforcing traditionally held beliefs. For example, the person wearing a beret (a symbol) is thought to be an artist, or that all Asians are Chinese (a symbol).

Investigating cultural elements involves a specific way of thinking, whether innovated or acquired; and that perspective should be based on the truth as known, that is, knowing the value and importance of culture as human beings. The culture of the symbol is a necessary part of the identification and preservation practice. The unconditional and objective value of culture is absolute; accordingly, it has many components that are recognized by symbolic references. Invented traditions, those that lack symbolic reference are viewed as routine, usually governed by overtly or tacitly accepted rules, which seek to instill certain values and norms of behavior. These activities suggest continuities that have past practices. They usually attempt to establish, where possible, continuity with an agreeable past.

Noteworthy objects, activities, or events of particular importance are often identified by symbols to invite interest. The symbols signify the variety or type of significance given to the object or event. Human feelings in most instances are likely to "see" or acknowledge the object or activity, denying the overriding authority of reason. In addition, even though the object or activity may be a duplicate (a symbolic exemplification), it is the relationship between it and the related conceptual image that grants it identity. Therefore, it has legitimacy and value. In this case, the feelings are emotions that cannot be seen, and in most instances, cannot be shared. People do not feel another person's feelings. In fact, most people have no way of knowing if a person has true feelings about a particular situation. Feelings are known, positive and negative, by acknowledgment.

Symbolism has a central function in cultures because people use symbols to define beliefs, needs, hopes, associations, and allegiances. For example, shoulder patches for the military or badges for the police. These symbols are designed to show membership in an organization. Symbolic depictions have sundry forms from the most unassuming to the most intricate. Certain symbols are generally known and only a limited number of people comprehend others. Culturally recognized figures and colors are augmenting symbols for differing meaning to people. Symbols are the nonverbal language for referencing the transcendent and emotional topics of most cultures. An example, the Georgian (the country) written language, has three alphabets—Mrgvlovani, Nuskhuri and Mkhedruli—all are used today. Mrgvlovani was the first alphabet from which Nuskhuri was derived and then Mkhedruli. The alphabets coexist thanks to their different cultural and social functions, reflecting an aspect of Georgia's diversity and identity.[13] Each alphabet is symbolic of a cultural affiliation.

Symbolized information is considered as being more meaningful than the identified element itself. This transformation occurs when the symbolized significance of the element is given universal status (this is not the same as a universal symbol). The universally important symbol is a symbol of the spirit and other valued concepts in belief. "The symbolic object appears as a quality or a higher form, and also as an essence justifying and explaining the existence of the symbolizing agent."[14]

The employment of symbols is a common human practice that is in every psychological activity and physiological act that energizes. (All written language is symbolic.) Subsequently, symbolic citation is a means for examining a cultural approach when studied in relation to underlying beliefs and the way they are intellectualized and configured. A part of theoretical rational is the skill to utilize symbols and to identify the concept that one person or object is signifying another. Even though most humans converse in languages with symbolized meaning, figurative symbology is also employed. Nonetheless, symbols are parts of exchange only if they have the equal meaning for both persons (groups). Generally recognized symbols, such as those connected with rituals (rites and sacred activity) convey acknowledged meanings and in that way inspire group recognition and reaction. Because nearly all speech is acquired by imitation, it is practical to think that the symbols connected with traditional rituals are also learned.

As an example, the circle is a sacred symbol. As a halo it is seen in art and religion as an indication of holiness. The circle indicates the ritualistic center of social order. It is found in ancient Rome and Assyria, and it exists in many social structures from the aboriginal peoples of North America and Australia to the dwellers of various locations worldwide. The circle is considered to indicate a sacred place or entity in the Eastern and Western worlds. "Circle" locations are usually considered as untouchable and separated from the dangers of the profane world. The circle, among the indigenous peoples of the southwestern United States, is symbolically associated with the universe. Another example is the Stone Circles of Senegambia in Gambia. The circle form, *enso*, is also important to Zen Buddhism.

The symbols as cultural elements reflect the interests, traditions, and beliefs of people. They may identify the special character of a group and that peculiarity is typically psychological. Practically every society has a symbol system that considers unusual objects and odd types of behavior. It is that each symbol system has a specific cultural logic, and every symbol communicates knowledge between members of that culture in much the same way as normal language. Symbols are an obscure reality that may be shared with others. They can be interpreted as what they are—that is, the image, word, or element they appear to be—or as that material explained to persons having knowledge of a particular mindset or emotion.

"Symbols ... convey feelings and attitude that have an objective existence outside immediate situations, and this development of self-consciousness is generally considered the greatest accomplishment of humankind."[15] It is possible to collate the symbolic attitude of individuals with the analogous products from their beliefs and practices, and with this information to interpret their "past" by establishing its context within the social structure of a particular people. This social expression reinforces the notion that the individual's thoughts, feelings, and behavior are influenced by similar responses in other persons. Whether those responses are a coherent body of precedents influencing the present as with "tradition" is a recognized factor.

John Kihlstrom, Jennifer S. Beer, and Stanley B. Klein contend that people have "no introspective access to their attitudes but rather infer them from observations of their own behaviors—just as they infer other people's attitudes from observations of their behaviors."[16] Kihlstrom et al., explain that "a related view is that our social behaviors are generated automatically and unconsciously in response to eliciting stimuli in the environment, so that the reasons we give for our behaviors are little more than *post hoc* rationalizations."[17]

A symbol can serve multiple ideas and may be understood in diverse ways, but usually has one exclusive meaning. This is not noteworthy inasmuch as the principal importance of the symbol and the idea with which it is connected is selected from several possibilities. Certain symbols are potent because they advocate the highest values, but symbols evolve in importance according to human need. Common understanding is ultimately conferred to the symbol because it is aligned with human interests such as those found in community endorsed practices, like road signs, number indications, and chemical markings.

The assumption is made that the meaning of certain words or symbols is self-evident and true. Self-evident can be principles explained as those ideologies that no orderly mind can refute. This does not mean that every person understands the symbol to be true, or even that everyone is aware it is (supposedly) true and universal, but it means that those who give the matter attention and take time to learn will see their true meaning. Truth (as noted) is not relative it is relational. There is a significant difference between tradition as an object and actual tradition. For instance, the simple statement "the person is smart" is subjective and means nothing because it does not establish a relationship. Whereas "the person is smarter than the others in the chemistry class" is objective and relational. It has meaning. The term "relative" is confused with relativism based on opinion and does not apply to this example.

Because it has a central role in life of every person and community, symbolism is important to most human societies. Symbols identify certain values shared by people and assists in maintaining an emotive obligation to that which was decided to be of significance to the group. Symbols increase the importance of artifacts without harming current or previous validity. Consequently, objects or activities as symbols have an immediate reality for the host community or person. That connection relates to the idea of a symbol signifying or prompting something to be remembered due to real connections or beliefs. Symbols, in this way, are an essential part of the cultural process. They are associated with concerns when conveyed in a ritual activity or informally implied by conditions and practices.

Symbols express meaning and serve to sustain an emotional responsibility to objects and ideas that are meaningful to a people or culture. Objects and events have an obvious symbolism, and a culture uses several symbols to transmit both positive and negative content. Objects usually take their symbolic reference from their association with social or cultural traditions or from the transfer of specialized ideas and qualities. Symbols identified with rites and rituals convey group acknowledged messages and thereby stimulate group affirmation and response.

Communication as symbolism reveals aspects of social and cultural information not provided by other elements. Tradition can be a symbolic looking glass that reflects the interest of people and divulges information not found in other practices. Personal or communal practices illustrate the distinctive personality of a people that is more than the physical aspects of skill and ability, but psychological and reflective of a reasonable thinking process. The people are the center in this exchange—the receivers and transmitters of information represented by symbols. The cultural context has a direct influence on recollection that influences both the perceptual and logical transmission of information.

Symbolism has an essential role in societies because people use symbols to express beliefs, affiliations, and loyalties. All types of visible expression depend on symbols as a means of informational transmission. As a result, symbol have many forms from the most elementary reference to the most compound statement. Use of symbolic elements may have conflicting meanings to people unaccustomed to certain cultural importance. Although symbols are employed to express ideas that may be beyond the scope of human perception, they are also used to strengthen generally held beliefs.

Each culture identifies its own symbols. The meaning of a symbol is enhanced by identification with other elements having similar values or purpose, and each detail in symbolic representation has importance. Symbolic thinking is analogous to early human communication. "It [symbology] came before language and discursive reason. The symbol reveals certain aspects of reality—the deepest aspects—which defy any other means of knowledge."[18] Symbols define ideas and aid in sustaining an intellectual and emotional commitment to that which is determined to be of importance to humanity. The symbols fulfill their function by illuminating the hidden meanings of cultural attitudes and beliefs.

Symbolic reference can be involved and assigned different levels of meaning depending upon cultural and intellectual influences; hence, the idea associated with a symbol is not integral to the symbol but may differ depending on cultural influences. "Concepts and words are symbols, just as visions, rituals, and images are, so too are the manners and customs of daily life.... Symbols hold the mind to truth but are not themselves the truth, hence it is delusory to borrow them."[19]

Found in all cultures symbols are not random designs but a response to an identified need. They fulfill a purpose by revealing the obscure meanings of cultural attitude and beliefs. "Social life takes place through time. It is the inevitability of change that causes society to endorse self-defining symbols to represent its heritage."[20] Symbolic inscriptions are associated with human cognitive skills, and these markings are a form of information that has cultural importance regardless of the mark or purpose. Symbols have a major role in contemporary social media and different animations including books. Science fiction books and movies are dependent on symbols to communicate what the viewer imagines they see. Much of today's television is illusion based on symbolic imagery.

The symbiotic relationship to information and people involved in fragmented knowledge and an attitude is an approach to existence. This approach includes the inclusive system of ideas and values that seem to acknowledge elements and practices within the context of personal and group perceptions. Although social tradition has personal value, it is not a concept that bestows meaning to all people. Symbols define values and assist in supporting an emotional commitment to certain objects or activities of importance to individuals and communities. Symbols give a different meaning to elements without influencing historical legitimacy. A viable symbolic representation may cause an object or event to be remembered due to associations in image, fact, or thought.

Symbols represent different aspects of human interests. The symbols associated with certain elements can be conventional or universal. The representative symbol may constitute a conformist acknowledgment. A universal symbol more closely identifies with the fundamental nature of the element it represents and has a universal nature. The symbol is a form of reality that is believable within qualified application but cannot be applied randomly and constantly without a synthesis of knowing and understanding. Most things in daily life have a symbolic reference, because symbols assist people to appreciate the various aspects of their environment and provide a foundation for decisions. When symbolic identity is assigned, it transforms the object or action into an "approachable" element. Symbolic identification acknowledges an immediate reality that changes the nature of an object or action into a universal phenomenon, that is, it is represented by a recognizable symbol. Symbolization causes the element to emerge from isolation from within its own existence into a system of connections and communication.

Symbolic representations are one way in which knowledge (true or false) is transferred. Symbols may require interpretation between their signification and the values they signify. The symbol is a depiction of which is seen many likenesses as conceivable between the object being studied and other perspectives that are already known. The symbolic references of a people when compared with information about the history and beliefs of a community may identify relative historical issues. Methods for integrating social expressions reinforce the notion that personal thoughts and behavior are swayed by the comparable reactions of other persons. That those practices influence "ways of life" is acknowledged.

A symbol is a proxy for an object or generally shared viewpoint, and consequently symbolism is an essential element of all societal communication. Even in those societies that take pleasure in utilizing the written word (words are symbols) through exceptional literature and progress in the arts, symbols are of critical significance. Although symbolism originated in ancient Greece, it was not until contemporary times and the initiation of psychoanalysis that stressed the research of symbolism that thinking was drawn to the function of symbols as a primary factor in cognitive development.

It is a fundamental concept of psychoanalysis that in the individual's mind countless beliefs, aspirations, and hopes are fulfilled. Every idea by itself is a symbol with more significance that must be placed in the proper context to be comprehended and applied. A person's belief adds to symbols and that practice is influenced by communal practices. It can be assumed that symbols satisfy numerous uses though memories and the imagination that can become intermingled causing the symbolic indications to be changed or manipulated. (Imagination and belief are both ideas that are symbolic.)

The symbol advances a recognition of a certain circumstance by supplying a regular reference to the situation in question. The associated symbolic arrangement develops and endures as part of a cultural arrangement due to constant use. The symbol can perform satisfactorily or unsatisfactorily, but unless it is identified and related with the proper act, activity, or event it fails to arouse interest. (For example, the word-symbol "FRAGILE" has more meaning when attached to an object or package.) The elementary quality of most symbols simplifies exchanges between people and confirms the stability of cultural signals. Symbols may be simple and straightforward; at other times, they are complicated and devious. Symbols are often shared cultural elements and are the means for transforming the circumstances of the human condition into imaginary terms.

The past is filled with symbolic meaning including symbols that identify ways of maintaining relations with other beings. A people's beliefs determined what people see, and what people see fortified their beliefs. Real life deals with daily existence and perpetuation of real history; that life is influenced by traditions and customs. Judgments (opinion) of perception about traditional things can be both personal and social. Deciding the "value" of traditional elements must relate to the idea of authenticity and ideals while remaining conscious to public considerations. Value-endorsed traditional elements must be considered although personal considerations often establish meaning. Judgments of perception are identified as requiring no clear notion of comprehension, but merely the plausible linking of ideas.

Representations are not the same as the originals. An element may be symbolic of a particular event and activity but does not symbolize all such events or activities. An element can be considered as a symbol of a time or a particular social action, or an element that recalls a symbol of a time or place without rescinding the authenticity of that object or action. "Symbolism adds a new value to an object or an act, without thereby violating its immediate or 'historical' validity."[21]

It is possible to connect the symbolic and collective attitudes found in personal elements of a group's history, beliefs, and practices. Patrimony uses information and by a comparative process, may advance a viable interpretation of the societal structure of a particular people and the significance of that tradition in the environment. This social expression reinforces the concept that the community has a purposeful role in defining and preserving the practices by which a people are identified. Group activities may be the basis for sustaining forms of communal recognition.

The chronicle of all humanity contains symbolic depiction, because devoid of symbolism (in some form), there is no culture. While early culture may not have been a combination of symbols, it was the purpose behind the symbols that joined the people into a mutual goal. The earliest documents of human existence emphasize symbols relating to magico-religious activity. They were intended to transfer knowledge to the individuals producing the symbols and to assist in the articulation of beliefs that avoided more ordinary forms of communication. The symbols were created from the human subconscious as an assertion of an inherent ability that could not be completely articulated in other means of expression.

Culture is the symbolic quality of humanity that signifies neither the past nor the future but is the unifying values of the present. The specialness of culture reflects its cohesion with people. The concerns of humanity are the same worldwide, but the responses to those concerns may be different. The differences in solutions are a display of the connections that define unity. If culture is only the object, event, or act and not the humanity it represents then it is unlikely to survive, however, all cultures have long histories composed of both tangible and intangible elements.

Things to think about:

1. Is there a significant difference between art as an object and actual art?
2. Do you think art and beauty are connected?
3. Is art a way of making beauty?
4. Is beauty and its depiction in art the same as philosophy is to cognitive understanding?
5. Can aesthetics explain why one work is considered art and meaningful and another work is not?
6. Who said, "beauty in art or the ideal of beauty in a higher

degree of perfection that real beauty. The ideal in art is not contrary to the real, but the real idealized, purified, and perfectly expressed?"

7. Is the creative process founded on the genius and work of individuals and that origin is not altered by time?

8. Are cultural elements symbolic—that is, do they have emotive as well as inspirational values for the initiating people?

9. Why is symbolism important to most human societies?

10. In what way do symbols define values and assist in supporting an emotional commitment to certain objects or activities of importance to individuals and communities?

11. Is symbolic representation a way knowledge is transferred?

12. Does the elementary quality of most symbols simplify exchange between people and confirms the stability of cultural signals?

13. What lays behind the symbols that joined the people into a mutual goal?

THREE

Culture as the Spirit
of Humanity

THE IDEA OF "HUMANKIND" has different meanings relating to politics, religion, and philosophy. It also is considered as countermanding the dehumanization of materialistic ideology. "Patrimony, or property, the total of all personal and real entitlements, including movable and immovable property, belonging to a real person or a juristic person."[1]

Human (humankind) philosophy is to "organize into a consistent and intelligible whole the chief elements of philosophic truth that it can find in the past or present and to make that synthesis a powerful force and reality in the minds and actions of ... [people]."[2]

Neither humankind nor patrimony is a twenty-first century concept since both have histories that extend into the distant past. Humanism as a concept is identified with indwelling values of people, and patrimony is a validating element for humankind. Both are about respect. Philosophers and scholars define humanistic value differently, but patrimony acknowledges the commonality of all humanity. The relationship between authentic patrimony and people is allied from the beginning just as the practical aspects of the past and present are conjoined. Like the concept of patrimony, the ideals of humanism have been arranged and rearranged over the years to fit different and often arbitrary purposes. As with patrimony, each change has offered a different view and a different perspective of humanity. The connection between patrimony and humankind throughout history is an indication of thinking as a people factor.

Many cultural elements constantly change (language, songs, food, and rituals are examples), but they retain the sameness of purpose or relevance. The procedure of change may include a sense of direction or placement that indicates the process of movement from one place, status, or condition to another. The concept of direction or placement can be measured in various terms, including time, space, duration, and context.

Authentic cultural patrimony fulfills a mission of unifying the past with the present and granting greater knowledge and understanding of different people, different beliefs, and different places. The unity accentuates other connective facets of a culture. Authentic patrimony, in that capacity, is a guide to other expressions of past and current humanism. "To some extent, and in varying ways, everyone experiences the tension between the necessity for the free access to progress and, on the other hand, the exigency of safeguarding our heritage."[3] Authentic patrimony (heritage) is intended to give a reference to the world in which humans live and a place and role for people in that world.

The idea of humanism stresses the values and achievements of people, and a preference for analytical thinking and affirmation instead of dogma or superstition. The word "humanism" was first used in nineteenth-century Europe, but the humanism concept is identified with persons from the earliest times. Greek and Islamic philosophers in the thirteenth and fourteenth centuries attempted to explain the world in terms of human reason rather than myth and tradition, thereby advocating humanist values in the years before the current era.

Humanism is identified with "a philosophical and ethical stance that emphasizes the value and agency of human beings, individually and collectively, and generally prefers critical thinking and evidence (rationalism and empiricism) over acceptance of dogma or superstition."[4] A word such as humanism may have no expressible meaning without an acceptable label. An element of humanistic thinking is the object of thinking, and that object is a manifestation of culture. William James (1842–1910) wrote in *The Meaning of Truth*: "The essential service of humanism ... is to have seen that tho [*sic*] one part of our experience may lean upon another part to make it what it is in any one of several aspects in which it may be considered, experience as a whole is self-containing and leans on nothing."[5]

People from the Yellow Emperor of China 2500 BCE to the end of dynastic rule have applied the word "humanism" to identify activities endorsing humanity. The name is often given to such concepts because people must give a name to an act or action so they can remember an understandable meaning.

Humanism and time have a sophisticated relationship. The issue of time and the division of human experience has been and continues to be a philosophical concern. The history of humanity is defined by measures of time no matter how time is determined. Events and objects acknowledge the "before," "then," or "back when" of people. The realizable value of culture as patrimony rests upon the ability of humans to identify with the symbols and signs of people or places, to endorse that recognition, and to express it in ways that other persons can share. The relationship of patrimony and society acknowledgment of humanity is a gauge of social awareness. "All rational knowledge is either material, and concerns some object, or formal, and is occupied merely with the form of understanding and reason itself and with the universal rules of thinking without regard to distinctions between objects."[6] Humanism and the basic traits of individualism share similar references to human experience, both in its everyday immediacy and in its extremes. The human-centered nature gives reference to humanistic nature as well as the individualistic thinking. This humanistic attitude precluded accepting dogma from sources that could not be questioned.

There are ideas that are basic to a humanistic view of the world and alteration of that view transforms all associated activities and perceptions. The actualities of today may have little to do with the realities of tomorrow. Beliefs about space, time, matter, cause and effect, may change because of a revision of the accepted concept of the universe and its relationship to humanity.

Humanism is a way of defining the principles of action found within culture. It (humanism) identifies humanity as the source of human principles that provide for correct and responsible actions. It acknowledges those principles that identify people as people, and for that reason, it is often described as conforming to anthropological philosophy. Humanity is the messenger because all patrimony involves knowledge and attitude as an approach to existence and the innate arrangement of ideas, values, and beliefs that characterize human conduct. "Every generation takes over some legacy from the preceding generation and decides, on its own, what shall be adopted as patrimony and what shall not."[7] Selected elements must be validated and explained for those persons seeking the security of a social as well as a representative sense of a cultural reference. Objects give evidence of a peoples' place in a social network as elements of valued relationships—the essence of humanism.

Material advancement is viewed as progress by some people at the same timeas it destroys traditional values and the basis on which life is understood and explained. "Remembering the past is critical for our sense of identity ... to know what we were confirms that we are."[8] People require reassessment of human values, and when the ideal of culture as an inclusive factor is projected beyond the immediate community, it prepares them to meet the challenges of their responsibilities and reasserts the most basic form of humanism.

The relevance of humanism to contemporary society is also not a new idea. That relationship has been described many times in different ways; unfortunately, it has been often viewed from a materialistic point of view. Respect for culture and its related importance increases as the practical connections with humanity increase. All things within human experiences and the potential of humanity are related. Humanism as a cultural value is a valid concept that gives greater validity to the ideals of patrimony and attaches a further protective layer to traditional values. Humanism and culture are sympathetic ideologies.

The humanist ideology includes fulfilling the possibilities that reside within the human idea of culture. The separation of humanism and culture may be overcome to promote a unified view of the potential of culture as a humanizing element that transcends time. The relationship between humanity and culture as a concept often seems subtle, but it is not. It is direct, true, and purposeful. However that relationship is often ignored. Culture reflects the genius of a people. It is a means of discovery and not a way of imposing history on contemporary thinking or productivity. Culture is a magic mirror that allows humanity to see into a past that can never be truly resurrected as evidence of history. The observer must enter the past in a true (real and meaningful) way and thereby establish a connection between the element and humanity. Viewing culture requires a sense of humanism that goes beyond subjective thinking (egoism).

An issue for humanism is how people interpret reality—the concept of "the real." Reality is consciousness of things as they are, instead of as they appear or are imagined. Reality is a way of thinking that includes all that is and has been, whether material or immaterial. Although the idea of reality seems simple enough, it has challenged ancient thinkers such as Aristotle and Plato. At the most basic level, one assumption common to people is that they are fundamentally unaware of the true nature of the reality within which their lives take place. Consequently, the majority of people live their lives limited by conditions that are not in harmony with the true character of their own reality. Reality is both a personal and social ideal that is fundamental to understanding patrimony and therefore humanism.

Humanistic psychology stresses individuals' essential ambition regarding self-actualization, the way of achieving and articulating an individual's abilities and creativity. It cannot be denied that humanism is a way of thinking, an attitude, and a way of viewing life. Culture as patrimony is an expression of the time and place of its origination and the values that represent the character of the related society. The specialness of cultural patrimony relies on the ability of humans to identify with the experiences of other persons living at another time and in another place. Culture often expresses those values in ways that people outside that time and place can share.

Humanity must view culture as a valued part of life, preserving elements, and attempting to reproduce both the cultural tradition and its attitude for the next generation. People seek examples of achievement and enlightenment as measures of "success." This type of success should be considered as determining humanist feeling towards a form of truth and defining a sequence of thought that does not require an extrinsic dictation of what the truth is to be. (For more on truth see Chapter Two.)

Humanism gathers the under-utilized resources of human knowledge and applies them to providing a refined vision of the human present and future based on a common recollection and consideration of the past. The humanism perspective considers every feature from the broad and inclusive view of daily activities to the individual lives enmeshed in those activities and from the questionable culture of the past to the possibilities of the future. Patrimony is about people, and while this seems obvious, it is a fundamental notion that is often overlooked. When the cultural element is genuine and when it has a universality of meaning it is because of an encounter occurring at a basic level. Humanism should be viewed as the relationship between people and the culture in which people are real, and a part of that environment is the historical elements identified as patrimony. Sir Julian Huxley (1887–1975) stated that: "Humanism thinks in terms of directional process instead of in those of static mechanism, in terms of quality and diversity as well as quantity and unity."[9]

Humanism is based on the idea that the people (individual and communal) are of foremost importance. Individualism is associated with humanist philosophy and denotes individual personality—distinctiveness. Individualism implies an attitude and an inclination towards self-realization instead of complying with established behavior. It emphasizes the value of the individual as a human being. (Individualism is not an illusion although all people are interconnected.)

It is nearly impossible to know the authentic ways of a people in an absolute way, simply because most people have only relative knowledge about themselves. The level of knowledge depends on the viewer's point of view and the symbols used to define the individual or community. The viewer must look at culture as a spectator viewing a photograph or a digital image that is further removed from actuality. Granted, the "view" of a cultural element may stimulate intellectual or even philosophical reactions, but as an individual process, it elicits a response that is little more than interest. These reactions remain abstract when they are separated from the realities that generate them and which they may modify.

The unity or non-unity of any situation or action is a measure of the agreement of humanity and the world. The principle or universal potential of humanism activated within the person is not manifest in this process. Such manifestation is the growth proceeding from a principle in some form in which the standards of value, ethics, and social responsibility, etc., become active. Humanism must then be a way of life in which authentic culture has a role whether actually or figuratively; however, the lack of a concrete reality challenges the impulses of the individual and hinders the concept of duty in the mind of most human beings. A person must judge themselves capable of dealing with social issues by means of reason, not in the future, but in the present, and while considering the past.

The ideas about the human relations with culture, as it appears and as represented, conform to a sense of reality although the patrimony may not be authentic. The tangibility of an object promotes the concept of truth as a feeling. The intangible elements often lack that feeling of immediacy and sense of understanding but convey an emotional aspect of humanism. Intangible elements exist in different forms of abstraction (ideas, beliefs, and preferences) that often require acceptance without true knowledge or appreciation.

Cultural patrimony identification is not just a process in which objects have an impact on humanism, but one in which culture has three objectives—(1) to patrimony as the passing from generation to generation, (2) to the histology that propagates an inclusive environment, and (3) to people as generators and believers in objects and events of value. The recognition of culture is not the expression of the needs of the times, but an expression of innovation relative to the recognized knowledge of human reality.

People may identify everything or anything as claiming to represent the culture of their community and people. The elements selected tell a great deal about the thinking of the selectors but may ignore meaningful information about the people or community. The selection may be viewed from the outside as questionable judgment, but from the perspective of the selectors, it is an assumed assessment of personal or communal value. These decisions, no matter how general, emphasize some elements at the expense of others, and are therefore responsible for the recognition of that determination of value.

In a communal location there are many limits for determining correct or incorrect actions; consequently, the decision is seldom a personal one. Every person, nevertheless, has an obligation to conduct daily activities in a truthful way. The thoughts that regulate observance of truth are intelligence and aspiration, and they are evident in the manner of choosing. It is a person who is eventually answerable for determining right or wrong in most instances. It is the wish to conform with the prospects of humanity that often stimulates logical thinking. However, truth means agreement to the concurrence between a person's beliefs and factual situations.

The study of human sensibility has broadened and become more comprehensive as anthropological studies have become more closely associated with social science. The scrutiny, in this context, for years has concentrated primarily on the urban areas in different parts of the world with a main interest in developing countries. This focus is changing to include more attention to communities in the developed world and their methods of dealing with change. Anthropologists also have divided the inquiry into different categories of research concerned with religious beliefs and praxis to the exchange between biology and social systems.

Ideologies of Particular Importance

Cultural patrimony, in philosophical terms, manifests itself in elements that place the producing societies and its people in a world context. The patrimonial elements are symbolic creations by which a culture is known, and often this production has been prized through history. The products of a people are valued not only because of their merit, but because they preserve the identity and character of their creators.

Cultural patrimony acknowledges an active refined past because things are done in the way they were done previously. Patrimonial elements often reveal the customs, practices, ideas, and beliefs of the time in which they were made and reference the history of their makers. Csikszentmihalyi (1990) wrote "...[O]bjects reveal the continuity of the self through time [it is the 'self' that makes the patrimony important] by providing foci on involvement in the present, mementos and souvenirs of the past, and signposts to the future."[10] Csikszentmihalyi continues this concept: "...[T]hings stabilize our sense of who we are: they give a permanent shape to our views of ourselves that otherwise would quickly dissolve in the flux of consciousness."[11]

A person, no matter their place in the social order, exists inside the culture of the related community. Furthermore, that culture survives because of the persons it includes. The people are the incumbents and advocates of their culture. This socio-psychological situation differs from group to group, but most integrated groups are composed of persons with related beliefs and interests (for example, book clubs, church organizations, and business associations).

People have the experience of relating to events and objects not by what is seen or remembered but by written or verbal reference. People do not recall events precisely as they occur. "They 'construct' a memory of the event, and this construction is influenced by many factors including the social and cultural context of remembering."[12] These recollections are often borrowed memories based on the testimony or attitudes of others who may draw their inspiration from a more distant generation of impressions. These remembrances, no matter how arbitrarily encountered, often have a profound influence on a people and a community. "...[W]hen recollection has been treated as a cultural rather than as an individual activity, it has tended to be seen as the recollection of a cultural tradition, and such a tradition, in turn, has tended to be thought of as something that is inscribed."[13]

Cultural tradition may be a basic means to connect an individual or a people with past elements, but the association is temporary. Substitute traditions identified as a communalizing practice often promote self-esteem and group cohesion by interpreting related activities in a way that maintains or reinforces group values. People are motivated to participate in or promote group activities when cohesiveness is high. This interaction gives individuals a sense of security and a feeling of personal worth. The ideas about the human relations with culture, as it appears and as represented to people, are conceptions of claimable reality. "Culture provides the grounds for developing ethical and moral norms. Philosophy is the power that supports culture."[14]

It is human nature to be attracted by the unusual, and one of the conditions inbuilt in such encounters is the compulsion to associate the unusual to the known. There is a propensity to consider the unfamiliar in the terms of the familiar. The typical result of this process is misunderstanding, whether dealing with objects, traditions, or customs. However, the unusual activities, may be easily understood when viewed from a culturally aware perspective. For example, Meddha is a kind of one-person story telling performed in front of a small group of viewers, such as a coffeehouse audience in the Turkish Republic. Relating the performance to the storytelling tradition of the southwestern United States or to the southern states gives a reference that is more easily understood. The connection is "comfortable" and "easy."

People affirm the arbitrary character of continuity by forming an acceptable opinion of the event or object. The cultural object is almost like something that is known to the viewer. The cause of discontinuity is often the result of the inability to comprehend different values or a search for absolute sameness. Abstract expressionism and surrealism are the same but different in appearance, just as the polyphonic singing of the Aka Pygmies of Central Africa and Georgian polyphonic songs are different forms of the same concept.

People assign importance to elements based on value (opinion). The enduring past's critical and prevalent value is to make the present known. It creates in the human mind the hypotheses that let people make sense of history. When a person has no knowledge of their history and makes no effort to know that history, the individual is doomed to a life without substance. "The Self is a mental representation of oneself, including all that one knows about oneself."[15] (Substance is describing the values and practices of those who came before. Substance is also a knowledge base representing the wisdom and understanding of earlier generations.)

There is a connection between the object perceived and the perceiver. Individual objects are often related by physical or intellectual connection with the viewer. The interaction between an object and viewer is established by physical, intellectual, or emotional conditions that link the object or event to the human thinking process and gives a means of connection with it, and thereby, (often a superficial) knowledge of it.

In the search for referential knowledge, people have attempted to bolster "belief" in the most rudimentary way, to appreciate the dynamics that shape the environment. There is always an area that is imprecisely known since it is probable that certain people will be driven to relate to their position in life in a general way. This place is an abstraction of the usual space allotted by direct involvement. It is also every person's mythical area. Things in the natural world including the sky and air and people-made objects are allotted their specific form of power or importance. Things of the natural world have a distinctiveness that exists on the inside, and in that form of authenticity, embody universal value for a specific culture. Such characters are a blend of form and substance, a joining of image and idea.

One of the older and most elemental beliefs is that the name of an object (or entity) represents the essential character of its essence. For example, Sowa-Rigpa, a medical practice of Tibet, is a centuries-old system that includes behavior and dietary adjustment, medicines composed of natural materials, and physical therapies to treat illness. It embraces the traditional Buddhist belief that all illness ultimately results from the three poisons: delusion, greed and aversion. The name calls attention to the practice. The difference between the name and the object (practice) is a philosophical determination. The physiognomies of the object (practice), in theory, are denoted in the name or its representation.

It is commonly thought that the naming of an item implies an essence of realities. This position comes from an understanding of basic knowledge. (Unfortunately, naming also limits recognition by categorizing the object, event, or activity.) It is true that a person can never know whether the things identified are identical to reality. Similarly, it is not possible to be confident that the words expressed are understood in the way as they are meant. Language often depends on social practice.

Naming objects, people, or events is a behavioral process according to John Dewey and Arthur F. Bentle (American philosophers) although what a thing is called in vernacular or colloquial terms has minimal significance. "If the negatives and the positives alike stand for something, this something is as thoroughly existential in the one case as in the other."[16] Some elements are called by different names, most of which are based on sound or image similarity; consequently, arbitrary naming often confound terminology. "Naming selects, discriminates, identifies, locates, orders, arranges, and systematizes. Such activities as these are attributed to thought by older forms of expression, but they are much more properly attributed to language when language is seen as the living behavior of men."[17] Identifying elements by name is important for humanity. This identification avoids misunderstanding and confusion; however, the name is not the element. Humans assign names for their purposes (usually organizational reference or to remember).

The symbolic name as identity is for more than daily purposes, it acts as a social or cultural marker; consequently, the Western world is festooned with names, titles, and acronyms. It is difficult for people to value a work of art or history unless a recognized name is connected to it. The name provides guidance and when there is no name as a point of reference, people are indecisive. The "name" may be synonymous with the "work" and as a result people may search for the name but give the work a quick look.

Words have meaning beyond communication. They reveal meaning not only about the context in which they appear, they also give identity to an objects or event. Words in English have different meanings just as objects have different identifying terms. (For example, a skillet is also called fry pan, frying pan, pot, cooker, and pail.) Words are not limited to one time, one place, or even one meaning. "A word transmits different and changing content or meaning in different cases depending upon the individual context in which it stands."[18] The recognition by "word" of a cultural element is a confirmation of linguistic capacity to communicate and reveal "things." Linguistic tradition is an important concern that is usually limited to the loss of indigenous language whereas, the corruption of major languages is often ignored.

Obviously, communication or the use of words to exchange information has much greater meaning when correctly understood. For example, Askiya is a genre of Uzbek verbal folk art that takes the form of a dialogue between two or more participants, who eloquently debate and exchange witticisms around a particular theme. Chinese calligraphy is the writing of Chinese characters as an art form, combining purely visual art and interpretation of the literary meaning. This type of expression has been widely practiced in China and has been generally held in high esteem across East Asia.

It may be supposed that deciding the precise meaning of each word will cause the character of the matter to be clear; in reality, trying to assess each principle, confuses the thinking process and causes a deficiency of comprehending instead of the reverse. For example, the words "good" and "bad" can be considered in comparative terms that must be explained before their purpose is known. Although moral decisions may not always have truth-value, they nevertheless, have a rational form. When decisions are a value relating to the idea of accomplishing good, and those decisions involve an essential, then good must have a coherent form. Although judgments do not have truth-value, they do have a logical form. Judgments (opinions) are deemed as a guide to activities in the idea that the person responsible for the judgment to do a particular act or not to do the act infers that the person declines the decision.

The designation (valuing) of particular words, objects, or events is a procedure that is central to linguistic activities. The word "fact," for example, is used to verify general exchanges of knowledge because the word implies something being known and what is known. The designation of an object as culture is also a verification of knowledge because the word identifies the element as a recognized (known) value. Regardless of intention, "...we can never know whether the things we perceive are identical to reality, we can also never be certain whether the meanings we express are actually understood in the same way as they were intended."[19] For example, who knows the right standard of beauty?

One name, location, or event may impart multiple messages, and each message may stimulate the interest of a separate group. Each group has a story to tell, and each may include a narrative (myth, legend, or story) relating to the element. One message—one purpose—is not more or less important than another, and each gives additional meaning and a valuable definition to the personal or communal cultural element. The "name" gives special acknowledgment to the person or item and separates it from other similar things. The more information provided about a particular element, the stronger the reference and the more meaningful the name. Defining the essence of an element often depends on the definer. The historic record of an element may have special meaning to one group or community and invoke no response from another.

Revealing cultural tradition, as with naming, is a multi-dimensional concept that is not limited by time, place, or practice. Names often make things what they are. They are reminders of human beings past and present and the events of humanity. The name is a reminder of an individual or a declaration of past events that is not forgotten. "Every name is very important to us," explains Dr Alexander Avram, director of Yad Vashem's Hall of Names and the Central Database of Shoah [Holocaust] Victims' Names. "Every new name we can add to our database is a victory against the Nazis, against the intent of the Nazis to wipe out the Jewish people. Every new name is a small victory against oblivion."[20]

"...[I]n our everyday interactions with the world, we relate to persons and things through mere names and concepts and engage in effective actions with respect to them."[21] Patrimony identification may use different but relevant names to refer to the same elements. The result of cross-cultural linguistics is an artificial construction of a personal design built around ideological suppositions that rely on imagination. "So, it seems that our very apparatus of naming things, and referring to them subsequently, presupposes the existence of identity, and involves the concept of identity."[22]

People relate to objects by name and interact with them as needed. Normative standards are not imposed upon basic communication, but on the ideas the message identifies. Language is a primary patrimonial element for humanity, and its use is an inherent part of human culture. Language in some form is not just necessary for communication; in addition, it has many other uses such as suggesting group identity and social stratification. Language is the symbolic storehouse of past meaningful experiences.

The languages of the world can be identified as being into one of two writing types: sound-based or meaning-based. "The sound-based system uses an alphabet, consisting of phonemes and syllabic signs, to express meaning that have no connection with their form. The meaning-based system, also known as ideographic writing, used graphic symbols to express meanings that have a close link with their form."[23] The cultural nature of language influences human perception of reality as well as what is important and related emotionally. Words express individual and community identity and belief. The communication system relating to patrimony is not just a way of sharing information, it is a means of influencing the thinking and attitude of others.

As an example: the Vanuatu archipelago in the South Pacific has a tradition of sand drawing. This form of "writing" is more than artistic expression and it is included in a variety of rituals. The drawings act as mnemonic designs to document and convey rituals, mythological beliefs, and oral knowledge about local history, kinship, and other issues. After the ceremony the writing is wiped clean. It is gone. The same is true of Tibetan sand painting. Once the painting is completed and the ceremony ends, the sand is swept together and the image is gone.

The relationship between the word "patrimony" and the object is an essential connection. It is through the identifying word that the patrimonial object reveals its true meaning. Although the word upholds the object and promotes its value, the historical appearance of the objects reveals a different time and place—a different truth. This is not a logical truth based on an assigned association but a reasoned relationship between thoughts and humans—a conforming of the abstract and the real.

In normal communication with the world, humans interact with people and things by names and impressions and participate in efficient activities regarding them. Hence, the standards of the world do not advance any ontological position over the things as implied by common exchange.

At birth a child can procure a language, but no one is born understanding a language nor are they predisposed to speaking one language. It is a learned ability. Nearly all human activities, from language to expressions of feelings, are learned. Social expectations that can cause people to hate each other because of race, color, faith, and beliefs are also learned. Social expectation causes people to place excessive value on the wrong concept (self, male, and imagination) and material elements (money, property, and objects). The values people learn as children create social expectations. However, social expectation is limited. It may bring social and cultural elements into harmony (or discourse) and is a means of identity (but it can become oppressive). Social expectations may be an unintentional unifying agent that leads to an enhanced sense of social identity and social connectedness. It may be a means for people to gain awareness of themselves.

Things to think about:

1. How have the ideals of humanism been arranged and rearranged over the years to fit different and often arbitrary purposes?

2. When was the word "humanism" first used in Europe?

3. What special value does culture have for people?

4. Explain how objects give evidence of a peoples' place in a social network as elements of valued relationships—the essence of humanism?

5. How is humanism a way of thinking, an attitude, and a way of viewing life?

6. Does every person have an obligation to conduct daily activities in a truthful way?

7. Why is teaching the theory of thinking not difficult but the understanding and use of thinking, ethics, or even passion requires more than knowledge (information)?

8. Do patrimonial elements often reveal the customs, practices, ideas, and beliefs of the time in which they were made and reference the history of their makers?

9. If the historic record of an element or objects has special meaning to one group or community, why does it have no meaning for another?

10. How does cross-cultural linguistics influence an artificial construction of a personal design built around ideological suppositions that rely on imagination?

11. Does every name have a limitation?

12. Is language learned?

FOUR

In Search of Cultural Reality

WHAT IS REALITY? That question identifies the philosophical basis for life and the culture of generations. The search for reality was initially identified with religious rituals, natural objects, and psychosomatic functions of humans and continues to challenge philosophers and theologians to the present. The question presupposes there is a diversity between what looks actual (real) and what is genuine; appearance is not adequate for its own actuality but is considered to rest on a higher reality.

Freudian psychology includes the reality principle defined as "the ability of the mind to assess the reality of the external world, and to act upon it, accordingly, as opposed to acting on the pleasure principle."[1] The pleasure principle is an emotional concept to balance impulse—cause and effect. The avoidance of reality influences the patrimonial recognition and speculation of individuals, communities, and nation/states. The individual may experience psychosocial problems by ignoring the reality of culture (loss of identity); for the community and people, the denial of reality can result in ruinous consequences socially and politically. Culture is the foundation of humanism and an essential element of social and personal identity. People should understand that reality depends on them, and when reality depends on people everything is correct (but not necessarily real).

The idea of "real" as it relates to culture and the "values, customs, beliefs, and symbolic practices by which men and women live"[2] can refer to the attitude of the person or group of people creating the objects or performing events. The activities of certain cultural events are intended, as are those of other creators or performers, to evoke culturally significant values. Creativity in this context is an expression of benefit.

Culture is a special type of reality. It is a means for rediscovering the valued elements of humanity. It foretells the social and ideological future of humanity and functionalizes the realities yet to be discovered. Culture as knowledge is not limited to consideration from the outside but is incorporated within the core of humanity. It can guide people to fundamental, albeit abstract, forms of social and cultural reality and these purposes remain abstract when separated from the realities that the element maintains. Education is the foundation of the reliability of humanity, and when it does not exist, truth cannot be found.

Reality is the manifestation of all that is real within a system, as opposed to that which is only imaginary, and in this context, defines a relative relationship with contemporary humanity. Reality and non-reality therefore may be the same. Confirmed by evolvement and enduring interdependence, reality is illusory not because it is imaginary but because the perception of reality deceives people into believing they are separate from the elements of which they are created.

The search for a fundamental reality "expressed itself in collecting from very early times."[3] In many areas of the world, East and West, much of the early cultural preservation was based on royalty and religious order. For example, figures representing deities were made as symbols of veneration and respect. In the Mogao Caves near Dunhuang, China, are examples of belief (religion) initiation and preservation. Cave embellishment was started in the fourth century CE and figures were added for a thousand years, creating a place of pilgrimage and worship for Buddhists. The culture within the caves is immense as documented evidence of aesthetic and religious practices over a long and continuous time. The Mogao Caves are being restored because they are the best known of the Chinese Buddhist grottoes.

Cultural elements may be inanimate with no innate ideology or meaning. "The earliest common use of the past was to validate the present ... tradition is the pre-eminent guide for behavior, especially if the precedent is believed, ancient, and constant. The past is an infallible [sometimes] source of truth and merit."[4] Contemporary society is backward looking even when planning for the future. People are limited by what they know, what they think they know, and what they remember from the past. The past often defines the present. The activities between the two extremes unfold in a familiar way based on past experience.

Idealistic observation views cultural elements not as they are but in forms that influence the senses, and thereafter only the emotionally influenced representations and not the objects themselves are considered. An archaeological site may stimulate emotional or intellectual responses for its historical importance that overshadows the tangible condition of the cultural element. Ideas about an archaeological site generate imaginary images whether there is familiarity with the location or not. "The popular notion is that a true idea must copy its reality."[5]

When truth and reality are absent the mind allows its imagination the flexibility to interpret.

Reality, conventional or theoretical, must have a basic cognitive foundation. Philosophical reality requires more than perception to justify distinctiveness. Philosophical realism is the opinion that portions of reality are ontologically separate from theoretical beliefs, hypotheses, and perceptions. Realism may be considered regarding the past, the future, the material world, and thought. "Realists tend to believe that whatever we believe now is only an approximation of reality but that the accuracy and fullness of understanding can be improved."[6]

The idea of "real" as it relates to cultural elements can refer to the attitude (thinking) of the person or group of persons creating or using the elements. For example, it may be "reality" that Guatemalans have in mind in the performance of the Rabinal Achí a Maya drama that developed in the fifteenth century as an example of pre–Hispanic traditions, or the "reality" of Baul songs sung by minstrels living in rural Bangladesh and West Bengal, India. These activities are intended, as are those of other creators or performers, to evoke culturally significant values. Creativity in this context is an expression of benefit.

Real is something that exists and not an imagined or idealistic impression. "...[C]hanges in form are perceived [but] this does not imply a change in reality unless a form has reality of its own. But, of course, form has existence only in dependence upon matter, for there is no form except in formed matter."[7] Though mainly psychological, there is also a cultural dimension to identify. Objects, places, and other physical and ideological manifestations reinforce individual or community identity but may not constitute true aspects of cultural or social validation. Each group (or person) must define its own history and the "things" that compose that history by unifying elements of belief, fidelity, and nostalgia.

Since the middle of the twentieth century attention has been directed to "reality, the character of meaning, the contrast between rationalist and empiricist approaches [as well as] the significance of awareness or unawareness in modes of thought."[8] The notion of rational reasoning is identified with the ordering of ideas. This rationality is concerned with the nature of the antecedents from which the reasoning begins, or with which it is associated. This premise recognizes that the thinking should be rationally or intellectually based.

The theory of reality addresses the state of things as they exist rather than as they may appear or might be imagined. This idea of reality contrasts with delusional phenomena. The idea of imagined cultural elements corresponds to myths and legends set in a timeless past.

Cultural value resides in its defining presence not just as an object but as a presence that defines the essential nature of humanity.

As the world's social values change, and historic indicators become expendable as much of the world has experienced the phenomenon of disposable history that is the symbolic aspect of social life. One thinks of the Sanctuary of Isis at Philae in Egypt[9] or the Medina of Fez in Morocco.[10] These locations are less difficult to conceive when relating the descriptions (whether written or projected) to similar locations that are familiar. Culture has a significance accessible to humanity for the common good, but people and communities have short cultural memories, and the ethos that remains is often modified by subjective and selective recollection. "[S]ymbolic culture is a product of past social action although its producers are not always easily identified."[11] When myth or fable is more interesting or entertaining than reality, the myth is remembered and transmitted.

Spectacles of the environment and the exploits of human activities are often pretenses but are considered to represent a reality. This form of reality may be sought outside the objects and activities identified by logic and motivated by all things expressed in time and space. This reality (true or false) is identified with a material-ordered system of existence, not intellectual or cultural. The change from a culturally patterned society to a material-ordered system has altered both the behavioral and cognitive response to the concept of culture as a valued reference to human existence. Culture is a source of identity and cohesion for communities and people disturbed by social changes and financial uncertainty. Humanism is possible when people are considered as conclusive instead of the hypothetical. When humanity is essential there is nothing superior to human judgment as the source of human principles. Humanism is a way of thinking (attitude) that endorses the principles for goodness and well-being, and these principles make human beings human and real.

Culture has a special place in the existence of humans. As a product of and for society, culture is in the mainstream of activities that include education, enjoyment, civic pride, and nationalism. Culture enriches social values and gives meaning to intrinsic ideals. It is the holder of memories that reinforces continuity and define group identity. Culture validates ideas so people can understand their surroundings and become secure in their communal settings. This joining of social elements promotes the remembering of social actions.

Consideration of continuity includes places or objects that establish a frame of reference. This qualification gives credence to the notion of patrimony as objects that are relevant to the continuity of identity within time. Time ensures the inevitability of change and the probability of society endorsing self-selected elements to symbolize patrimony. "Social relations as reproduced, and identities are formed through movement in space as they are played out through time. ... Human beings are involved in sets of relationships which are constantly mobile through both space and time."[12] The meaning and purpose of culture are defined by the authority but acted upon by people. All societies have mechanisms that include different ways for enforcing or regulating judgmental formation. Social values provide only a reference for various activities. The correctness of specific beliefs or attitudes may be questioned. People respond, in most instances, to circumstances or situations in ways that are culturally patterned. These responses reflect individual as well as group values and beliefs.

A Timely Existence

Philosophically there may be no past, present, or future but for the authentic cultural element, it may be argued that it manifests all three aspects of time. Social patrimony as a representation is essentially a virtual likeness, in that it is close to being something without being it. Patrimony is often an opinion of the present and viewing an element reinforces the idea of the element but does not necessarily authenticate or validate it.

Psychological continuity is an important principle of identity and a primary ingredient in the notion of true patrimony. There is, however, an illogical nature to the notion of continuity in reference to time and place. This concept requires that the place remain consistent for an extended identifiable time (although time may not be real). The requirement is often addressed by associating the continuing cultural ideas with an object or system of objects embodied in a place. Thus, any consideration of continuity includes persisting places or objects that establish a frame of reference. This qualification gives credence to the notion of cultural patrimony as "place" is relevant to the continuity of identity within the time continuum.

It is said that time is a voyager of the past. The past is a time (in this instance time is identified a measure of duration not chronology) that is difficult to define because it is whenever and wherever a person wants it to be. It is a time without restriction. A person can choose any time that they wish. The past society does not impose itself on the person whereas in the present society people have a defined position and distinctiveness. The flow from past to present acknowledges a wholeness that confirms the significance of all activities within the context of time. That there is a clear separation between the events of the past and the activities of the present demonstrates a continuous movement of elements that reflect "then and now." Every action depends on physical or mental recollection. The things with which humanity deals daily are either "passed" from previous generations in the form of social and cultural patrimony or learned by comparative steps using past knowledge. In contrast, social patrimony allows people to draw upon their past and to arrange those elements in ways that make sense in the present.

The happenings of the past, whether distant or recent, are recalled through the filter of time. Time is a common factor in social and cultural transformation. The objects or events can be markers of communal activities and identifiers of changes in contrast with the uncertainty of memory. Advocating social and intellectual cognition is part of communal activities and sharing that aspect of the community's enterprise with the others is a responsibility. This shared aspect is true whether the object is a rumor, gossip, or fiction.

History as an idea happens while it is being considered. The present is minimal and the immediate past is a moving point in time. The elixir of life, the peach of longevity and the dream of immortality were to stop the progression of time. Centuries of alchemic study and practice were unable to alter or control the movement of time. That life takes place through time is the inevitability of continual change causes society to endorse self-defining symbols to represent its social history. Although the symbols may be arbitrary, they are often qualified by time. The concept of "then" and "now" allows the past to validate the present and the present to project the future. Situational necessity promotes the invention or rediscovery of culture, or as it may be called "situational patrimony."

Situational patrimony is defined as the patrimony developed to meet a specific cause or circumstance. It has no time designation and is not based on historical evidence other than ideas expressed in the community or nation/state. It is created to meet the needs of the "situation." It often tells of the heroic deeds of a person or group of people in the service of the nation/state. (Situational patrimony is found in war museums or cultural spaces portraying local history. The war museum is often a place to find false or exaggerated situational patrimony.) The past is difficult to validate, therefore, true knowledge of actual events is limited or unclear.

The present is the only one of the three divisions of time that appears to last longer than the other two since the past is gone and the future is yet to arrive, however, the present is the shorter time—not even one day or one hour. Saint Augustine wrote, "In relation to the first hour the others are future; in relation to the last the others are past; and any intermediate hour comes between the hours which precede it and those which follow it."[13] The Buddhists contend that the present is the second between the past and the future.

"The present is an indivisible instant, whatever duration we assign it; the past is a length of time. Length lets us order and segment the past and hence explain it."[14] Events succeed or precede other events, making the concept of time an integral part of all patrimony considerations. Humans define their activities and events according to their relationship with other events and connections with the past.

Verified cultural elements have in common the factor of time as a part of their formation and the identification of elements is defined with reference to the value of time as well as space (location). Social patrimony, in contrast, may identify with time as an element of history; that is, the patrimony may be defined by its historical reference.

Time is a human-designed technique used to organize and regulate several activities that transcend human concepts like infinity. A nonexistence past does not preclude a relationship with the present. A social element is identified with the past because of its relevance to the present. The element may define history. "What characterizes these factors as temporal is precisely that they are never, like things of objective intuition, given to the consciousness simultaneously."[15] The ambiguity of time is an issue for cultural patrimony. The concept of an earlier time is personal and usually local because recollection is influenced by experience as well as knowledge.

Although the idea of time is essential to human life, the time duration process is theoretical instead of real. Life is measured by events and organized by the hypothetical concept of time. Consequently, the passage of time depends on other means to determine its progress; time is only a related factor. Things often occurred earlier or later than remembered. Events may be real or imagined, therefore they are frequently confused. The symbolic meaning and emotional significance of time as a cultural feature is implicit in many elements of daily life. People seek reassurance that time as reality transcends daily activities.

Conscious consideration (thinking) of cultural elements is an acknowledgment of time. That social culture as patrimony emanates from a time before now is understood, and that it is preserved for "now" is realized. Neither time nor space can be experienced, yet no other experience can be practiced without acknowledging their presence. Nevertheless, neither nature nor humanity can divide time into three separate and clearly defined dimensions. The three aspects of time—past, present, and future—are interdependent, and none can be correctly identified without the other.

Human beings who reflect historically should not think according to a generational lifespan but should plan in terms of a future that is not known by the current generation. The world requires a view of history that asserts the scale of humanity as a measure of social achievement. The cultural element recognizes a human measure and delimits the connection to the people to a particular culture, and therefore, the scale of that culture to the humanity.

Investigation of consciousness by Professors C.D. Broad, H.H. Price, Andrei Linde, John Smythies, and others question the presence of a "time" identified as "now." John Smythies wrote in an article in the *Journal of Consciousness Studies* (2003): "Contemporary 'common sense' thinks of the world as a collection of material objects [including patrimonial elements] extended in three-dimensional space and enduring in a separate Newtonian time."[16] Professor Smythies also stated: "*Special Relativity* unifies Newtonian space and time into space-time. It does not recognize any special universal 'now' of time."[17] Philosophically, the past and future do not exist, and physiologically the "now" does not exist. The activities of the world, nevertheless, may be based on belief, faith, speculation, and science that consider the "now" experienced as the past once removed. "The true nature of the present reveal[s] itself; it [i]s what exists, and all that [i]s not present did not exist. The past did not exist. Not at all."[18] (The wristwatch is a reference.)

Regardless of chronologic value, time has been inserted into the cultural tradition consideration process and maintains itself as a way of articulating meaning and importance. Time may indicate that something happened "then," and gives special significance to a vague distance from the present. The time reference implies whatever took place at that time and place no longer happens. Culture cannot rely on either time or space for validation, leaving only the values assigned by people.

Past activities and events are usually recalled through a filter of vaguely remembered time, whereas objects are true indications of community activities as opposed to the ambiguity of recollection. "Bringing culture back to a world suffering from the depleting effects of acculturation, in which entire generations have forgotten their past, is one of our greatest challenges."[19]

Time and space are necessary conditions for the identity of physical objects. Time and space are also associated with the history of a people, and therefore, it is reasonable to speculate that historical affiliation and collective memory are means for people to orient themselves to their past. Culture and history have similar roles (from an external perspective); however, culture has greater representative significance than the object, time, or place as identified by historical reference.

"[S]pace and time seem distinct from substances because they are causally inert, causally inaccessible—their aspects or properties cannot be altered by interacting with any other substance—and imperceptible."[20] Julian Thomas wrote in 1996: "Neither time nor space [can] be directly experienced in themselves, yet no other phenomenon [can] be experienced without postulating their existence."[21] Time comes before or after an identified event, but few people know when those times start or stop.

There may be unusual times when looking at a cultural element so completely different and unfamiliar that it avoids being immediately categorized due to cultural prejudice and assumption before analysis and identification. Once a cultural element is separated ideologically from its location, it no longer has a place in history, but may be said to embody all history. Examples are the rock drawings in Val Camonica (Italy) and the Gaudi buildings in Barcelona. They express an encounter between the real and the imagined (fanciful). The past is defined by the element and its origin and any change in either will influence the other. The element delineates the future as a type of unqualified present that reinforces its enduring nature. The difference may be defined as the degree of intensity, that is, the quantity of emotion.

Professor Julian Thomas contends "...that without time, we could not be conscious of other phenomena at all, and that no phenomena could exist outside of time."[22] This kind of thinking is fixed in Western space, and space is ambiguous and impersonal regardless of its presumed location. Time, as related to life, is not a social fixture because life itself is not a measure of time. This perspective of time is relative to the notion of a "radical separation, which much of the western tradition has maintained between the outer world of things, and the inner world of the soul."[23]

"...[It] is essential to recognize the distinction between the space of perception and the space of physical, and between phenomenal objects and physical objects."[24] People identify with both space and time, but both are relative and abstract. "Distance, for example, is made abstract by emptying out whatever is particular in the concrete intervals—it is reduced thus to a sole 'difference,' a difference of 'place,' which is a logical or salutatory distinction, a so-called 'pure reaction.'"[25]

Cultural elements are placed into categories of time, space, and type in which dates and place note each element. The characteristics of elements are classified and the material evidence of each object, event, or location is identified, interpreted, and registered. The descriptive information gives a special focus on the significance of when and where the activity or event occurred, and is therefore, a necessary part of the true patrimony of the element.

Certain actions may be defined as intuition when in reality they are feelings. The human brain recognizes intuition (knowledge acquired without proof, evidence, or conscious reasoning) as an accumulation of information stored for future use. The information is held both consciously and subconsciously and may be accessed as needed; however, feelings are personally valued and subjective. Feelings of this nature have no intellectual foundation but are based on emotion. This type of feeling should not be confused with the physical sensations based on prior knowledge, and a form of relational truth.

The changing nature of the cultural element is shown by what it means to see a world of reality; however, that reality vanishes each time we concentrate on it. A cultural element does not simply communicate with people it also conforms to their way of knowing. The mind is therefore in a practice of developing and re-developing the known world. World culture is molded into new experiences with new possibilities of having value in and for itself. Among those possibilities are the assignment of higher and lower degrees of value, the higher values being assigned to those elements which are more vital or involve a greater degree of perfection. This idea describes the evolving philosophical nature of humanity as a worldview, which seems appropriate to reference culture.

Revealing culture transforms the impression of another time and place. It is an objective self-defining concept in that it represents a level of knowledge and understanding. The cultural element enhances the subjectivity of the otherwise seemingly objective process of assessing humanity—value, purpose, and benefit. This reality may be the same for culture where age, use, and relationships can be projected with reasonable validity.

The belief that things evolve and endure interdependently describes a fundamental nature of existence that is not conditional on relations among discrete entities. The interdependence of the individual existence is an abstraction from existing relational dynamics. This conception of reality corresponds with beliefs of interdependence and impermanence. This approach can be understood, suggests Karl Potter of Washington University, "as a principle of psychology and habit. Karma seeds habits, and habits create the nature of man [people]."[26] (For the practitioners of Buddhism, the term "Karma" refers to the principle of cause and effect wherein the actions of the individual influence the future of that person.)

One action may be identified as better than another on a relational basis for assigning values. It is possible to assess the relative good of the cultural element based on its relationship to people and the beneficial service provided to humanity. Individual cultural values identified with established practices are less likely to cause a negative outcome than those chosen randomly or for personal reasons.

Cultural values (not monetary) may be assigned or rescinded, and self-interest is a precedent. Neither logic nor social responsibility guides human thinking, in such instance, when considering the idea of "right" or "meaningful." This attitude reflects a personal value system. Value is an indication of individual consciousness, and consciousness is the recognition that comes out of the idiomatic stress between possibilities and imitations.

Things to think about:

1. What is reality?
2. How do people know reality?
3. How is Freud's conclusion about the reality principle meaningful?
4. How does reality, conventional or theoretical, have a cognitive foundation?
5. What is the meaning philosophically of there may be no past, present, or future?
6. How is the ambiguity of time an issue for cultural patrimony?
7. Does a cultural element communicate with people, or does it conform to their way of understanding?
8. What is meant by the interdependence of individual existents as an abstraction from existing relational dynamics?

FIVE

Truth Is More
Than a Way of Thinking

THINKING CAN TRANSPORT THE MIND into the distant areas of the world and beyond and into limitless places where everything is wonderful or in total confusion. Thoughts seem very true, and they are, as thoughts; but when they are expressed, the truth becomes less valid and less rational. Truth should be absolute, contemplated, and objectified. Consider the role popular myth plays in many social and cultural activities. All things are ideal. Ideas about almost every aspect of life are influenced by preconceived notions based on myth and misconceptions. Stereotypes, clichés, generalities, and fabrications abound in most communities and people, and truth does not enter their thinking.

Truth must be a relational term because there is no "absolute" truth (as already mentioned). It is important to realize that truth regularly pretends to be false just as fallacy can pretend to be fact. Each statement of truth must be considered in the situation of use before the meanings are fully understood. True and false are usually identified with circumstances where value judgments (opinions) are required. Firsthand data may be evidence of truth, but perhaps it is only a gauge of what is reasonable to humans. "In its most unrefined form, truth appears as a regulative idea, as the task of unifying knowledge both from the side of the object and from the side of the subject."[1]

Truth is important to humanity, but technology is making it easy to disbelieve what a person hears or sees. Technology allows the production of false images and sounds or the altering of images by the touch of a key. Little is real. Communication by internet is a standard procedure. Copying and duplication of text and images is common practice. The idea of respect and personal integrity is overlooked or forgotten in favor of expediency. Although words and ideas are not labels and values of a transcendental idea of reality; they are an actual portion of reality and that is ignored. The correct understanding of reality is essential.

Socially defined truth is not absolute (the inclusiveness of a concept may turn it into untruth). The idea is "true," but the conditions are diverse. It is often stated that truth and good are synonymous, but the notion or meaning of "good" or "true" can be questioned. Truth can simply be what a particular people believe to be factual—what generates understanding from their limited point of view. Like truth, people attribute meaning to a variety of determinations they make every day. All these judgments involve resolve. The quest for truth is an endless process. Truth is a value, and there is no standard for truth that applies to everyone. Traditionally the two concepts good and truth have been linked, that is to say, the idea that something is good if it is true. But is that a fact? A false statement can appear to be good and serve the interests of those concerned just as a true statement may be bad (or not good) for all involved. It is assumed that the natural tendency of humans is toward good. If individuals respond to their true nature, their actions will have a predisposition toward good. It can be presumed that the idea of honest principles is founded on knowledge and experience, and usually make no claim to promoting absolute truth because people depend on their habits (good or bad).

Truth cannot be assigned to cultural elements but to the human assessment of those elements. The cultural ideal is inanimate and possesses no ability to be true or false. Culture as a part of the historical record of people has a value for the pursuit of truth. "Truth is not just a property of statements, propositions, or beliefs, it is a quality of being, of human beings and human activities."[2] Truth is based on knowledge. Truth as related to knowledge and the act of knowing is demonstrated by attitude and shared values. "[T]ruth is a relational property involving a characteristic relation to some portion of reality."[3] The reality of any situation is the result of compliance with established norms or of relying on pragmatic data. Individuals with no sense of reality are disinclined to be value motivated; therefore, they are unwilling to endorse the value of patrimony as a meaningful human reference.

Judgments are a part of all facets of a person's life. Decision making entails choosing between values. (It is not possible to exist without valuing people and things in some way.) Value implies the amount of significance (truth) of an issue, action, or object with the intent of deciding which activities are correct or which method is right to live by, or to explain the importance of various action. Value systems are based on beliefs as much as opinion (they are not usually based on fact); they influence the proper conduct of an individual or are the source of their calculated behaviors. A value decision is a personal belief. Usually, essential values are resilient and subordinate values are subject to modification. The simplest judgments involve good and bad values. In most circumstances, the options are discernible, and the conclusion is easy.

Socrates thought of truth as the highest merit and identifying truth with patrimony (personal history) as a challenging societal function. Truth in this case is "truth in value," a relational truth defining a culturally meaningful element. It may be correct that there is a psychological relation between the idea and object, although "abstract" stands for tangible or intangible connectedness. This relationship is subjective but is represented as objective. The idea of an object may be separated from its meaning to manifest an ideal. "They [objects or events] become memorable because of the experiences people attach to them."[4] The idea maintains truth because it is true to the object, whereas the object may or may not represent a concrete reality. "The maximum conceivable truth in an idea will seem to be that it should lead to an actual merging of ourselves with the object, to an utter mutual confluence and identification."[5] The assumption of this convergence is it brings together the idea, memory, and belief, to form a complete concept.

Truth is a universally maintained value that is acknowledged and endorsed by most people. (Most people realize the significance of truth although not all actively endorse it.) The primary impetus for truth is respect. The idea of truth is very challenging to describe as an intellectual fact. Truth as a theory fulfills an understandable requirement yet it is most easily defined by concepts that are the opposite. (Truth the opposite of falsity.) Truth validates an act, idea, or statement by attaching it to a larger or more recognized source. Many academics argue there is no criterion for truth that pertains to everyone. Most can agree there is truth as an idea, specifically thinking about something (as an idea) is believed to be true. An idea can be said to be true because it is formulated in the mind of a person and reflects conceptual thinking; however, once the idea manifests itself as a form of reality, it is no longer personal and may become false. Thinking is unencumbered by proof and is impossible to prove. It is an abstract process. The essential truths are not representations—not, that is, ideas, propositions, or symbols that can be separated from their source. Instead, the truths are lived, felt, and acted upon. (More on truth in Chapter Two.)

The pluri-dimensional nature of truth was realized at the time of the Renaissance. It is by this historical process that "the problem of truth pertains to the very movement of our civilization and lends itself to a sociology of knowledge."[6] It is the unification of truths that ideas, activities, and responsible actions bring together that influence culture and humanity. Truth in its various manifestations is unified under a banner of belief both clerical and philosophical, and the formations of truth influence the identification and adoration of cultural elements.

Truth is principally a link between two items, an idea, on the one hand, and an actuality separate from the idea, on the other. Reality in this unification is not an opinion. Many people acknowledge the value of truth identified in this way, but each interprets it differently thereby defining reality in a different way. Like truth, reality is not always real. The idea in truth is to identify the concept and subsequently to connect it to the purpose it represents. This connection can relate to the associated objects, a belief, an impression, or memory. The identification and approval of objects, including the emotional and sentimental elements, are a personal or communal issue, and can only be achieved by inclusive opinions. The object or event verifies itself through social inclusion, but this inclusiveness may focus on the object or event for only a limited time.

Truth is a value acknowledged by people because it represents something they (at least) know and esteem. There is for most people a desire for truth and a sort of perfection that can be acquired (for them) through tangible (material) things. They believe they can change their lives and the lives of others in their community (or family) through their activities. They learn that activity for the sake of form or activities that end in themselves are often senseless and unintelligent. The result of an act or action must be to support good in some way. Most people are alike, but they deviate because of practice, and when they lack self-respect or respect for others, they have no reason to be honest. Understanding and respect are central to truth. The challenge to truth is more than "lying" or "misrepresenting," as untruthfulness is an offence to social value. Words, ideas, and beliefs have minimal communal importance without truth.

Philosophically good and evil, true and false may be considered relational concepts. It is normal to consider "truth" as corresponding with fact, but there are facts both right and wrong. Often a person believes a situation is right although it is wrong based on personal belief. The concept of truth in role responsibilities means conforming to accepted principles. The human psyche has a need for truth, and truth is considered consistent with fact or reality. Truth establishes a sense of reliability and is given special value when activities go beyond the normal restrictions of society. Experiential judgments establish the foundation for humanistic purpose and practice.

Truth of this type is described as relational, that is, it is determined by the situation in which it is used. The obvious difficulty with relationalism is that there is no logic or reason for definable truth. Each situation can claim truth as authentic based on local or individual justification (opinion). The "agreement" concept of truth is individualized and does not transmit across social or cultural boundaries. The relevance of authentic culture as an element of truth is lost along with cohesion. There are aspects of culture that require assessment for truth because common agreement identifies those objects. Ideas and concepts are considered true only so far as they lead back to the world of intellect.

Truth is recognized in many different forms, and in this way is relational. (For example, the concept of up and down does not exist. They are relational values.) Freedom of thought about truth as a concept of correct thinking is gained through knowledge. This approach requires a reliable means to acquire correct knowledge and eliminate wrong thinking. False knowledge is often the result of unawareness, whereas correct knowledge promotes overcoming misconceptions to understand truth and reality. Correct knowledge and understanding are different from reflexive cognition in that correct knowledge is based on reality and not on an expression of reality.

As stated, truth has different forms. There is the truth of right and wrong, truth that defines reality, truth that has no meaning beyond the immediate exchange, and spiritual truth that has a meaning that is universal; however, truth is not always true. "Truth may mean conformity to fact or the agreement between one's thought and objective conditions. Truthfulness is the agreement of one's words with one's thoughts; it involves the intention and the responsibility of the person."[7] For example, a person can lie and believe it is true. Each truth is different in its application but the same in its origin; it represents respect. It is right to expect truth in culture as an inclusive humanity, but truth should not be based on the expectation of return, it should be a value unto itself.

The search for absolute truth is seldom pragmatic, it often becomes a question of which "truth" is to be accepted. People think the idea of truth is fundamental, and they are unable to justify words that are easier to comprehend than the concept of truth itself. An acceptable answer must depend on the facts that support a particular truth. Beliefs are important to social patrimony because they are only supported by ideas regardless of the topic, they do not actually identify with truth—only acceptability. Concern for the past, real or imagined, emerged from the infinite number of ideas and ideologies, which loosely compose what is thought of as modernity.

To establish truth based on matching fact is a rational method when it can be used, that is, when the conditions offer a suitable accurate reference. Some "ideas," especially those concerning an individual's beliefs supposedly founded on historical, cultural, or spiritual concepts, are difficult to substantiate based on factual knowledge. Traditional convictions often displace facts and amend the means of establishing truth. A person who is unequivocally certain that their opinion is the correct one is often unreliable. Such thinking precludes the person from acquiring different truths. For example, the rituals and practices associated with Kit Mikayi Shrine concern the Luos people of western Kenya. Legend tells that the Kit Mikayi Shrine is associated with the good fortunes of the Seme people and other Luo ethnic communities who live around the shrine.[8] This belief is based on legend and not fact and may not be true.

Truth is about perspectives based on shared values including the concept of consistent conditions. Truth is a part of everyday life but is not easy to accurately identify. "Tradition defines [truth] as an agreement, an agreement at the level of our power of judgment (of affirmation and negation), an agreement of speech and reality...."[9] Traditions give a measure of truth and stability to most activities. Such traditions may be invented and not as verifiable fact but have a value of truth based on unity of thinking and therefore represent the social patrimony of a community.

Objects of patrimony exist because they agree with the thinking of the group (community or individual). Conventional reality relies on analyzing the view of an object and comparing that assessment with available information. An object and its understanding are collectively related. One does not exist prior to the other, nor does one possess an ontological repute superior to the other. Items endure in relation to assessments, while understandings occur in relation to the articles.

The thinking about true and false is not restricted to words but must include actions as well. People pursuing a personal search for information often come across not one truth but several truths. Consequently, they are aware of a conflict in the conformity of ideas, in that to approve one truth is to deny another. The logic for this is that most acts denote meaning at some level, and if they are true—that is, they relate to what in fact is real—they are ethically accurate. This is if people presume truthfulness is the agreement of one's word with one's thoughts and actions. It concerns the intention and the reliability of the person. Therefore, it can be assumed that a statement or act that does not agree with fact, is false.

People may try to be honest, but when they follow the way of least resistance, they act in ways that are unreliable and can result in an undesirable action. In this sense, right (true) and wrong (false) acts reflect the predictable reaction instead of unbiased assessment. This position becomes more difficult when the action is founded on presumed conventionality. Common human pursuits may be in reaction to two forms of motivation. The first is those undertakings done as a means to an end even though they may not be pleasant or gratifying in themselves. The second is behavior influenced by commitment. These activities are realized even when there is no pleasure and no favored result.

Truth does not always conform to the standard of a rational truth defining a culturally meaningful element. (Remember: there is no absolute truth.) The importance of an action does not identify anything desired based on universal need and meaning. Values influence and are influenced by the way individuals (community) respond to circumstances. When culture is viewed as an idea as well as a social achievement, then the notion of describing culture becomes more complicated because personal ideas are not subject to collective consideration—relational truth—until presented to others. Culture concepts (in this case) are part of a method. The system is intended to present cultural considerations as fact and the outcome of qualifications, instead of as an arrangement of ideal objectives. This concept is expressed in the idea that what is true today will probably be true in the future. Truth about culture depends on several factors, few of which are unambiguous.

Truth is a subtle concept made difficult by the changing circumstances that affect personal standards. Truth is usually determined by accrued knowledge and respect. It is identified with situations that correspond with fact or actual occurrences. The validation of truth, regardless of the method used, should "define a standard" that has consequence for comparable situations. Whereas belief as a cultural phenomenon is described as acceptance of an idea without knowledge required to determine its truth. Knowing something is true simply requires believing it is true.

A measure of truth can be identified in many activities that appear unique regardless of their factual nature. Culture as a humanistic element represents a range of truths as determined by the circumstance. Social culture has its own unique form of transcendental truth. Each truth has a measure of value that reflects the related human element. The truth of most socio-cultural traditions may lay in the minds and imagination of individuals or communities although they are presented as including all humanity. However, truth does not always transcend time or memory. Memory helps project situations into the imagined future. The abstract reality of culture is to create the object representative of the people; thereby, the people may be comparable with others.

The objective of the subjective mind may be quasi-reality and not truth, and although truth is often defined as equaling reality, the two are separate entities. Truth is usually related to different defining aspects of a particular situation. Social, religious, and personal morals (social ethics) as well as laws and practices represent a form of reality but offer no verified truth. Social elements may be of unique value although they do not always represent truth, other than truth as known from subjective reality. Both truth and reality are in relation to the situation, and should not be considered separately; even so, the mind should focus on the truth.

When circumstances provide the appropriate factual reference, it is reasonable to determine truth based on corresponding information; however, this does not verify, for example, real versus social beliefs. Such information is founded on experience as well as practical understanding; but neither experience nor education ensures knowledge. "Truths ... relating to individual beliefs based on historical or cultural significance are difficult to validate. Traditionally held beliefs often supersede facts and complicate the process of determining truth."[10] Beliefs are determined to be real (true) when they satisfy the interests and needs of the people. There may be little difference between the secular and spiritual worlds for some people. Beliefs once accepted galvanize a societal energy that is both emotional and physiological.

Communication is a mode of truth corroboration. Honesty corroborates a degree of trust but communication is impartial for creating a feeling of trust. This is not to say that people are always honest when they send or receive messages, because they lie (for example, on the Internet). Lying is a socially permitted condition but lacking the belief of the honest utilization of words. The capability of people to perform in a verbally oriented society would be impossible regardless of the language spoken or written. (Most people lie regularly. They validate those lies as "white lies" and believe they are socially necessary.) There are limited general statements that relate to all persons in every culture, but there are several universal statements that pertain to most adults in most societies. In all cultures there is an assumption of truth.

Truth relating to beliefs is not easy to validate. Belief often displaces facts, thereby complicating the process of ascertaining truth. Although truth is a basic requirement of human interaction, it is based on shared values including the concept of consistency. Because truth is a recognized value acknowledged by most people, the ideals of truth do not transit social belief. The search for truth is an endless process. Most people say truth is important, but truth is defined as a personal or communal consideration.

There is an assumption that most people endorse certain truths; however, major differences often influence individual and group practices and attitude. People in a communal environment are considered more inclusive in their problem-solving methods, whereas persons in individualistic societies often view situations as personal and unchangeable. Different attitudes about group identity and the relationship of the past to current social and cultural values often results in disregard of traditional elements. Different values are entrenched in cultural practices and subsequently influence fundamental sociological and psychological processes. An assessment may be thought true for different reasons; that is, "because it has been empirically certified, or well corroborated, or because it is the best explanation, or the simplest and most conservative inductive projection of the data."[11] Practices relating to truth may appear flexible as circumstances influence the significance of decision-making; however, the meaning of truth is constant.

Culture can have truth as a point of reference that identifies continuity; therefore, the need for reality (the real) would be relevant. It is possible for culture to have a greater impact on feeling with truth as a factor. Knowing and understanding becomes more complicated when believing is a matter of personal importance. "Has the meaning erased the sign, or has the sign abolished the meaning?"[12] Cultural activities may modify the participant's sense of reality. This type of sensual modification is most common in professional activities involving aesthetic manipulation.

Expressions as Truth and Untruth

Belief is a world-wide phenomenon, as is the multilateral arrangement of the universe with heaven, earth, and purgatory (or their equivalents). People sanction some form of psychic devotion as a way for dealing with the social, physical, and emotional surroundings. Belief is an element of the biological process. Human beings are what they envision themselves to be, and those assumptions are dependent on their cumulative intellect and understanding. The relation between theory and practice is true only for the situation prevailing at the moment. Subsequently, that relationship can be replaced by new beliefs that agree with the perspectives to which those beliefs exist.

Belief in the spiritual that occurs separate from the factual world is a principal part in the enhancement of the human psyche (think about revered beliefs). All cultures embrace some form of expression devoted to belief in the spiritual realm. People have always needed to believe in something, a spiritual phenomenon or an object. Cultural affirmation of faith as a psychologically satisfying concept has had an essential role in the beliefs of people from the advent of known history. The spiritual also accommodates those times when humanity requires release from a state of being that is too restricting. Therefore, those beliefs relate to human freedom from any restricting form of life (prayer and the ecstasy of belief).

People have always had concerns about where they came from, where they will go when they die, and the environment in which they live. (See more on Life and Death in Chapter One.) Traditions, myths, beliefs give expression to those concerns that play upon the psychological agenda of all humans and fall within the accepted social patterns of group mentality. The evolution of culture is the outcome of people pursuing those factors of life they value and that reflects a condition of social progress. It is culture that joins the facets of human survival and gives those activities meaning. Culture also verifies how a people relate to their environment. One of the major developments in human existence was self-awareness. People became conscious of themselves and their relationship with the entirety of nature, and they began to change that expanse to meet their objectives. Out of that effort came the awareness that human survival was based on many factors, several of which were beyond the rule of people. This understanding conveyed the notion of hope and fear and formed the basis for an ideology of belief.

People in various societies are directed by beliefs and traditions that developed from former times. As stated, people frequently believed beliefs and traditions to be true. Ceremonials and rituals are often related to the acquisition of knowledge (as with the handshake, kiss, or graduation ceremonies) or the pursuit of knowledge that is associated with influence. The transfer of power to preserve cultural stability is accomplished in different ways corresponding to the practices and values of the community. As with most community-based pursuits, there are no firm peripheries that constrain the traditional influences. Societies change just as people change. A basic purpose of tradition is to protect habits and practices and thereby to encourage community character and union.

Social patrimony can be identified with communal activities such as the rituals and social celebrations as defined by the traditions of a society. Rituals remain as a constantly changing continuance that is a part of the rites. Rituals identify the relationship between the ritualized performance and the performers. The funeral ceremony is an example of a ritual activity for community members wherein the family, friends, and associates are the participants. The rituals may be different, but the concepts are the same.

Organized belief systems define the concept of truth in ideology, words, activities, relationships, and personal attributes. These truth formulations may be identified with social elements. The temporal process of truth unification includes many of the same elements. These elements are temporary, unstable, and changeable and therefore are not true patrimony. When it is realized that nothing is implicitly patrimony the proposed ideas and the facts become unreliable.

Particular pursuits are seen as positive whereas others are deemed negative for group harmony. Such an activity of harmony is Buk log, an elaborate thanksgiving ritual system. This behavior is viewed as normal for Subanen people in the southern Philippines. Behavior incompatible with group norms is generally opposed by social morals because they encourage constancy by acknowledgment. The moral significance increases as diverse groups and distinctive objectives are founded to support special interests. Group comprehensiveness and the capacity to adapt to group subtleties is a way of recognizing and conserving communal values.

The ritual is a basic element of communal consolidation. It is centered on a desire to understand the powers that motivate social life, and it reinforces social pride as human beings and managers of their fate. To illustrate this unique happening, the Fiesta de San Pachi, celebrated by the twelve Franciscan districts of Quibdó, Colombia,[13] is an observance of the community's Afro-descendant Chocó character, and fixed in popular religion. This ritual reinforces Chocó identity and encourages solidarity in the community, while encouraging originality and creativity through the revitalization of traditional knowledge and veneration of the environment. Countless ritual events are planned to permit individuals to triumph over the struggle between their wants and the behavior expected by society.

Cultural activities such as rituals and ceremonies are often community manufactured and represent the ideas and materials necessary for a viable society. Cultural deeds of some nature pass through several stages of evolution before arriving at their current standing. They usually occupy the stages of change successively without losing their identity as unique entities. These changes are temporary and constantly in flux. This transformation is influenced by the cognitive structure represented by members of the host community.

A great deal of life is about change, and events are held to indicate the changing of the seasons, coming of age, graduations, marriage, and other special events in the lives of people. All these events are circumstances for rituals. In these deviations the human body may be changed from one description to another by painting, piercing, and other forms of disfigurement. These self-imposed acts from pierced ears to circumcision are designed to enrich a person's life or to alter the "natural form." Some of these physical alterations including piercing ear lobes are common. (Male circumcision is the most common form of mutilation in the world.) Beliefs and tradition often dictate the conditions for physical change and embellishment. For example, cosmetics, plastic surgery (eye, nose, and lips alteration), bust enlargement, and even hair transplants are changes endorsed by society.

The ritual is a method of amalgamation and transmission that causes people to gather and to focus on a certain issue. This practice is a way for people to handle a celebration or crisis. Regardless of the kind of issue, rituals create sources of stability known within the people. Rituals are the verification of the constant upholding of traditions started by antecedents to act as patterns for human activities. For most people, rituals are a way of cultural diffusion developing for replication and imitation. Fraternal organizations of all types are examples that include various rituals and ceremonies that are passed from generation to generation until the actual meaning is lost.

There are at least three concepts about rituals and their function. The first idea is that rituals are achievement-concerned happenings because they cause something to occur. The second opinion supports the notion of rituals as demonstrations of belief and that they achieve their function by realizing a portion of the belief scheme. The third view endeavors to evaluate every ritual based on its task in a specific community, discounting category. The first two meanings could designate a ritual subject to how it was conveyed by external appraisers. As neither the foresight nor projected results of various rituals is realized, the inclusive method noted by the third choice seems the most functional. Rituals are a means of giving expression to feelings. These opinions maintain the psychological importance of rituals. In general people endorse rituals because they need them.

People acquire an enhanced sense of history by taking part in the ritual events associated with tradition and by creating activities that demonstrate a knowledge that has an educational as well as an expressive element. Ritual behavior enhances the people's perception of who they are. Traditional ritual activities grant an enduring nature to the culture of a society that otherwise would disappear in the fluidity of mindlessness. Memory reinforces and augments perception, which becomes more comprehensive to include several related reminiscences.

The ritual is a central part of communal conformity and a method for realizing and upholding shared solidarity. It confirms the idea that people are continually aided and influenced by the deities (as exemplified by the Škofja Loka Passion Play of Slovenia,[14] based on the ancient works of a Capuchin monk, and Buddhist lamas chant of the monasteries of the Ladakh region of Jammu and Kashmir, India). Though ritual events may be an unwarranted practice for certain individuals, the ceremonies impact the activities of many persons and confirm the convictions of the group as shown by their prolonged continuation.

Because the ritual world is basically of its own creation and dominated by the requirements and beliefs of the people for which it was developed, it is a way of prompting a group endeavor. Rituals cause people to work for a prearranged objective and to realize a predicted outcome. They are considered to have a definite function in the host community or nation/state that is consistent through time. Such rituals are overtly related to beliefs. Rituals of this kind can be identified as an arrangement of symbolic activities that are centered on procedures endorsed by groups for specified purposes (for example, religious services, fraternal rituals, and social ceremonies). The ritual practice develops within the culture, promotes the pursuit of cohesion, and reflects the established customs of that society. This type of rituals is meaningful because it reinforces the ties that unite the advocates to their activity, and bonds the person to the society of which they are a part.

The ritual is an essential element of social unification for many communities. It is based on an aspiration to control the dynamisms that impact humanity and to substantiate the self-respect of human beings as controllers of their own destiny. A principle purpose of rituals is to stimulate peoples' enthusiasm and to remind them of who they are. Many ritual undertakings are devised to permit participants to challenge the encounter between instinctive wants and the demeanor expected of humanity. The characteristic of the ritual is exemplified in nearly all sacred activities. For example, Saman (the dance of a thousand hands) is one of the most popular dances in Indonesia. It originated from the Gayo ethnic people from Gayo Lues, Indonesia. It is normally performed to celebrate important occasions.[15]

In many ritual activities there is an element of make-believe. That characteristic is true whether the event is sacred or secular. Such emotional measures apply beyond the range of human understanding because the existence of a system of beliefs for personal conduct that follow the requirements of society are included in ritual practice. The structure of a social system embracing dramatic productions that involve the consistency of the society are the items of that system of beliefs. For example, the differences between Eastern and Western thinking about sacred activities. Western people are generally material-bound, and unmindful of the essence of their own being. Eastern humanity, in contrast, generally acknowledge the world of essentials, and their thinking is fixed on the fundamental nature of being.

The ritual is a chronological connection that relates the past to the present and the current to the future. It is a means for the amplification of time and place. The anticipated result of a ritual is the corroboration of belief and a reassertion of the power (authority) by intensifying the importance of the extraordinary world. In the ritual act, there is a merging of the ordinary and phenomenal worlds in ways that create understanding between the two realms, and for the advocates' truth and belief to be connected.

As an established practice rituals often explains and validates those issues that promote social harmony. They usually celebrate the ways of "those who came before" by addressing situations in a prescribed manner. Ritualized activities are the primary occasions for displaying the objects and costumes associated with traditional activities. The ability to attach special meaning of these objects because of their connection with other persons is essential to the ritual processes. Rituals (and ceremonies) for most people involve several aspects of cultural significance and are strong factors in the maintenance and continuance of cultural solidarity. These activities regularize social and cultural ambiguities and are the means for expressing and reinforcing social unity.

The ritual in group practice can cause normal life to be postponed. It is thinkable for ritual activity to reinvent the underlying connection between mortals and immortals and to reorganize that relationship. The movement from secular to sacred time created by a ritual also implies a provisional affiliation, as the liturgical time is a lengthening of the time when the ritual (of a sacred nature) was previously enacted. A ritual is an allegorical portrayal of the necessary components connected to human life. Rituals are often a contrast between construction and demolition, pleasantry and tragedy, and the sacrosanct and secular. Those subjects are so intermingled that it is often problematical to identify their presence.

The lives of people are impacted by rituals. The ritual sphere produced by a culture is basically of its own creation (as stated) and dominated by its understanding. It is a way of motivating a group endeavor. Rituals bring together group members for a prearranged reason and to accomplish a predictable outcome. Rituals as confirmations of group consistency are methods for accomplishing and sustaining stability. An early example of ritual observance is shown by the anthropomorphic figures located in Les Trois Frères cave in southern France.

The motivation of various rituals, irrespective of the place, is to emphasize accounts of the cultural events of past times. (As examples, Khon masked dance drama of Thailand that depicts the glory of Rama, the hero and incarnation of the god Vishnu,[16] and the ritual journeys in La Paz during Alasita to procure "good luck" miniatures associated with Ekeko, the god of fertility.[17]) These activities were brought forward from the past and were implemented as a celebration. They were granted traditional importance and integrated into a scheme of ideas that passed from generation to generation as topics of social reference. No society has been discovered that such traditional ideas were not observed in some form.

Human sentiment is strongly associated with rituals, and though it is an important part of social activity, it is not a true basis for the ritual. Once the expressive attributes of the event are in the command of participants, the ritual comes to an end and the affair turns into an expression of sentiment. Because rituals are communal endeavors, they need a certain orderliness, and too much passion hinders performance and management efficacy and permits the partakers to engage in personal activities.

Rituals originate underneath the basic aegis of humanity and are obsessive inclinations caused as a reaction to communal or nation/state situations as well as other external stimulus. Nevertheless, it is obvious that people want and need rituals. It is evident that cultures perform rituals to safeguard the welfare of people or to achieve social unity. Rituals based on tradition make use of the inventiveness of both those presenting and those watching the enactment.

Rituals often depict myths, even though the connection is not plainly described. Sometimes the myth is the literal script of the ritual action, while in other situations the myth is only a stimulus for the ritual. Early dramatizations with mythical foundations generally related to the daily needs of the people (food, sex, social activities, family life, religion, and life in general). However, some dramas have no mythical or sacred basis and are only dramatizations of social activities that have popular acceptance. These dramatizations changed with each enactment while the basics of the story remained the same. Dramas of this type often included statements of acceptable moral practice and are intended to validate or teach a social or cultural custom. Regardless of the source, human sentiment is closely affiliated with rituals and, although it is a crucial component of the activity, it is not the origin of the ritual.

Giving voice to a social or cultural myth is the sharing of an inner knowledge relating to the past that has as its objective the identifying of semi-remembered practices and procedures. The positive part of an externalized myth is the sharing of both the knowledge and the past. The remembering of the myth gives authenticity to the historical element as a real (although usually imagined) activity and promotes a communizing reaction. The value of this assumed reality might change when the myth is exposed to logic or reasoning; nevertheless, the idea of culture is sustained.

The myths of a people often provide the models and programs upon which internal identities are molded. Myths, whether stories, legends, or tales, are found in all cultures. Creation myths in different culture usually have similar features including the "in the beginning" element that identify the creation of the world and the origin of humanity. (See also Chapter One.) The myths are believed sacred and honest accounts of the source of humanity and are essential elements of most religious traditions. Myth is a means of conveying the "imaginary but powerful world of preternatural forces into a manageable collaboration with the objective facts of life in such a way as to excite a sense of reality amenable to both the unconscious passions and the conscious mind."[18] For example: Cheoyongmu is a Korean mask dance centered on a legend. It is also considered a shamanistic dance because it is performed at the end of the year to drive away evil spirits.

People have identified cultural elements that relate to beliefs and myths. The idea of beliefs is multi-faceted and include traditions, personal, and community activities. Such ideas are indispensable parts of all cultures. Myths glorify, fabricate, and at times provide a degree of truth that defines or explains human attitudes and practice. The meaning of a myth includes the basic character and social significance of the story and the relevant culture. This process identifies the incorporated human values and traditions acknowledging that myths are shaped by time and prevailing beliefs and practices.

The myth can be viewed as a demonstration of the knowledge of culture. A myth may require the entirety of the mind to find its meaning instead of simply the intellect. Myths are a part of the spiritual development of humanity that often deal with the actual instead of the ideal. "The ancient myths of every culture tell the same story of our search for wholeness. As the mind explores its own depths, it uncovers archetypal images that sustain and guide the journey inwards."[19] Myths often emanate from an indistinct time (past) and are believed to express accepted social history. "Myths are messengers of social and psychological exchange from person to person and from generation to generation."[20]

A myth is a means for bringing the imaginary to fruition but compelling the nature of extraordinary circumstances into relationship with an identifiable situation to stimulate a feeling of reality agreeable to both an objective (outcome) and the conscious mind (reason). Fables are different from myths. The fable is a story and does not provide rational logic for identifying and interpreting patrimony, but it makes visible something from the imagined time and place of people (examples are Rumpelstiltskin and Pinocchio). The fable resides within imaginary history and often has patrimonial meaning because it describes elemental values. (The fable often includes animals, legendary creatures, and imaginary objects, but they usually have a moral.)

Instead of focusing on the details of the sequential progress of the group (or community), myths supply the necessary stories to explain the measures that caused the people to unite. Myths also describe in symbolic expressions the circumstances of the social environment that permit the group to recognize and advocate that relationship. Myths of association are a critical subject of the mythological arrangement because they verify the distinctiveness of the group (or community) and define the limits of an individual's life.

Myths are a critical means for considering the complications of social transformation. An important function of a myth is causing a situation to be seen as accurate, different, and separate from everyday events. Myths in most cultures interest the people by expressing cultural opinions or by frequently expressing sentiments. When a community has little true history to justify its survival, there were abundant myths to call upon for endorsement. A myth, in the majority of cultures, narrates a time-honored anecdote that describes an incident, routine, or belief germane to the social solidity of a community. They are usually detailed stories centered on opinions (or beliefs) instead of verified evidence and related to the exceptional events of a certain group, society, or culture.

Most socio-cultural myths have a purpose in their originating location, and by using marginal information about related events or circumstances they are believed to be important. Determining value by speculation or imagination is problematic, since the time, ideas, and the influences in the real world often make factual identification difficult. When basic facts are absent from the model of understanding, or do not identify objective qualities, the element often has minimal cultural importance.

The idea of correct and incorrect human activities is by no means an original concept. It has continued unchanged for years; nonetheless, a difficulty often arises when people do not comprehend the idea of good as a comprehensive way of thinking. As moral reasoning, expressions such as "good," "value," and "truth" require attention not as subjective considerations but as inclusive ideals. Culture is about equality. It has no divisions based on ethnicity, gender, economic status, belief, or age. It is inclusive of all people. Though culture may be a thought-provoking social issue because of the exact concept of equality, it maintains that people are equal but not identical. The essential idea of equal is respect with equal dignity of all human beings. It is a social normative that everyone deserves the same respect and consideration, including the possibility to make the most of their lives and talents.

Things to think about:

1. What is the nature of reality?

2. Is truth as it relates to individual beliefs based on historic or cultural significance truly that difficult to validate?

3. Why is there an assumption that most people endorse certain truths?

4. How is it possible for there to be more than one truth?

5. Can the idea of an object be separated from its meaning of an ideal?

6. Why is a myth about imagination?

7. Is there a ritual connection from the past to the present and the current to the future?

8. Do creation myths in different culture usually have similar features including the "in the beginning" element that identify the creation of the world and the origin of humanity?

9. How do myths provide a degree of truth that defines or explains human attitude and practice?

10. Are myths a part of the spiritual development of humanity that deals with the actual instead of the ideal?

Six

Ways of Cultural Recollection

THE CULTURAL NATURE OF human beings consists of various elements, but two of the most noteworthy are memory and symbols. Memory is the foundation of tradition, focused thinking, and sustaining stability. Symbols unite ideas into identifiable impressions to fortify memory and thinking. The record of culture is a kind of related memory that involves a collection of events and objects arranged in a way to explain the physiological, sociological, and emotional tradition of a person or group. "...[E]verything we know involves memory."[1] In this array of semi-tangible components are the schemes and measures for uncovering and describing the past.

Mnemonic words or actions are a memory aid used to distinguish aspects of the past. They help in remembering an activity that relies on the event-story, not the event. A shared memory can contrast two features, real and imagined; consequently, the concepts of memory vacillate between two worlds. Differentiated to the extreme, the individual memory dwells in either an enchanted or disgusting place. The enchanted memory world has wondrous nature and fantastic things; whereas, the disgusting memory may include heroes and villains is a comparatively dark world, but individuals may wish to belong to both worlds. The two worlds exist, side-by-side, but have different realities and different perceptions of associated meaning. People seldom have a clear idea about past things; therefore, the true world is often located between the two extremes of the real and the imagined.

"Memories label a diverse set of cognitive capacities by which we retain information and reconstruct past experiences, usually for present purposes. Memory is one of the most important ways by which our histories animate our current actions and experiences."[2] Memory is an element of personal identity although recollections are often inflated by emotions and may be influenced by feelings caused by affection (caring), sorrow, or social obligations. Memories influence decision-making, both for the individual and for a community. Memory is a factor in

97

moral and social life because human identity is fixed within time, and it gives meaning to human-defined elements. It is a significant factor in the human/time relationship; therefore, a person with no memory can be said to have no temporal reference.

Memories are a reservoir of past information, but they can never be as detailed or factual as reality. Memory, knowing, and belief are associated in this concept, but each is difficult to validate. Communal history is usually a recollection of illusions. "The distinction needed ... is between the illusion of a collective memory and illusion within the collective memory."[3]

The past is a constant part of the present in the form of tradition or dogma. People are often reminded of the time "back when Grandpa was young." "When we remember any past event, the memory flows in upon the mind in a forcible manner, whereas in the imagination, the perception is faint and languid, and cannot form for any considerable time."[4] A memory is a feeling that is located in the past. The memory preserves the original form in which its elements were presented, and that wherever people depart from this memory in recollecting anything, the process is falsified. Concepts are often stimulated by false memories that result from persistent beliefs or repeated misinformation. The generation effect of the intellectual obstructions is an acknowledged experience where repetitive exposure to a belief, suggestion, or false information is better remembered by each subsequent generation. "When the ideas suggested by something are widely shared, those suggestions become implications. When the suggestions are not widely shared, they remain suggestions or 'free' assumptions."[5]

The past relies on memory; therefore, "...the things of the past are never viewed in their true perspective or receive their just value, but value and perspective change with the individual or the nation/state that is looking back on the past."[6] Remembered and preserved events comprise the historical record of a people and place. The role of history is to find information that will add to the formation of an acceptable view of the past. Patrimony may be historical evidence and a means of reinforcing memory.

The characteristic and importance of certain elements may differ, may not conform to the ideals of people or community. The memory of events is often distorted giving different values to real or imagined actions. It is difficult for people to retain memories of isolated events that relate to similar times and places. Memories may require connections to assist in the remembering process, that is, connecting the familiar with the unfamiliar. The practicality of memory is confirmation of the past.

Avishai Margalit (professor of philosophy) wrote: "A shared memory of a historical event that goes beyond the experience of anyone alive is a memory of a memory, and not necessarily a memory that, through the division of diachronic labor, ends up at an actual event."[7] Professor Margalit emphasizes, "This kind of memory reaches alleged memories of the past but not necessarily past events."[8] Memory reflects "knowledge from the past,"[9] but it is not necessarily knowledge about the past, nor is it necessarily true knowledge. Memory provides the information that may be believed, but belief is not the foundation for truth. Memory may recall interesting and socially acceptable information, and it may lead to valid (or interesting) information about past events. Social beliefs are usually only communal traditions or memories, but they are ideas or customs that reflect knowledge of the present as well as the past.

The different types of memory are the most studied area of cognitive development. Memory is the "primary form of mental representation from which all other forms, including concepts, categories, schemes, imagination, and plans, are derived."[10] Memory of traditions is encouraged by two separate but interrelated methods. One recollection inducement is verbal notices conveyed in speculative expressions. This method includes ceremonies and rituals and consists of a scholarly and frequently evocative semantics. The other way is the use of images that include representations and different figures of material as exemplified by the objects related with the idea. For example, the idea of the Central Garden of Cuenca, Ecuador, or the night market of Liujia, Taiwan, are less difficult when relating these locations to similar places that are familiar. The idea of physical conversion presents both a verbal and graphic reminder that identifies its foundation to a former time.

The past may be defined as the events or activities that happened before a given point in time. It is contrasted with the time defined as the present. The idea of the past is based on the linear methodology in which humans experience time as accessed through memory and recollection. The past is determined by two points of view—the definite and the theoretical. The definite approach intends to discover and describe the actual happenings, and it requires the adjustment of ideas into a rational system of understanding and endorsement. The theoretical approach is often identified with "good" (ignoring the bad or unacceptable), that is, it insists that unless an event or activity is related to a measure of good it could not otherwise be achieved and would lose its rational authority.

Time in all cultures is separated into different realities, and people are a small portion of the secular domain but have a larger importance in the material realm. People identify with the present, but socio-culturally they acknowledge the preceding time and look forward to the future. In contrast, ethereal time is constant and infinite by concepts of past, present, and future. Ceremonies and rituals connect the two times and allow a stability of the people. Cultural events and places join time and place. The cultural occasion carries a look or idea that people think they know from the past. It is an idea (reality) people value and trust more than the hypothetical.

Memory is an element of time associated with all locations and activities; however, it is limited in its capacity to recount history. The events stimulated by memory are often less real or more irrelevant than experienced. Personal or communal recollections do not transfer to others seamlessly or with equal importance from generation to generation. New methods have altered the way locations, people, and objects are viewed, although old ideas (memories) and old things continue to be fascinating.

Time (real or unreal) is an essential factor in the relationship between event and memory. The longer the event and recollection are separated by time, the less factual the recollection. Memory as a short-term event quickly loses details. Recollection must be regularly reinforced to maintain integrity. "[T]here is an important qualitative difference between experiences at the time of their original occurrence, and at some time when they are either remembered or anticipated by the imagination."[11] This relationship of time and thinking has a universal nature and influences memory regardless of how people may be culturally and socially aligned. There is a tendency to exclude the past (memory) and future (hope) in various cultures relying on context for temporal reference. This approach to measuring time relates to the nonessential nature of time.

Recollection refers to what is remembered, whereas memory pertains to both the ability to remember and what is remembered. A collective memory is the means for people or communities to orient themselves to their past. The process of remembering should at the same time acknowledge that all aspects of presumed reality are subject to change. The collective memory of a people is of particular significance. It is the chronicle of a people and a record of former activities. The use of symbols or images, including photographs, to give a reference for the recall of words or activities is necessary for most people. Imprinted upon the human mind are the stories and activities that define the group (community or family), and this prompts the recollection. The symbols and images aid in recovering the correct (or semi-correct) information about a specific occasion or narrative. References can encourage the recall of many words or a complete story that gives meaning and clarity to social activities. For example: The Byzantine chant of Cyprus and Greece is a vocal form that has endured for more than 2000 years. It is passed on acoustically across generations and uses different techniques to highlight the syllables of certain words.[12] It helps people recall the past.

The memory process requires incoming information to be encoded, stored, and available for retrieval. The storage process maintains the information for short periods. A part of the memory process is the retrieval of stored information requiring the location and return of data to the consciousness. Retrieval may be easy or demanding depending on the type and complexity of the stored information and the complexity of the encoding process. Time and memory are interconnected in the encoding, storage, and retrieval process. However, people neither encode nor recall incidents exactly as they take place. People fabricate a recollection of the event, and this creation consists of numerous factors including the communal and cultural framework of recalling.

Memories are not new or necessarily authentic. They are transformed every time they are accessed. Each time a memory is recalled, it is then re-encoded in a similar, but not identical way. Memories are not stored in an inactive state and then reclaimed with believed perfect clarity; thereafter, they are available for reentering the thinking process. Retrieved memories are usually stronger; however, the re-encoding can influence how the information is remembered. Facts may be changed, and certain parts of the memory may be strengthened, weakened, or lost depending on which element of the brain is activated. The idea of memory and change is exemplified by Radif, a collection of melodies preserved through generations by oral tradition in Iran.[13] Radif is a collection of old tunes that are passed from masters to students. Eventually, each master's interpretation added new songs to the collection. The continuation of these songs is contingent on each generation's memory because the melodies are conveyed by oral tradition only.

Certain thinking exists in the present to call the past to mind; however, there is a tendency to project current understanding into the formative time. Memory is constantly revised where it is influenced by current source material and past actions. "...[E]vents of the past cannot be kept; the events of the future cannot be caught. But the mind is too easily possessed by such images."[14] The past has its own historical motivation that is unknown to contemporary people. Tradition as a remainder of previous life suggests the possibility of survival—that is, going beyond the current state of being. Traditional objects epitomize memory and dreams. People worldwide endorsed this same dogma as a part of their history. "Afterwards" as the life beyond is a primary concern for people in all nation and all beliefs.

Remembering is a necessary part of the social and cultural environment. People like to remember the past and to guide the collective memory. It is an ideal primer for the remembering process. The collective memory does not maintain the same importance in all times and places. Although these references should not be forgotten, remembering and forgetting are equal aspects of the memory process.

A person has two aspects of the memory process—one individual (personal) and one collective (social). Maurice Halbwachs (1877–1945, French sociologist) maintains individual memory is reinforced when others remember the same or similar objects, events, or activities. There are numerous reasons to substantiate the parochial nature of memories. Just as people are affiliated with several groups at the same time, so the memory of the same fact can be identified with different agendas, and memories are connected in a person's thought in various ways. The "collective" recognition of past circumstances allows the individual to reconstruct a body of memories that are recognizable. The person has one memory process that reinforces individuality, and a second process that declares objective recollections of relevance to the group. The social memory can be relied upon to fill the gaps in individual recollection when needed.

The memory relating to perception expands to accommodate additional information, ideas, and images. The concept of expansive recollection and the influence on perception has a logical foundation. The mind holds many images and ideas that are stored in the subconscious, and they may be called upon to add dimension or clarity to an issue. The same perception occurs for other locations formulated in the thinking process. The assumed recollection stimulates the process by bringing images and ideas together to form an often-new perception. Eventually, the perception and the person or location blend until there is no separation between them. The imagined view of the element is as strong and real as the actual person or location. Reality is obscured.

Memories are curious in that the person can change the memory to be as pleasant or appalling as they wish. A memory can be as dramatic or dreamy as the individual desires. What makes memories common to a group of people is that they (memories) are a part of the totality of thoughts common to the group. The same process occurs when attempting to localize memories. Common local social activities identify shared memories for a community and people.

Communal memory may not transcend generation gaps, and education does not define or clarify such pseudo-cultural events. Local history books are changed, and memory is distorted by emotions. Reality and fiction are easily combined. An informal and less restrictive means for narrating informal history is the source of much communal memory. This exchange is called "gossip" (hearsay) in its basic form, or it may be represented as a factual recounting of events. The narrator is known and believed, and subsequently the stories (unfounded information) are repeated based on memory, and become unrecognizable after a number of re-telling.

Persons outside the group may not believe the same stories as persons within the group. The difficulty with this is that group invested value is not transferable—the emotional attitudes cannot be assumed by persons dissociated with the sign, symbol, or activity. The results of this disconnect is the appearance of disrespect that can result in destruction of group venerated objects or ideology. This decline is inherent with the gradual dissolution of traditional practices.

People often identify and elaborate different viewpoints when telling of events, acts, and beliefs regarding persons living outside their community. These opinions are usually intermixed with current historical and social references to supplement relational and sometime irrational information and experience. This process uses current thinking and relate elements from another time and place. It is difficult to think about the past without implying a relationship with the present.

Beliefs handed down within a group often have symbolic connotations rooted in the past. While it is often believed that beliefs have dated pasts, many are created intentionally over a short time. However, belief is a necessary part of social memory for focusing people on a subject. Performance verifies communal significance based on formalized activities that are believed to repeat the practices of the past. Repetition adds importance to the practice. Traditions and customs are repeated for the benefit of communities and social groups, but they are not true patrimony. The Otomi-Chichimaca people who live in the semi-desert area of the state of Querétaro in central Mexico are an example of this practice. They have established traditions that express their special connection with the area topography and ecology. These practices are not true to their history or the universality that proclaims a traditional event that is new.

Belief is social action even when the belief originator is not known. When belief is more interesting than reality, the belief is remembered and transmitted. "Belief systems are cultural, but acceptance or rejection is social, and it is often myth that influences the individual and society in the decision-making process."[15] People endorse beliefs that make their life easier regardless of the source of the information. Belief reinforces ideological acceptance that something or someone is true or real. This notion of reality bolsters the psychological validity of the belief and amplifies the importance of believing. Beliefs may change the nature of reality. William James wrote, "Beliefs are really rules for action, and to develop a thought's meaning, we need only determine what conduct it is fitted to produce; that conduct is for us its sole significance."[16]

There are numerous beliefs that bolster everyday life to advocate the idea that the merits of the world are basic on the parts. The daily undertakings of many people are augmented by ritual events that are honest or dishonest. The ritual enables a sociological and physiological stability by equalizing the emotive needs of a people. They advocate established beliefs and at the same instance make them accurate. The preservation of beliefs is an indispensable part of conserving community memory and rituals have a central responsibility in that activity because they are older than the people who present them and remember their origin. That condition acknowledges the tradition of the ritual actions that are created on beliefs and memory and forwards them from generation to generation devoid of accrued learning.

Many social activities are based on repetition. Certain acts are repeated regularly, and those recurring elements are often the basis for erroneous beliefs. When certain elements (objects or events) and societal activities are frequently repeated with the same expected outcome, they are remembered. For most people, repetition reflects a certain commonality, and the group response to the cultural element is situated on emotion-stimulated experience. The people in those circumstances observe not the cultural element but themselves, and the truth of that observation is affirmed by an interplay not founded on reason or logic but on social committal and expectation.

Social recollections represent an individual's past experiences and constitutes the largest part of an individual's memory. Memory is a means for stimulating actions and activities. The nature of memory is fundamental to the human capacity of recalling past experiences and is a primary characteristic of an individual. There is a relationship among remembering, perceiving, and imagining although remembered experiences are different from perception because the memories are not of current events. Memory is not the same as imagination because remembered events and elements essentially happened although the factual nature of memory is inaccurate.

Social traditions are emotional and can be assigned to a range of symbolic activities. This approach allows a tradition to evolve and to assume different forms without disallowing previous examples.

Language, for instance, changes while remaining the same—an accepted form of communication within a particular group. Language can help reduce rigid presumptions that are obstructions to understanding. Social traditions are developed, changed, recreated, or destroyed; and in all cases, the emotion attached to that expression of socio-cultural viewpoint is unchanged. Tradition reflects markings that accrue cultural impressions embedded in the individual psyche and activated by group response. It is not history or symbolic reference that damages a creation, but the need to show the value of the object or events. That value does not depend on feeling, but on the combining of its subject with the way it appears. The work's importance and probability of lasting exist in its quality, irrespective of the maker's plan. The creation represents the value and feelings as well as the activities of the maker.

The power of the past to shape perceptions of the present is fully appreciated by history. History occurs when people rely on their knowledge of the past to comprehend the present and when they must consider the facts and events that foretell their time. When past connections are known, the present is no longer inexplicable and irrelevant. History is a perspective that joins the present with the past. It is incumbent on each generation to confirm the relevant truths by appraising the past to understand those truths as reality. Confirming those truths implies a sense of knowing beyond the realm of simple recognition.

No matter the perception, culture is not easy to clarify as a communal phenomenon without delving into the subject of social psychology. There are, however, matters to be considered, because culture, in most communal uses, is something that is a composite of elements partly real and partly imagined that people rely upon to deal with the challenges they must address. Cultural practices are transmitted by means of imitation, social conditioning, and instruction. "...[A]ll memory is shaped by the social environment and derives from social interaction. In other words, the social world is a constituent factor in the construction of memory."[17]

"Preparing" or priming may be needed to activate the relational memory or cognition process. The concept of "preparing" is using commonly related words, sounds, or images to generate memories. Words may activate memory by causing the recollection of a particular good or bad experience. "To think, to decide, and to act wisely require full access to our vast memory library—old memories and new, verbal and nonverbal memories and intellectual memories; ... without memory our very identity disappears."[18]

Memory serves a special role for people. People maintain memories of different times and events in their lives, and those memories are continually reproduced although people may not remember exactly when or where the event took place. Through a relationship with memories no matter how vague, a sense of identity is established. Memories lose the form and the appearance they once had because they are repeated and repeatedly acknowledged in different systems of thought. Their origin cannot be determined but they have the characteristics they once had.

The "real" may be a byproduct of memory but unless defined as a specific objective, it is bypassed for pleasure—remember the best and forget the rest. Impulse response requires no premeditation, and no attention to the outcome of an action other than the immediate (positive or negative). The avoidance of truth may influence the recognition and investment of individuals as well as communities and nations. The question of authenticity may cause problems by ignoring the reality of the past for the community (or group) because it is the foundation of humanism and an essential element of social identity.

Recollection as Social Orientation

Recollection is a means by which people orient themselves to their past, and many of the elements of the past, both real and imagined, are chronologically organized. The markers, in most cases, are not imposed artificially but exist, albeit of lesser consequence, within the socio-cultural or political process and are given enhanced status. The purpose of the markers is to codify history, and in many cases, they are to provide a conceptual basis for patrimony. Memory is frequently a communal procedure, one that includes shared effort to put the past into words.

Memory is an appraisal of history, and although history may assist in identifying the present and envisaging the future, it often reduces a person's capacity to react to a certain situation in an imaginative or attentive way. Memory is a means for accessing history that offers opportunities for humanizing. Without a social memory and a community identity, the values of a humanistic nature are marginalized. "...[O]ne of the roles of memory is to act as a guarantee against the fragmentation of personal identity...."[19]

Memory is often used to validate personal identity. People constantly invoke the past to explain who their parents are, where they lived, and their work history. John Locke (English philosopher, 1632–1704) considered personal identity to be founded on memory, and not on the substance of either the soul or the body. Locke wrote: "identity and selfhood have nothing to do with continuity of the body or even continuity of mind. Selfhood consists entirely in continuity of memory. A person who remembers nothing of his or her past literally has no identity."[20]

The sense of continuity is meaningful for people. Ceremonies, rituals, festivals, and similar activities are demonstrations of continuity that are usually called traditional. However, the expressive aspect of communal culture maybe overlooked or simply viewed as something picturesque or quaint. The ceremonies are for fulfilling the beliefs relating to a particular purpose. These annual events are performed for the community and celebrated as special occasions. Documentation about these cultural events may assume they exist and that almost everyone is aware of their existence. The need for continuity perpetuates the documentation of family or community history (genealogy), as well as the interest in identifying and preserving (social) culture. There may be other reasons for interest in history and culture based on individual or group initiatives, but the concept of continuity is a foundational motive.

A presentation of the past, as it is assumed to influence (true or false) the present, can be a meaningful part for all social life. Objects and activities assembled as expressions of the past reinforce group identity, however, they might not constitute true elements of history. Memory, for example, often reflects personal or group interpretive priority. This prioritization does not mean that individuals or communities cannot use collective memory to understand history better; however, collective memory is usually limited in its ability to record factual history. Such history-related activities, whether true or false, are often determined by time and place, and the certainty of change can cause people to recognize self-identified elements to denote group practices. These elements are usually arbitrarily selected, but they gain endorsement and validation by time.

History is often distorted, and the truth subverted, for various reasons, including intellectual exploitation, with the transmission of factual truth relegated to future generations. History is an element of the collective memory and is an essential part of human self-knowledge. History is meaningful in defining social identity. Knowledge, whether theoretical or practical, is necessary for a person to progress beyond the daily routine. Mindfulness of history also enriches communal and national character, legitimatizing a people in their own judgment.

No one living today can trace the beginning of most historical records. The obvious observation of that record is partly memory and even that is questionable unless it is passed from previous generation to the present in a reliable form (which it seldom is). "One of the most striking characteristics of our time is the fact that history is made without self-awareness."[21] History does not define itself; that responsibility resides with humanity. "Since the past is no more, since it has melted away into nothingness, if the memory continues to exist, it must be by virtue of a present modification of our being...."[22]

The history of things begins in the past (when they were created) and extends in an unchangeable order until they disappear and are forgotten. Deleting facts shortens the memory of society to a collection of factors that support a predefined and self-serving idea. This is not to say that all retained memory is individually or socially supportive or holistically self-endorsing. "Endurance ... distinguishes historical knowledge; whereas most memories parish with the possessors, history is potentially immoral."[23] There may be more to human personality than self-importance. Certainly, impertinence is not an element of people's mindset at birth. It is a learned quality.

This idea of the identity of self with truth offers the basis for the way of release that represents the realistic core of a pragmatic philosophy. It is a view which considers the different things and procedures of the world as expressions of a greater truth that is whole and unlimited. In this unlimited wholeness is diverse levels of certainty, separated by the intensity they share in truth and being of essential reality. Because of this union of being, the influences required to realize liberty are accessible to all humanity. Therefore, self-knowledge is imperative. According to Friedrich Nietzsche (German philosopher and cultural critic), "The self is not a constant, stable entity. On the contrary, it is something one becomes, something, he [Nietzsche] would even say, one constructs. A person consists of absolutely everything one thinks, wants, and does."[24] The self is both the object and the objectified aspect of human cognition. The human view of "self" is a visualization of social memory.

Defining communal or personal history based on memory is a meaningful feature of identity; however, memory as a self-generated process may be viewed in different ways. Speculation does not have the facility to generate a valid identity but may introduce imaginary (but believable) characteristics into the individual or group thinking. This process is usually tempered by emotional and social circumstances. The view of the self-as-memory is based on our ability to reproduce our experiences from memory; whereas others believe the self is based on our ability to reconstruct our experiences in memory.

Self-gratification has a dominant role in most peoples' lives and this attitude dominates social thinking. Reality is seldom the primary motive for recollecting the past. For example, the oral tradition of the

Mapoyo in Venezuela who live within the ancestral region include many stories that constitute the recollection of the people. It is emblematically connected to a number of places within the territory of the community along the Orinoco River in Venezuelan Guyana.[25] This oral presentation may stimulate the memory of other activities whether true or false.

Memory manipulation may be used to influence decision making, just as using images to direct the viewers' thinking or emotions. A combination of elements may be incentives for emotional reactions rather than subliminal stimuli. Truncated indicators such as sounds or symbols may stimulate memory and cause an occasion or situation to be recalled. The mnemonic references may be minor in certain instances, and the recollection indirect. The notion of memory, like the ideas of will and belief, relate principally to individuals. It is not the experience of the past remembered but the pleasure the memory induces that causes personal or group reaction.

Although human responses to most issues can be described as the spontaneous outcome to circumstantial conditions, the implanted attitudes have a socio-cultural basis. Assuming all human behavior that is not a reaction, the recognition of memory, personal or communal, is a "true" manifestation of a social response. The human capacity to assimilate group memory is expansive and directly influenced by the spatial and temporal circumstances in which the person resides.

Although not a reliable resource for identifying past events, the memories of images and ideas the human brain creates are often interesting. Social recollection is usually unwilling to depend on memories without looking for different connections between past event and current references. An individual must commit to understanding the historical event memory recalls, a process not required when dealing with traditional shared memory. Persons living within a tradition believe the memories of that tradition are true. Again, as in the situation with belief, truth is suspended because memory matters more than reality.

Culture has been separated from the regular practices of humanity, and refereed to a sterilized idea which, in its established structure, is often used to make valid the ideas of innovativeness and progress. This process of validating culture is by the learning processes of enculturation and socialization, which is demonstrated by the range of cultural times throughout history. Culture may be used to exhibit the genius of individual creativity to convince others that the acknowledged human nature never varies, and that social and traditional life is holistic and recurrent. Whereas at another time, the representation is reversed, and viewers are informed that various social and cultural expressions distinguish one people from another, and that the described differences are the very essence of a discrete activities.

Although memory may be a valid way of looking at communal history, memory and truth have little to do with each other. Memory is closer to an idea or belief. It helps people envision a situation and lets them see the consequences. "Truth is not just a property of statements, propositions, or beliefs; it is a quality of being, of human beings and human activities."[26] Assuming this transitional form of memory provides the foundation for such matters, then it denies the truth in belief, idea, and tradition. "We cannot affect the past; we cannot undo the past, resurrect the past, or revivify the past. Only descriptions of the past can be altered, improved, or animated."[27]

Truth is an essential element, and a basic part of life. (As reported in Chapter Two.) It is more than a notion of legal or ethical accountability. Trust is the foundation of positive relationships, both inside and outside the social (or business) environment. It facilitates a sense of intellectual and emotional security based on respect.

Memory is associated with many locations and activities, but it is limited in its capacity to recount history. Memory as an identifiable source of information is an important factor in social and cultural activities; however, although declarative remembrances may intend to report true statements, that intention does not verify how often memories of the past are true. The remembering memory is identified as "episodic memory," and the primary feature of this type of remembering is placing a person into contact with the actual past event that the memory is about and that causes the recollection.

Memory may allow the objects or events to be visualized in their uniqueness, but often the realness of the element is more as a social symbol or an ideological concept. Shared memory is presumed to consider a certain relationship among all humans; however, it may also acknowledge a special type of reality as an "idea-object." The object may be real, but humanity may never comprehend anything about it except by means of description and specialized work. The object appears to be a determination of a culture that was once a vigorous element of humanity. This process immobilizes the object while beforehand was always changing.

Episodic memory is the ability to recall events, or an event related to time. The recollection consists of memory and impressions is valid and therefore true because they represent realities within social consciousness. These memories and impressions when considered outside of social consciousness may be false because they cannot be shared, repeated, or verified. The idea may manifest itself in a viable form that "passes for true," but the "truth of our mental operations must always be an intra-experiential affair."[28] David Hume (1711–1776) wrote extensively about knowledge and the processes of knowing. Hume maintained, "...the imagination is not restrained to the same order and form with the original impressions, while the memory is in a manner tied down in that respect, without any power of variation."[29] The processes of knowing (possessing knowledge, information, or understanding) reside within experience. However, knowing might not be a knowing of ideas but a knowing of things; therefore, it is possible to consider thinking as a misleading activity.

Imagination is the forming of impression in the mind, which can be recreations of past experiences such as memories, or they can be completely fabricated. There is a clear distinction between fact and imagination. Many elements of communal or personal culture are based on faulty memory and opinion. Unfortunately, transmission of false patrimony eventually puts on the façade of myth and is integrated into the collective memory of the community as truth. "Nostalgia distorts the past by idealizing it."[30] For example persons observing the Day of the Dead celebrations in Mexico may consider the event entertaining with the masks, sugar skulls, and trips to the cemetery, but knowledge acknowledges the religious and traditional values of the celebration. These "traditional" celebrations are "re-enacted" each year.

Episodic memory has a significant connection with personal or communal ability to recall past activities. A primary component of episodic memory is recollection—the process that retrieves information in relation to a specific event or experience. A person or group may recall an object (or event) from the past, but not recollect when or where it was viewed. Although a current situation may cause recovery of a previous experience, that is, the person or group may feel a relationship with an object or event that is influenced by memory and not facts. An attribute of episodic memory is it permits a person to believe in moving backwards in time. Memories may nevertheless be made difficult to retrieve due to related memories.

Shared memories are important to collective existence. Episodic memories are common to a shared recollection of the people and a community. They define specific times and events in the chronicles of the community. Social and cultural situations promote the discovery or rediscovery of those events and times. Communities promote shared memories that reflect a common past—an inclusive/exclusive history. Although shared memories may be false, they are socially or politically induced to generate different emotional or physical responses.

The reinforcement of a shared memory is achieved through

institutions such as churches, schools, and archives, and communal mnemonic devices, such as monuments and stories as well as social activities. This type of reference enhances recollection although the person may simply have an obscure impression about previous events. The responsibility for maintaining a viable shared memory, such as group recollection, is incumbent upon each member of the community, but it is "not an obligation of each one to remember all. The responsibility to see to it that the memory is kept alive may require some minimal measure of memory by each in the community, but not more than that."[31]

Culture as retainable objects or events relies on visualization because many objects are beyond the immediate environment. People tend to imagine and often claim to know what they cannot see or understand. However, in theory it is impossible to visualize something that existed or is in another place or some other time. What is envisioned (or imagined) is an idea or memory and only that. As examples, a person imagines participating in the Kumbh Mela (festival in India) or taking part in the Škofja Loka Passion Play in Slovenia; the imagination is as close to real as the person can get no matter how vivid the image. The recall may tell a great deal about the person but little about the event.

The culture "industry" often promotes a vicarious experience that depends on using objects or locations as a means of entering or living in the past. Ludmilla Jordanova wrote, "Visitors are required to assent to the historical authenticity and reality of what they see, while they simultaneously recognize its artificial, fabricated nature."[32] In the same article Jordanova states, "We understand the past, not by spuriously re-experiencing it, but by turning over many kinds of evidence relating to it and by generating from this an understanding which inevitably has a strong intellectual, that is, abstract component."[33]

People remember different events that tell a part of the communal story. Each activity has a value that differs according to individual memory, connections, and emotions. Community recollection tends to focus on commonly recognized local values. These recollections are identified, selected, and placed in an institutional environment to immortalize by these means the spirit of the community past. Nevertheless, most assessments are subjective and based on perspectives that are far removed from the actual people or events—a form of social make-believe.

Communities are not only founded for reason and necessity; the priority of all social systems is an arrangement of beliefs and the related rituals to insure the continuation of a vested ideology and dogma. Certainly, knowledge and reason have roles in furthering these objectives, but they are secondary. When there are conflicts between reason and belief, the usual human tendency is to affirm those assumption that are elements of their tradition. People act according to the examples given to them by their history and to the examples inscribed in their social order. This tendency is true for the economic, social, political, and cultural life of a people.

The culture of a community (whether large or small) resides in the memory of the members of that community. Members of a community relate to the memories, and the group remembers the memories of their progenitors and so on back until the event (object, activity, or circumstance) occurred. Personal or communal culture is based on the memory of first-generation experience, and that occurrence may or may not be true; furthermore, each generational transfer of memory allows revision, exaggeration, and redefinition. Rituals, for example, are considered a part of a community or people, but rituals are often altered, relocated, or abandoned based on changing social conditions. The remembered and transmitted culture of a ritual has no identifiable starting point to serve as a reference. The memory is of dubious quality where actual knowledge of an act or activity is non-existent.

People with common ancestry may share a sympathetic association with past events or objects although the current generation has no direct connection with the artificial recollection resource. This association is embedded in the collective memory, and it is often possible for affected persons to remember in detail, activities, events, or objects that are described or identified by others. People say, "I remember...." When they do not, in fact, remember. There are many examples of this phenomenon, and among the most common are those found in self-perpetuating ceremonies such as religious ceremonies, fraternal organizations, and procedural affirmations. These elements, though intangible for most societies are aspects of the collective memory and routinely (although incorrectly) associated with authentic events.

The idea that human beings recall information from a previous life, instead of attaining it in their present life by means of experience was endorsed by early philosophers, including Plato. This thinking is associated with transmigration and is like belief in reincarnation as identified with Buddhism. The transmigration believes the soul is immortal and passes from person to person when the body dies. People of different ages and locations have different motivations for relating to cultural elements. Each person or group may have a special reason for remembering an event, activity, or cultural element, and that memory is often a recalled experience that can be described as transmigration. It is impossible to say that a person (alive or dead) transfers their thinking to another person. While it seems unlikely, all people have experienced an event that is remembered as having happened before.

Such knowledge often relies on a relationship between the expected and the experienced, and many memories depend on this symbolic reference. The information may be the signifier of communal phenomena and the notion signified may have great value to one people and be of marginal interest to another. An easily recognizable symbol-associated memory is more quickly assimilated into the vocabulary than one that defies understanding.

People hope to repeat the meaningful events of the past, but seldom do memories stimulate the same level of response, physically or emotionally, as the original event. It is usually the same with patrimonial elements and human associations. The current generation may know nothing about the Temple of Preah Vihear in Cambodia dedicated to Shiva. (They may not even know who Shiva is.) They have no actual or imagined recollection, however, because of the patrimony identification, an assumption of importance is associated with the Temple. Observation and thought acknowledge of an identity that is marginally familiar, but not relevant. People usually recall what they feel comfortable in remembering.

The collective unconscious is a part of the unconscious mind shared by a society, in an interconnected system that products common experiences and concepts as science, religion, and morality. The collective unconscious differs from the personal subconscious that is particular to each person. The collective unconscious is also recognized as the source of the knowledge of people.

Things to think about:

1. Why is memory the foundation of tradition, focused thinking, and sustaining stability?

2. Is it reasonable to say that a mnemonic is a memory aid?

3. How does communal memory transcend generation gaps?

4. Why is episodic memory, the ability to recall events or an event related to time, important?

5. How is the memory basic to a person's capacity of recalling past experiences?

6. Is memory a means for accessing history that offers opportunities for humanizing?

7. Why is collective memory limited to its ability to record factual history?

8. According to David Lowenthal, why is preserving knowledge of the past one of history's prime reasons?

9. Why are many elements of communal or personal culture based on faulty memory and opinion?

10. What is it that community recollection tends to focus on?

SEVEN

The Critical Nature of Culture

VALUE CAN BE DESCRIBED AS a subjective assessment of an activity, object, or event. It is often described as doing what is right and evading what is wrong. Value judgments are often assumed to have cognitive status, that is, they represent a determination based on intellectual assessment (opinion). The cultural element is often influenced by contradictory thinking, philosophical dialectics intending to determine the truth. Dialectic reasoning is integral to ideals in which the values are in constant motion, and each value contains a facet of its opposite. An inconsistency between cultural elements and social understanding usually occurs due to a failure to understand this special attribute. Life requires meaning, and culture aids in establishing a verifiable reference.

The value and truth of cultural elements may be determined materially or intellectually. For example, the Joya de Cerén Archaeological Site in El Salvador is an example of the chronological dimensions of culture. The site contains the remains of a pre–Hispanic farming village that was covered by a volcanic eruption in the seventh-century CE. "The ... volcanic event led to the remarkable preservation of architecture and the artefacts of ancient inhabitants in their original positions of storage and use, forming a time capsule of unprecedented scientific value that can be appreciated in present times."[1] The Sangiran Early Man Site is another equally important location. It is one of the key sites for the understanding of human evolution. The values of these sites may be based on different aspects, but each includes unique cultural value.

Theoretically, the idea of value is not new. The definition of the word "value" is extremely flexible. It is utilized as an alternative for "good," and at times it is used for a range of evaluative terms. (It is sometimes used to describe the meaning of culture, as stated in the Introduction.) The concept can be expressed to mean different objectives and each of those manifestations refers to some aspect of goodness. Value can be described as a subjective judgment. Value judgments are therefore assumed to have cognitive status, that is, they represent an evaluation based on logical consideration. A positive outcome is the true measure of both people and culture with the focus on the receivers of judgment instead of the providers.

Value as a theory defines activities that are meaningful on a social or cultural level. It is an instrumental good that is a means for achieving a meaningful socially or culturally enhancing result when used in this way (a viable judgment). Culture as value also must be viewed as an instrumental good. The instrumental nature of culture is identified by the responses to this question. Cultural patrimony has a purpose beyond simply identifying a state of being.

As is often the situation, the theory of value depends on the meaning assigned to a word or idea. Personal values are inevitably self-defined and may change; however, social and professional values are often predetermined and require conformity. The extrinsic merit of culture is an example of the nature and genius of humanity. Culture has humanistic significance. It is reasonable to wonder whether that "value" is permanent or temporary based on human action. Culture in the sense of symbolic practice is part of every activity. Each generation places value on culture, causing elements to be added or removed to their cultural agenda; in addition, elements are removed from cultural resources due to destruction by humans or nature. The fact that forthcoming generations will define (or redefine) the culture of their people makes it more important that the ideals and importance of culture are explained on a knowing and understanding level.

The theory of value places importance on truth and ethics that goes beyond the idea of common sense. The truth meaning of an object relates to the reality of the object and the idea it represents. (See also Chapter Two.) The patrimonial element may verify itself through public judgment, but the public focuses on the object for only a limited time. The truth of a cultural importance may be flexible as world conditions, but special interests modify the importance placed on patrimonial elements. There are undoubtedly different opinions about values as relative concepts that reinforce or weaken ideological, as well as sociological perspectives. All opinions should be given consideration.

Humanity is made aware of value through the conscious and education, and at the same time, is drawn into a way of thinking. The values associated with different people are influenced by emotional as well as social and cultural ways of thinking; however, the attitudes do not explicitly differentiate individual responses to external influences.

Humanity should have the ability to recognize objects or events of value and their obligation to act in accordance with those merits, and to apply those meanings in active decision-making. Value decisions are a form of rational behavior; therefore, the valuation or devaluation of a particular cultural element should include an intentional awareness of the people represented. An unmediated presentation of social patrimony, presumably with the intention of being true to the elements and culture, is characteristic of many interactions, but it cannot be called an effort of social benefit when it denies the significance of the elements to the originating society. Too often the origination people or person is ignored. Societal integrity implies a perspective involving the esteem and fair repute that follows the correct fulfillment of a public role.

A cultural resource requires the specification of a time and place relationship and universal value. Without the universal meaning or logical subjectivity, recognition is not obvious. The cultural element must be thought of as maintaining its identity although that is a process of change. Culture exists in a person's or community's mind if it retains an aspect of value. When it loses the sameness with the community, it ceases to exist not as culture but a cultural resource and subsequently cannot be in any associational process nor can it change.

Culture has universal value and attaining the universal position is generally considered to be a high achievement. The inclusive concept of culture endorses a worldview of elements and humanity. This acknowledges that culture changes, and each manifestation has and deserves universal value. There is no assurance that culture remains constant. The next generation may question the importance of the Buddhist Monuments in the Horyu-ji area or Lake Malawi National Park no matter how culturally significant. Each generation defines its own culture and it might not include the culture of past generations.

Consideration must be given to the differences between the absolute and relative meaning of the circumstances that precipitated the tradition from which the cultural element is derived before values are assigned and endorsed. There are individual values and group values. Group values are promulgated from the issues that are part of a group's social surroundings. Group values are often described as "social ethics" because they are often broad based and relatively inconstant. Group values often result in both positive and negative actions because they guide both the perception and interchange with others. People think and act in patterns, and the influence of cultural patterns (the inclusion of values and beliefs) often results in patrimonial damage and destruction.

The unity of substantiality and subjective values include the distinctiveness of many cultural elements, and by this fact, an objective determination of value cannot be made on individual objects or activities. There is a fixedness of tangible character that identifies an element of culture, whereas intangible or hypothetical culture has no fixed character. Variation or improvisation is an inherent part of much intangible culture. It is likely that no persons or groups perform an activity repeatedly without variation. A song, dance, or ritual is important to a culture because it allows indigenous expression; the objective is consistent, but the method varies. An example of this type of event is the Tan-Tan Moussem, an annual gathering of tribes from southern Morocco in Tan-Tan, a town in southwestern Morocco. The *moussem* is a type of cultural fair.[2]

The value of cultural expressions is secondary to symbolic or mnemonic allusions. Vague or personal as these references are, they stimulate a response that implies understanding. The cultural value in most circumstances can be regarded as identity through time, and as such, that identity verifies culture as being important. When a people have a time and space relationship, there is an innate notion of identity, and with that identity, the related culture has validity. Real or imagined culture manifestations are viewed as elements of continuity.

The true value of an idea resides outside the person, although most people are inadequate in critical self-evaluation. All people are inclined to believe in something whether that belief causes action or conjecture. Belief is a state of mind and to deny a belief results in a contrary state of mind causing doubt and uncertainty, whereas an idea may result in action for verification. William James wrote, "The truth of an idea is not a stagnant property inherent in it. Truth happens to an idea. It becomes true, is made true by events. Its verity is in fact an event, a process ... its verification."[3]

Elements of human activities, including cultural recognition, are measured by value (meaningful), and determining what has value is to decide that an action or act is true. A person may be objective or subjective when assessing values; however, truth (respect) supports an objective, consistent, and predictable approach to value. The values of a cultural element originate within the individual (or individuals) most often as a subjective assessment that includes mostly practical considerations; nonetheless, determining the value of such a patrimonial element is important. Values (meaningfulness), although subjective, are related to the search for ideals, and high values are believed to equal "good quality." The true value of cultural elements need not be fully recognized or appreciated. Values assigned by a special interest group often compromise the merits of a cultural element. The projected value is made complicated by considerations of current verses future thinking. These influencing factors may not be right or wrong but may obfuscate value considerations.

Value is a subjective assessment of culture—it represents a determination based on intellectual, emotional, and aesthetic consideration. Value judgments (opinions) are the result of interaction between humanity and a situation, as well as the cultural element. A value judgment should be an attempt to identify truth, and to reinforce the ideals that are central to a relationship between the people and culture. The values that define truth are derived from collected knowledge source in humanity. The search for truth identifies the options that are the most appropriate for the actual situation. Determinations are based on values; that is, decisions consider which option provides the greater good.

Social, intellectual, and historical values (of culture) are measures relating to the importance of culture, and the difference between elements and their merits are central to this consideration. Objects and memories pervade human understanding. "Every artifact is the product of human intentionality, but that intentionality itself is conditioned by the existence of previous objects." Each piece of the past eventually expires, but together they are unending. No matter if it is acclaimed or entreated, focused or unnoticed, the past is pervasive, a cultural value abstractly envisaged as a reference to an image to be acknowledged as a manifestation of importance. Humanity seldom comprehends the way diverse elements cause the past and the present to coalesce and have no understanding of what significance elements have or how and why those meanings may change. When the past is valued, that value permeates the past's physical remains.

Values influence the way people respond to specific circumstances, the ways they determine practices, and often the ways in which they assess truth. Humanity has a fundamental need for truth because truth is believed to be consistent with fact or actual circumstances. Truth relates to a positive value and may be given additional status when activities go beyond the normal margins of society. The situation identifies the importance of the need and defines truth as a proportional value. Truth, in this context, may have no inherent meaning outside the situation in which it is applied.

A cohesive system of cultural values is based on thought and meaning, and such a system has internal and external features. The internal part reflects the sphere of inner experience, as images, ideas, feelings, and emotions. The external part of this value system includes elements such as: objects, events, and activities. "These external phenomena belong to a system of culture only as they are the manifestations of its internal aspects."[4] The relationship between the internal and external aspects of cultural is significant because the realm of the mind controls that part of the cultural process. Everything is dependent on something else—this notion is the issue determining intrinsic and extrinsic values. "There is no independent self-entity, no self either in ourselves or in the phenomenal world around us. There is only conditioned existence."[5]

Judgments about the value (not monetary) of cultural elements is personal. Deciding the "value" of cultural objects or events should relate to the idea of honesty (difficult to access) while remaining consistent with comparable considerations. The merits assigned cultural elements, because they are personal, may have no viable meaning beyond the immediate. These judgments require no inclusive impression of agreement with anything but are simply an opinion.

In this world of progressively more indistinct societies, it is natural to warrant agreeable relations between people and groups with different and assure cultural uniqueness as well as their willingness to dwell mutually. The act of preserving culture, whether real or imagined, is an expression of resilience and an announcement of sustainability for a community. Preservation of established values is an effort to serve people, the environment, and creative endeavors to prevent deflation into mediocrity. It is a cumulative effort to save humanity and its allied history. This concept relates to all humanity equally (inclusively), and cultural activities are an important part of preserving and verifying community identity, as well as countermanding the devaluation of culture and the meaning of humanism.

"Both complex and simple communities may be inclined to regard history as the decline from an initial order that those living in the present strive to replicate, or as a cumulative sequence of development."[6] Collectively, cultural tradition is viewed as the result of human activity before the present, without the material objects that define current social life. The developing or defining of humanity through objects is mostly imagination. According to this way of thinking the truth is not necessary.

The issue of cultural tradition meaning is not just a question of physical or intellectual fact or what may be called metaphysical fact. The importance of "meaning" (the meaning of a cultural element) must be understood at a level above the concept of right or wrong. Just as a biological specimen has minimal consequence without the related recovery data, the cultural element is incomplete without the relational information. The meaning of a cultural element has absolute merit and must be preserved to give true significance to the associated objects.

The social and political endorsement of cultural tradition acknowledges that the cultural community is considerate of the needs of society and justifies a valued position of communal endorsement. Society grants cultural responsibility for preserving the legacy of humanity, but that responsibility must be accomplished in accordance with the liability to the people for whom patrimony is being preserved.

Every society has presumptions (social expectations) about what a "member" should believe and how a person should act. Some of these expectations become (nation/state) laws, some are held as moral judgments, and others are socially enforced. These social expectations change over time, and often have different meanings for different social and cultural groups. The value transmitted across time is the stimulus for understanding practice and traditions of an activity. For instance, a cultural activity may be valued due to its exceptionality in combination with its unity of purpose and effect. A social value system defines the work of a particular element and locations it within the communal context. (See also Chapters Four and Eight.)

When the public attempt to define an event of cultural proportions, it is necessary to assign its various portions to the delineation of collective time. Such temporal apportionments are imposed upon the public because the event as a cultural resource might not reside in any single memory. This measure of social time (a collective) is external to the lived duration of contemporary society and beyond the grasp of the individual. A situation of this nature differs from a historical event that has distinct temporal limits.

Each cultural element has an emotional aspect, and, in every case, the emotion is relevant to the element's form and meaning. Such an example as the fourth-century Christian Necropolis of Pécs[7] in Sopianae, Hungary, is valued by some people and is not so important to others. However, most cultural elements have a meaningful relationship with humanity. They are not simply visual adornments but expressions of human values—expressions of spiritual, intellectual, and temporal significance. The notion that culture is "relevant" for humanity as a concrete element detracts from its emotive importance and limits its aesthetic (creative) value. The emotional merit associated with culture is an independent reality unlike that of other emotions. It is not possible to separate the sentiment from the object. The viewer must subscribe to the meaningfulness of the cultural element, just as to its emotion and value; in other words, each element must be experienced for what it is itself. The joining of the impression and the object to form an endorsable cultural importance.

What is observed creates a short-term image in a person's mind—an impression. That impression is stored and available for recovery. The separation between the observer and the observed is not extreme; consequently, the related judgments are usually subjective and have no universality. Both the protection and destruction of cultural elements may be enacted based on social validating determinations.

The significance of communal cultural elements may be determined passionately, personally, and intellectually. The merits may be based on different aspects of the elements including ideals, attitudes, and social mindfulness, as well as presumed cultural or merits. This is not to say that one perspective is inherently better or more valuable than another.

Things great and small have special value for the world's population. Many elements continue to survive because of the culture designation. Cultural elements endure because they have meaning, but unless people adopted a more moral and responsible attitude, that protection will not withstand the destructive energy of materialism.

The idea of value is associated with ethics. The question for most people concerns values that are not as clearly classified as right or wrong. Normal determinations often involve seemingly good values, and this circumstance calls for a knowledge of ethics. Decisions with minimal value are those judgments that are good only because of their good result.

The Universality of Ethics Thinking

It is not possible to teach thinking or passion because they are aspects of attitude. Teaching the theory of thinking is not difficult because it is a skill but the understanding and use of thinking, passion or even ethics is more than knowledge (information) it requires knowing. Knowing is a personal understanding that goes beyond simply hearing and receiving the information (knowledge). Often ethics is considered an issue of right and wrong, but it is seldom so simple. A better way to describe ethics (not social morals) is right and not-so-right rather than wrong because the issue may be correct (right) in either way of evaluating it, but one way is "ethically" correct. Both ways may follow the principles, but one way conforms to the attitude of ethical correctness. (Morals, social ethics, normally consist of the rights and wrongs people are taught when they are young.)

In considering ethics, it is usual to encounter the diversity of the opinions represented. This circumstance is due in part to the intricacy of life, and partially to differences between attitude and beliefs. Human disposition is diverse, and existence has different values. Ethics tries to attain and devise standards that inspire people to better comprehend and conduct their lives. Ethics recognizes attitudes of acceptable conduct to act as positive influences for individuals and communities. Therefore, ethics relates to values and facilitating ways of strengthening an attitude of intelligent, logical, and honest opinions and actions.

Cultural separation is regularly considered as an obstruction to the transmission and performance of ethical practices. In some places any change is a possible hazard to the prevailing practice and the traditional practitioners. Ethics as a theory brings together assorted parts of a complex society. It is based on fact, experience, values, and beliefs, as well as caring. Ethics is also based on a belief in service. Belief may define the thinking for a community although some places have supporting ideals to recognize their distinctive nature.

The ethical person is an element of meaning in an ethical society, and unless they have value in themselves, no community of such persons can have importance. Consequently, when a person says they have done the best they can do or they are dishonest and nothing further can be expected. Obviously, that thinking is inadequate. Such an attitude should be different from the community's expectation and separate from a person's will. If the expectation is unknown, the person may believe themselves correct, but because of community judgment they are wrong. It is not enough for a person to be truthful, that is, true to their opinions; they must also agree with communal beliefs to be judged correct. Ethical correctness is the more significant because it includes honesty and good will, but communal acceptability is important, as without community investment the action may not be valued.

Ethics for people is about value judgments, as well as doing the right thing. Ethics is attitude. The inclusiveness of ethics refers to its universal nature because belief in the universality of ethics is fundamental. Ethical responsibility is identified with truth and trustworthiness as well as social responsibility. Ethical practice must form a complete basis of understanding within the community and beyond. Ethical thinking is not simply concerned with correctness and incorrectness, but with an interest in many different types of social concerns.

Ethics identifies appropriate conduct. It also creates a unity of purpose and practice for persons performing together. (People do not devote a great amount time to thinking about ethics activities.) An ethical act ought to be a sensible act, and for an act to be sensible it must have a reason beyond itself. Acts for the sake of form or acts that end in themselves are senseless and unintelligent. The result must support good in some way. The responsibility is to act in some "good" and sensible way that results in beneficial (meaningful) change. Thinking about ethics produces ethical proficiency.

All ethics have a space (area) for collective objectives, human rights, and special or unique obligations. Ethics may vary in the extent of the rights and duties limit and in the correctness bestowed to aims greater than human rights and human rights more than obligations. Ethics differ in the language of whether they consider aims, or obligations, as more basic. Obligation-based ethics are involved with the importance of personal deeds, with the compliance of personal action to a code of right behavior. The ethics takes priority over individuals, their fancies, or routines. Right-based ethics, in contrast, guards the value of individual thought and belief. Individuals' goals, and habits take priority over any idea of the appropriate ends or ways it is "natural" for people to organize themselves.

The primary purpose of ethics is to clarify the practices of the community and to define activities in relation to that group. Ethics and the community are jointly supporting, and due to this connection, transmission of ethics in the community should reflect commonly endorsed principles. Truth fills a certain logical need by verifying an act, idea, or statement by relating it to a more accepted source. Decisions made about events or actions are considered true in similar activities even thoughts there is no proof of legitimacy. Borden P. Bowne (American philosopher, 1847–1910) wrote in *The Principles of Ethics* (1892), "Positive truth must always depend upon the matter itself and the reasons offered for it."[8] Bowne believed the final arbiter for human action must be "our actual mental insight."[9] An ethical mind, is meaningful. What one does is important to other people, but what one thinks and does, as an ethical person, is important to the individual themself. A person must be ethical from within, not from something imposed from outside.

Such intellectual perception goes to conditions beyond the presumable where people can imagine whether a circumstance is correct or incorrect. The significance of an act is not simply derived from the ends it attempts to accomplish, but also from being in accord with the attitude of the community (group). Contemporary thinking must reflect the contemporary organization in that the standards and practices may be altered to correspond to the situation of the community. However, it should be specified that the standards (principles) do not change. (The principles remain the same although the practice may change.) They can be used in a different way or extended to accommodate current issues, but the principles continue unaltered.

People insist there are no common ethical interests that cross from person to person, and that an individual may have a totally different ethical understanding than another. Granted, there are many variances between one person and another, but most have a sense of responsibility. Since right and wrong are considered in all things; things must be viewed in their diversity. For example, people believe in Xooy, a divination ceremony among the Serer people of Senegal,[10] and others believe that taking a picture of someone steals their soul. Central to this thinking, it may be assumed that certain kinds of physical labor is irrelevant or that photos are hazardous to a person's well-being. Instead, it is presumed that all cultures are unique.

Although human behavior is either learned or modified by social conditions, and the fulfillment of desire is often the motive for invented social patrimony (personal history). This approach reinforces group agreement on the value of its members as a part of the physical or natural environment. A composite of activities, described as culture, identifies a person individually and collectively as a member of a specific group or society, and the environment in which they live. That collective setting is an aspect of humanity that includes the "...objects [that] often symbolize significant community or local meaning, the great cultural wonders of the world, and provide witness to human aesthetic achievements."[11]

Social patrimony may be the core of the debate about identity, social cohesion, and the development of a knowledge-based society. The identification of social patrimony can make almost any object or event present in the intellectual context of the present time. This method of identifying patrimony is a way of expressing time. It may offer the individual something totally known, but the individual lacks the ability to recognize, or in some instances, the courage to acknowledge and divulge that the element is a part of their life. It is not that those items are constant reminders of the past, but that they exist for reassurance as needed.

Logic and reason are two actions that motivate thinking and decision-making. Laws are devised on logic but ethics is an achievement founded on reason. Once a community (or group) invests in thinking, they can decide to respond to a greater standard than that advocated by cognition. There is no standard for every subject that may be encountered by a community; consequently, the people must accept the task of responding to each situation in an intelligent way based on thinking. The appropriateness of principled thinking can be assigned to many actions. It can be presumed that people know correctness and incorrectness by intent, but truth and reason should be elements of ethical deliberation.

Things to think about:

1. Do value judgments have cognitive status; that is, do they represent a determination based on intellectual assessment?

2. What is a cohesive system of cultural values based on?

3. If communal culture is everywhere in both touchable and untouchable form, how can it be so important and what are the advantages and disadvantages of preserving and protecting it?

4. How is it possible for culture to exist in a person's mind if it retains an aspect of value?

5. How are obligation-based ethics involved with the importance of personal deeds, and a personal code of right behavior?

6. Do standards (principles) change or is it that people change?

7. Why is value a subjective assessment of culture that represents a determination based on intellectual, emotional, and aesthetic consideration?

8. Is ethical thinking important?

9. Why must a person be ethical from within, not from something imposed from outside?

10. If ethics is founded on reason, why is it so difficult for people to understand?

Eight

Knowledge
and Cultural Thinking

CONFUCIUS IS REPORTED TO HAVE SAID, "If you learn without thinking about what you have learned, you will be lost. If you think without learning, however, you will fall into danger."[1] Culture as education—as learning—is an inclusive concept, but people, including those within communities often think of education as an activity for others. Education, however, is not for one person or one group that justifies its activities and unites its relationship with a community. Learning is a lifetime activity. All people are involved with culture as education. The activities of daily life are within the domain of culture, and cultural education is common for all people and all arenas of life. Cultural thinking is a part of every decision and is fundamental to interaction with other members of the community and the public. Inclusion (including education) is a necessary part of culture.

The philosophy of education is concerned with the methods of being educated. It is the part of education and applied philosophy addressing questions about learning (instruction) as well as the ways of knowledge. Ideas related to education do not necessarily dwell in the minds of a specific society. It is the impression that these ideas are the influence of an emotional reality. Rarely it is understood which thoughts guide the community (people) to a certain idea, but it is practical to presume that they are of perceptional learning importance to society. It is also logical to think that the idea of education is a believed valuable given the criteria of the time and place.

The philosophy of education is part of practical philosophy focused on the ideals of education. Since education is widespread in societies, it is an inclusive field embracing topics in ethics and social philosophy. The philosophy of education is concerned with both theory and practice and includes all issues relating to educational practices. Education is the foundation of humanity, and when it does not exist, truth cannot be found, but meaningful education is not adequate to modify culture. Only cognizing that has been incorporated into peoples' thinking can cause such a change.

The idea of education is a concept as old as humanity. Education began in prehistory as training in the knowledge and skills considered important in society—survival. Storytelling in pre-literate society was a means for passing knowledge, values, and skills from one generation to the next. (Storytelling is a part of all societies.) Education is not limited to any racial group and is certainly a basis for personal theoretical ideals. Education is an element of culture.

Education succeeds or fails based on the truth or untruth not simply on belief. The word "knowledge" in almost any concept is too vague to identify a single intellectual achievement. There are various elements contributing to the concept of knowledge including the method of knowing by identifying (naming) as in the case of cultural spaces. (It is also relational.) There is a level of knowledge associated with the concept of identified persons or locations even though they may be unknown by actual contact. Humanity often has no actual knowledge of the named locations apart from a naming to such extent that it can be used as corroboration. (See also Chapter Three.)

Knowledge is a kind of certainty; the greatest type of certitude related to people's comprehension. Seeing, understanding, and knowing are separate processes that require different skills. (Much of people's traditional understanding is being replaced by a new form of technology. Seeing is no longer believing.) Although thinking influences the senses of humanity, the response to traditional thinking is influenced by social or intellectual consideration. Tradition is often representative of the thinking of its time, as well as the attitude and politics of the identifying process. Basic time references are only relational categories for understanding tradition.

The authentic culture of a people involves knowledge as a holistic approach to existence that includes the environment, the sciences, technology, and the arts, as well as a system of ideas and values that define the world. "To understand what people are and what they might become, one must understand what goes on between people and things."[2] Knowledge is then the basis of culture because knowledge of the object cannot precede the object itself. Society may consider culture according to the dimensions of history, vast and diverse, whereas such patrimony provides a perspective of the world that defines the role of people.

Education is an attitude as well as an inclusive concept. It is the knowledge we have or do not have; it is people's intellect; and it is their emotions. (For example, the digital camera has made everyone a photographer. It has replaced most of the skills needed for photography but not the creativity or passion.) Education is humanism and a necessary part of human rights. It gives people a sense of identity. Intellectual resources have emotional and cultural appeal since they evoke a sense of pride. People intend to produce a milieu where they can gain a better understanding of the merits that exist in humanism, consider a past they can appreciate, and believe in a future to which they will consign the culture of their own existence. The danger lies in assigning social or cultural values to simulacra of a marginally defined past. The consequence of such misalignment is cultural entropy and emotional confusion.

Humanism is viewed differently in different areas of the globe, but each culture includes values that are elements of world culture. All things are relational. The humanism of China and India may be expressed differently, but as with all areas of the world, they are equal to that of Europe and North America. The European belief of importance in the humanist field is baseless guesswork. Culture is the outer shell of humanism that contains the logic, reason, and the essence of individuals and nations.

Culture gives meaningful importance to knowledge and knowing because of its humanistic relevance and significance. The localization of culture does not deny its meaningfulness. An essential part of culture is preservation of ideas to understand experiences in ways that display familiar patterns. For instance, participants in the Bumba-meu-boi of Maranhão, Brazil, perform a ritualistic activity that includes music and choreography in which the groups' connection with the sacred is represented by the shape of the ox. The performance includes certain elements: the cycle of life; the mystical-religious universe and the ox itself. Each year, the groups reinvent this activity.[3] The examples of culture identification and preservation are indications of human attitude that are not measured by an individual's lack of knowledge.

Knowledge is elemental to appreciating truth because truth relates to thinking and the idea of knowing. The truth people believe is the truth they know. It is about assured ideas based on common values, including the belief in consistent situations or accounts. Truth often (too often) is a social creation. Truth in its various forms is of generally understood merit that is recognized by nearly all people—recognized but not always endorsed. It is commonly understood that the principal motive for truth is respect. Persons with no self-respect or regard for others have no concern about being dishonest. Values may be personal, but they are values of items real to people, or subject to their decision.

"Throughout [much of] the world education is seen as the key to progress and success.... But buildings and hardware are not much without good teachers and interested students. Knowledge and understanding are the foundation for all accomplishments."[4] The concept of "good teachers" and "interested students" is relative. There are many good teachers and just as many interested students. However, an individual may possess ability whether they (as teacher or student) know it or not; talent (ability) can be assessed in a person whereas creativeness can be recognized only when a work is undertaken. The facility to turn information into knowledge is ever-present.

The acquisition of knowledge is a characteristic of humanity, although true knowledge has no explicit form in practice. "Human beings generally seek knowledge, especially some understanding of humanity's place in the universe as a basic good."[5] Knowledge may be identified as circumstantial or as referring to specific information, its corresponding value, and associated reasoning. True knowledge is acquired as the direct understanding of a particular situation. The North American philosopher Richard Rorty wrote: "The eventual demarcation of philosophy from science was made possible by the notion that philosophy's core was 'theory of knowledge,' a theory distinct from the sciences because it was their foundation...."[6]

Culture is the essence of contemporary insight into identity, unity, and expansion of a knowledge-based connection with people. An acknowledgment of education as culture as a universal factor brings humanity closer to an inclusive social understanding while ambivalence leads away from a humanistic affinity. People may respond to the destruction of culture without knowing what is gained by preservation. It is important to know why one approach is correct and in contrast, the other approach is incorrect. Regarding cultural preservation the question should be not how to preserve, but how to stop destruction.

Culture reflects the capabilities and needs of time. The assumed specialness of cultural elements is often because people have forgotten the meaningfulness of previous achievements. Culture, as education, may be represented in ways that do not conform to current values.

People may accept culture superficially but fail to respond to it as a whole experience (educational). The more familiar the element is, the easier for people to place the element within a more general context. Humanity must first contextualize the cultural element into an acceptable experiential order—in other words, the encounter must relate to what is already known for acknowledgment. "This is not surprising if we remember that universality is a characteristic of significance; the greater the work, the deeper and more general its significance; the more general the significance, the easier it is to apply it to wider varieties of particular experiences...."[7]

Culture is an active participant in the educational process not just as object assessor. Knowledge is partly represented for that physical contribution, but also communicated in specific attitudes signifying technological activities and influence which could not be lacking from cultural expressions. It is this information-sharing mission of a cultural location (space) that is to identify the meaning of objects as well as relating the myths and stories associated with their history. There is a need to view culture not only as objects of the past and present, but also as something valued for discussion and investigation that confers a distinctively humanistic factor. Objects or events may be explained and used to increase the knowledge about human beings and cultural achievements in a time before the present. Cultural spaces should be repositories of knowledge. They should share that knowledge and make the meaning of that knowledge accessible to everyone.

David Lowenthal (American historian and geographer, 1923–2018) stated, "Preserving knowledge of the past is one of history's prime *raisons d'être*: both oral accounts and archival records have long been kept against the lapse of memory and devouring time."[8] A chronological continuum is to give things a place in time. It provides the past an orderly form, thereby allowing the current generation to define their lives and emotions in reference to past events. It is normal to think of tangible patrimony elements as being of the past. "Preserving historical knowledge, including that of things, is to allow for critical knowledge of our own society."[9]

Identifying and confirming tradition may be recognized simply as "putting things in order." It is possible to bringing the past into the present or identify the present with the past. The validation of "world patrimony" is probably a political action and a reflection of national ego, but if viewed from the human perspective, it is usually considered that knowledge, as a working practice, is more sustainable than tradition. Psychosocially the concept of patrimony originates within the framework of tradition, which, in turn, involves the collective aspects of mental activities and their results. It can be stated, therefore, that the concept of patrimony depends on the "knowledge" of critical meanings. For example, the Royal Ballet of Cambodia, Chinese calligraphy, the Tsuur end-blown flute of Mongolia, Daemokjang, traditional wooden architecture of the Republic of Korea, and Romanian Horezu ceramics are culture activities that have meaning (value) based on knowledge as well as tradition.

The concept of knowledge has a historical foundation that should not be separated from the social merits. Information and the way in which it is obtained is an important element of human existence. Knowledge in traditional thinking, for instance, is something that originates from social contents and that is inseparable from social practice based on a holistic viewpoint. Knowledge is an important factor, "necessarily and inextricably linked to human activities and the implementation of social practice; any separation of knowledge and (social) practice was equated with the separation of human beings from the world in which they have found themselves."[10]

Although the acquisition of knowledge is a fundamental element of human existence, the concept of knowledge has no specific form in practice. Knowledge has proven importance, but that value of knowing must be realized regardless of its possible use. Knowledge in traditional terms should not be viewed as an end in itself but as a means to other ends. People seek greater knowledge to discover phenomena that are accessible regardless of circumstance. It imposes unity on an array of information, and thereby, uncovers knowledge (truths) that transcends social, cultural, and political differences.

Knowledge is a necessary aspect of everyday life, and the foundation of many activities although it may be difficult to define, describe, or identify as the theoretical or practical understanding of a subject. "The word knowledge will be applied only to a claim that is certain, a claim which could not be said to be true today but false tomorrow, or even possibly false tomorrow," according to Plato's philosophy.[11] It is equally true that intuition, opinion, and instinct cannot claim certainty; therefore, those abilities must be excluded from Plato's concept of knowledge.

Culture reinforces knowledge, ability, and physical effort, but it is not a substitute for personal or group initiative. Knowledge is a review of what is known, how it is known, and what it implies to know something. Defining knowledge is important because it is not adequate to believe, without a motive for that belief. Knowing, in this process, is more than intellectual adroitness. It constitutes understanding in a thorough way, and the ability to comprehend the significance of a particular cultural object or activity.

Knowledge as "knowing" does not refer to intellect in scholarly terms. This kind of knowing may be experiential or intellectual, as well as insightful and traditional. The cultural factor includes the "totality of experiences, concepts, beliefs, and their consequences. It provides the determining context in which language finds its meaning."[12]

People seek knowledge as a social achievement, and consequently the level of knowing (complete understanding) is often exaggerated. People have a natural attachment to history; hence, the risk of being mistaken about fact and dates can be rationalized by the claim to search for truth. It is possible, therefore, to hide behind history and recollection and to acknowledge nothing on one's personal account. The practice of historical exaggeration influences the recognition and appreciation of cultural tradition, but at times, gives a basis for communal beliefs and fanciful tales.

Robert J. Ackermann wrote in the *Theories of Knowledge*: "...it can be said that the senses yield only the appearance of things, but not their reality, so that in order to have knowledge about anything, we must know it through some other means than the senses."[13] The senses cannot be trusted because of the influences of opinion or lack of information. The senses' impressions may be accurate but, in some instances, they communication faulty data.

The role of the knowledge in the continuity of civilization as a socially and culturally viable entity is meaningful and necessary but not always understood. References to the past are often symbolic reminiscences of the people who created them. People recall objects, events, and times in their mind so the activities can be reclaimed in their uniqueness. Communal traditions may reflect the history of a location; however, the significance of specific elements may not have the same value to all persons regardless of how the elements are considered. "...[O]ur experience of the present very largely depends upon our knowledge of the past.... We will experience our present differently in accordance with the different pasts to which we are able to connect that present."[14]

Understanding, Logic and Expression

The act of seeing and knowing an element is not limited to simply reviewing the information associated with past experiences. When a person sees something, seeing is not simply a visual experience, but the act of seeing implies the influence of something "on the mind." The impact of direct knowledge of anything requires more than simple assessment but complex understanding. The simplicity of observation is insightful, but the complexity of understanding must define the observed by references from past experiences. Preserving cultural tradition requires both knowledge as a sense of inclusiveness, and recognition of human values. These are universal values that are a part of all knowing experiences although such values may be determined by what is held to be important by the individual.

Knowing as a process connects an idea with a reality. An objective instance of knowing is recalling from a personal memory, and such a recollection includes the idea and the object as well as the process by which the individual is guided from one to the other. "...[W]e know an object by means of an idea, whenever we ambulate towards the object under the impulse which the idea communicates."[15] The person understands the idea is not the object but a means of connecting with a conceptual reality even when that reality is an abstraction. The tangibly realized element is often identified as the object always considered because the idea that represented it (the object) has an inclusive identity, although that identity may not conform to reality.

It is important to understand that knowledge is derived from different and often extraneous sources, including recollection, fable, legend, belief, and local stories. People constantly adjust the past to validate the present. The verbal transmission of traditional practices involves the concept of communication, and communication only has importance when it has meaning to the speaker and the receiver. Every specific subject of language divulges and conceals the truth of reality. It is at the same time both an uncontaminated meaning and an indication of something else. Language is not simply a means of interconnecting it is factual that language also influences humanity. Language is the receptacle of the important practices of humanity throughout history. Meaningful exchange allows language to function as a conveyer of information. The forms of communication employed express a view that may originate from personal or social history.

The objects with cultural and social significance and having special meaning are often lost due to people's lack of knowledge; however, education does not give meaning to many cultural elements. People may assign different meaning to a culture based on their beliefs and experience. Although culture may acknowledge world importance, the meaning may differ based on individual assessment. "This is not surprising if we remember that universality is a characteristic of significance: the greater the work [of culture], the deeper and more general its significance; the more general the significance, the easier it is to apply it to wider varieties of particular experience...."[16]

Cultural identity is often based on knowledge of similarity. "Similarity is an important notion in the theory of knowledge. Our knowledge of the world is dependent on our ability to identify similarities among things."[17] Similarity is also an important factor for tradition, considering much patrimony is beyond the recollection and often the perception of contemporary humanity. Imagining is less difficult when relating the descriptions to similar locations that are familiar. Similarity allows the viewer to categorize the traditional element as a knowable type.

Culture has a foundational purpose regarding the activities of communities that gain meaning through objects and activities. Cultural elements may be identified as referential knowledge, and such knowledge is dependent upon information that was first assessed by application. Application suggests understanding, and theory identifies the underlying methodology of knowing. Henri Bergson (French philosopher, 1859–1941) commented about two ways of knowing; intuition and intellect are "two profoundly different ways of knowing a thing. The first implies that we move around the object: the second that we enter it. The first depends on the point of view at which we are placed and on the symbols by which we express ourselves."[18] Bergson maintains that intellect "neither depends on a point of view nor relies on any symbol. The first kind of knowledge may be said to stop at the *relative*; the second, in those cases where it is possible, to attain the *absolute*" (Bergson italics).[19]

The limiting aspects of communication have direct implications for all aspects of the community. The methods and practices of anything are influenced by information (knowledge) transfer. Contemporary society associates knowledge with "knowing," but they are not the same. Either knowledge or knowing may exist independent of the other.

Analytical thinking attempts to rationalize life and knowledge on an elevated plane. It is the intellectual practice of vigorously and dexterously assessing data collected from understanding, logic, or common expression, as it influences belief and action. Analytical thinking involves the investigation of those elements that involve reasoning, problem solving, and atypical ideas. Analytical thinking differs according to the reasons motivating it. When devised for egotistical reasons, it is often expressed in terms of service to a person's special interest. As such it is usually defective, no matter how practical it might seem. However, when based on honesty and fairness, it is normally better, although it may be called "idealistic."

Analytical thinking about culture is a necessary part of thinking and discovering its value. Thinking about cultural issues allows objectivity, but endorsement requires an increase in inclusive understanding and the ability to accept emotional and intellectual growth at both quantitative and qualitative levels. Analytical thinking is the analysis of facts to make judgments; about culture, it is multifaceted and has many interpretations that generally include rational, skeptical, and unbiased analysis, or evaluation of factual material. It is a judgment to determine the authenticity, accuracy, worth, validity, or value of something.

This approach to thinking about culture establishes the predetermined method and suggests that the relevance of referential knowledge is a formula fixed process that is not definable as either subjective or objective. Identification and selection of analytical thinking must be based on a heightened level of knowledge. René Descartes (French philosopher, 1596–1650) places an emphasis upon the individual and this way of thinking supports the humanistic ideal. His philosophy is clearly individualistic and stresses human independence and the importance of individual self-reliance.

Various acts involve the appropriate associated sanctification (as examples of the force of words, prayers are said before eating or going to bed and oaths are sworn before joining a club or profession or giving testimony in court). Such happenings are a request for help against the influences of the unspecified negativism that is life. The associating of words and actions enables the connection between the human-originating appeal (request, prayer, or plea) and the powers qualified of realizing the requested action.

Communication in all its forms is an important part of all human relations; consequently, it is often unnoticed as an influence on the realization of activity goals. The intellectual effectiveness (knowledge) of the communication process is not easy to appraise. Humans as language and symbol users have a responsibility for truth—the truth of correct linguistic meaning and purpose. Immanuel Kant contends language originated from emotions, but others believe that it came from rational and logical thought. Regardless of its origin, communication is based on knowledge (see also the Introduction).

Because people are a mixture of ideas and emotions that are well developed, they include certain assumptions and expectations. Consequently, they may not be amenable to adding to their knowledge about culture or other human and natural activities. People may not learn or respond to the same intellectual or emotional stimulants in the same way. Nevertheless, some additions to cultural thinking can be achieved, while association and validation are required to reinforce other ideas. The willingness to accumulate information (knowledge) has a measurable influence on the mental and visual reception and response of the average person. A receptive attitude can be a link between the individual's life experience and their intellectual and spiritual growth. Successfully implemented, this connection may influence the quality of life of the person.

Ignorance or non-thinking is confusing because it causes individuals to act (react) without understanding, reason, or knowledge. People are influenced by ideas without thinking there is a different way to look, act, or feel. The authority of most things is included in the word. When a person speaks a word and knows how to use it, that person has gained a certain power over the idea associated with the word. Consider how many ideas and feelings are influenced by other people and the ideas they express. Some individuals are believed knowledgeable because people call them "intelligent" or "smart" as opposed to "dumb." The words people use are not only a means of exchange of ideas, or ways to articulate ideas; they are as insightful and discerning as the people that use them. Etymology is the storehouse of the happenings of humanity, and, as such, it influences individuals in the activities of existence.

Things to think about:

1. How old is the idea of education?
2. How is culture an all-people educational activity?
3. Why is seeing no longer believing?
4. If the acquisition of knowledge is a characteristic of humanity, why is it a basic schooling requirement?
5. How does education allow people to engage with objects or events, and with other people?
6. Why should a person understand the idea is not the object but a means of connecting with a conceptual reality even when that reality is an abstraction?
7. Are words forceful?
8. Does ignorance or non-thinking truly allow individuals to act without understanding, reason, or knowledge?
9. How does naming something or calling a name influence a person?
10. Who was Confucius?

NINE

Cultural Spaces
and Social Inclusion

THE HUMAN PHYSICAL (anatomical) structure has not altered appreciably in centuries, and daily life continues mostly unaltered (faster paced, more technological, but much the same). People calculate their life from birth to death by markers that are generally understood. A prevailing issue in the collection of human interests is the determination of personal standing within the complexity of the universe. Probably people do not think in theoretical terms about this issue but normal conditions are thought to produce common responses across different societies (responses like love, hate, envy, and remorse). The individual response to sociological inducements is usually prescribed by habit.

"Civilization is now a matter of fact, while culture is a question of value. In this sense of the term, culture now appears to lie irretrievably in the past."[1] (See also the Introduction) Many of the world's complexities were in place by the mid-nineteenth century, and in some locations, that condition occurred much earlier. Therefore, it is better to view patrimony not as validated historical truth, but as reasoning to explain the nature of things to people. If it is assumed that patrimony has no empirical reality, then the process of identification is greatly simplified.

Values, beliefs, and attitudes are fundamentals for cultural space. The loss of worth may cause the parts of the space to no longer work in unison. Attitude is a major factor in measuring the true meaning of the cultural space. Attitude whether individual or institutional is formed through contacts with individuals, social groups, or institutions. "Attitudes are constructed in which a certain type of relationship exists between an individual (or institution) and a specific social-cultural referent."[2]

The value and non-value of a cultural space may amount to a difference between aspects for which there are no predetermined qualifications and those for which there are reasonably specific characteristics.

One space may be based on traditional human reasoning that has multiple functions, and another may be viewed as functionless. The issue of function is extremely relevant to cultural space meaning and identity. Decisions on space are functionality assigned by persons far removed from the time and place of the originating creator. A change of function alters the meaning of the space; subsequently, a much-valued element may be considered functionless when it is separated from its true meaning.

Cultural spaces are a range of locations dedicated to the enactment, housing, presentation, or preservation of culture. They can be theaters, museums, galleries, churches, temples, and even some department stores. (A theme park is not normally an authentic cultural space.) A cultural space may be as small as a studio or a home office where true "art" is created or as large as a museum or historic site. It can be a coffee house or bar where poems are auditioned. Cultural spaces may be a philosophical concept. It is a reaction to basic human requirements. It contrasts with practical places that are dictated by intellectualizing and rationalizing, it dispenses with the ideas of exclusion and ambiguity. Reasonably a defined "space" should have one focus, but cultural spaces can have many different centers of appeal. The cultural space is composed of different locations, each with its own place, parameters, and purpose. The parts are important for the identification of the concept of cultural space, but a part does not reflect the whole in scope or spirit.

The objects in a cultural space (if objects are included) may have distinctive status in the related social environment. They (the objects) may represent a time in human history that is unlike other times; nevertheless, the objects represent history and not necessarily the culture. "In human history, the actuality of the object, as opposed to a reproduction, draws people in and gives them a literal way of touching the past."[3] Commercialized culture has objectified human achievements and has made common "the patrimonial objects." Cultural patrimony is consequently identified with the object and thereby the cultural and philosophical value are marginalized.

Cultural spaces are formed around ideas as well as elements that reflect the interests and beliefs of the place in which they are located. Recognition of cultural and social activities can serve as the basis for social interaction in all forms. The cultural spaces are often in locations that consider and acknowledge human issues and concerns as well as tradition. Such places provide guidance and support for the present as well as information about the culture of yesterday and today. Cultural spaces have an increasing role in society as places of humanism that redefine concepts relating to public interaction and learning.

Cultural spaces (including institutions) are guardians of people spaces as well as interpreters and protectors of patrimony (human identity). They are places for the study of cultural and natural materials, and expressions of societies and communities. Cultural spaces also include the spaces where people live and work like libraries and studios. Cultural spaces are basic to the agenda of humanity. The opportunities for cultural spaces are great and the characteristics so diverse that although meaningful contributions may be anticipated, the way of achieving them is time-consuming. Cultural spaces are agents of change and proponents of truth, human dignity, and responsible stewardship—humanism and the facets of life. The accumulated elements endorse an environment where people can gain an awareness of the continuity that exists in human creation from the past to the present and obtain an equally meaningful view of the nature and the resident creatures.

Localized culture adaptation may occur when social patterns outgrow the practices brought forward from the past, thus affirming the need for a new scheme of socio-cultural interpretation. This transformational need occurs in most societies as a reflection of group identity and growth. It is recognized as the fundamental nature of a community and a part of civilized progression. Expressions of adapted (pseudo) heritage can include multiple and contradictory elements; that is, there can be more than one message with essential qualities because societies are composed of different attitudes and experiences.

Culture spaces are unlimited. They are everywhere. They include traditional spaces such as museums, concert halls, and places of worship, dance studios, recital halls, as well as heritage sites, theaters, libraries, cinemas, parks, community centers, clubs (some), yoga centers, dojos, zen-do, and on and on. Culture spaces are locations that practice the knowledge and skills that people acknowledge as part of their cultural life. Culture is constantly reinvented in response to history, and the natural world. It provides people with a feeling of specialness and stability, thereby advocating social diversity.

Identifying the role of cultural spaces in society as locations for holding, studying, viewing, or enjoying culture, and how they address the evolving needs of a dynamic community is a challenge for people. Cultural institutions have changed and will continue to change, particularly in relation to interaction among objects, education, and the people. Although cultural places continue to be viewed as object gathers and keepers, the collecting of materials, which was for years a primary part of their mission, has truly lost its hold as the foundation of institutional work, as people become more sophisticated and more demanding. Displays often rely on objects of differing quality and importance, and less on institutional collections requiring the principles of institutions to expand in service to society.

Education has become a force within the cultural community causing cultural spaces to develop new and better educational programs. Personal and program practices are in a constant process of renewal. Many educators reach back to the early years of the twentieth century to borrow from innovative cultural pioneers who promoted centers for education. Culture is an all-people educational activity.

Cultural spaces, including locations that have service responsibilities, share social and scientific information, correct misconceptions, improve attitudes, and influence cognitive skills. Cultural spaces are called upon to address the physical and metaphysical questions about human existence. They have an essential part in actualizing personal and group identity. The introduction of new technology has altered the way cultural information is shared by both the center and the public. Organizational vision, as a viable and realistic view of the center's service possibilities, is an essential part of cultural places' thinking and planning.

Many cultural spaces, as a form of social interaction, are responsible for transmitting cultural information in all its forms. Society's endorsement of such places, and the special role of those centers, is conditioned upon fulfilling their responsibility to promote truth as a patrimonial value. All culture spaces develop and maintain the means required to ensure the objectivity and value of their role in society. It is likely that many definitions will describe instead of define cultural organizations. Regardless of the preferred definition, cultural spaces have a duty to consider the effect of each activity related to the space and the people. Cultural spaces balance specialized interests and group dynamics with genuine concern for humanity and the interests of society.

Culture is for everyone, and the cultural space is inclusive. It excludes no one whether the physically or mentally challenged, caregiver, or senior. Cultural places maintain time-honored values while considering public expectations, changing demographics, advancing technology, and governmental regulations. The idea of culture is not considered as unchallengeable; however, the value of culture is not questioned because it is subject to the same failings and flaws as humanity. The challenges for culture increase when it engages in international activities including object gathering and presentations.

Culture enhances people's lives and enriches their mental and physical health. Culture allows people to engage with objects or events, and with other people. The cultural space brings people together and generates a sense of collective understanding through cultural activities. Community activities or neighborhood centers have extraordinary potential as active facilitators of social change through helping people understand the concepts of disability and having a chance to meet people with physical and mental challenges.

Cultural spaces are centers for learning and information exchange, and they fulfill this important role by talking about the past and presenting current topics. These centers have an increased role in society to influence the appreciation of elements of everyday use, and the level of respect and understanding for humanity. The objects and events in a cultural center communicate beyond the surroundings in which they are located. The activities cause people to visualize positive ideals and stimulate thinking that will cause future generations to have similar inclusive feelings.

The cultural space is changing as it gains foci and significance. The space is viewed admiringly by some people and totally unnoticed by others. Culture influences awareness. People see what they want to see, not what is present to be seen. In theory, the cultural space should be considered in a circular and not linear perspective. It has a larger, more inclusive view that is inclined to repeat itself. The repetition is not that a single manifestation is repeated, but that the same values are found in more than one location. Time in the East has a cyclical quality, but since the fifteenth century, time in much of the Western world has gradually lost its recurring nature and become linear. The view of time as a circle has given way to a straight line.

Cultural events are normally considered in terms of activities. Many cultural events have different objectives to serve different constituents, thereby making every activity unique and the service provided of special value to the respective group. The gathering of special objects follows the development of social investment in culture as a part of a community. Culture is often distinctive, and the community served gives such value to the activities as respect, caring, and social merit. Culture has a role in maintaining the identity, beliefs, and values of people. Their responsible is the continued investment in a positive response to challenges to the attitudes and practices, values, and beliefs of current and future generations.

Cultural places are most beneficial to communities when attention is given to objects or activities in terms people can understand—not just words but meaning. Cultural spaces attract visitors and arouse curiosity that leads to questions and thus promotes true learning. The social identity of a people requires a comparative assessment that views culture in inclusive terms. A comparison is required to demonstrate the distinctiveness of the reference group's cultural tradition. This uniqueness is verified by culture. (This is a facet of inclusion.) The designated culture must be recognized, perhaps most importantly, as having universal value.

Personal or communal cultural tradition is most likely socially transmitted behavioral patterns and products of human work, beliefs, and thoughts. The personal culture of each human is a product of the incumbent traditions and social environment, and that totality identifies a person as a member of a certain culture. Group activities are influenced by the concept of tradition, which continues practices from a previous time. Multiple issues are involved in determining the traditions of a society, of which value is one. Belief and other factors endorsed by community members and the environment are also significant.

A person or a people may choose to disregard their past and the related culture. People may try to adopt new customs and practice without the cultural background or traditions to support those activities. This type of de-actualization often leaves individuals and communities baseless. (This de-actualization is happening with some immigrant communities.) The loss of cultural affiliation takes away the values of the past and denies a people of their foundation. The practices to identify social values are reinforced as they are transmitted from one generation to the next. This integration of nontraditional activities alters the coherent whole of the group and challenges the validity of uncorroborated practices allegedly based on communal objectives. Patrimony is often defined to accommodate new ideas. That kind of disruption damages individuals, families, and communities. People are denied self-respect and a sense of wholeness.

Cultural tradition is an expression of the singularity of a group (or community) that defines its uniqueness and prevents combining that group into a uniformity of thought and practice with other similarly motivated and defined groups, people, and societies. Culture presents itself as a unity of discrete and functional (true) meanings. The underlying reality of culture is that it seldom persists unaltered through circumstantial change unless it is maintained in a non-contextual environment, much as an artifact in an institution.

Cultural spaces can give meaning to the idea of inclusiveness. The attitude of caring, whether individual or institutional, is formed through contacts with individuals or social groups. "Attitudes are constructs in which a certain type of relationship exists between an individual and a specific social-cultural referent."[4] People with different backgrounds and different needs can develop relationships in the cultural space. Cultural spaces are also places for people to establish positive attitudes toward persons with a disability. They are places to clarify concepts and to remove prejudices.

Cultural spaces are places to assist the communities to meet their social obligation. Human ability creates inequity and alters the existence of thousands of individuals and their families. Eliminating the physical barriers assists one segment of the audience, but it has limited meaning for others. The elderly, mentally disturbed, and clinically depressed persons normally do not view culture as a part in their life-pattern, although cultural locations can be locations where they feel safe and secure in the knowledge they will be treated with the same respect as others.

Society must change from reliance on traditional attitudes of life to more adaptable life choices. Cultural spaces provide a range of opportunities for persons with either physical or mental limitations and their caregivers. "Allowing older adults to actually remember, not only cognitively but through all senses, is important and help retrieve forgotten memories. It enables communication between generations and creates well-being."[5] Societies must be inclusive.

Inclusiveness is a part of the idea of personal significance, yet people with special needs are often forgotten. Mental health is an essential part of personal well-being. People often experience a degree of stress when experiencing new situations. This can be disabling. Suffering from social anxiety disorder is a condition that is often misidentified as shyness.

The assumed social stigma of mental illness is an issue that cultural spaces can help communities understand. Studies show that many people with mental illness are unwilling to let others know about their condition. They fear discrimination, a negative impact on their work environment, or loss of friends. Families prefer to hide the mentally ill from relatives to avoid possible embarrassment. Public information, programs, and displays can aid people in understanding the importance of receiving proper mental health care. Instructional programs are for the everyone, not just those suffering from uncertainty.

Cultural spaces can provide information that will reduce misunderstandings about mental illness. They can offer educational programs for caregivers as well as persons who are dealing with social, economic, or personal issues that cause depression or reliance of alcohol or drugs. "Mental health is a state of well-being in which an individual realizes [their] own abilities, can cope with the normal stresses of life, can work productively, and is able to make a contribution to his or her community."[6]

Disability is both a common but personal experience that exists across the entire globe. It has widespread economic, cultural, and political implications for society as a whole. People with physical and mental disabilities are everyone's neighbors, friends, or family members.

Cultural spaces in many locations seek methods to serve humanity while preserving and disseminating the character of the cultural tradition. Cultural space values emanate from a clear understanding of what is to be achieved, how it will be achieved and how achievement will be determined. Humanity should understand that culture is not merely an expression of the tangible world in which they exist but also represents the world of everyone. It is not that those objects or events speak to us or for us; they conform to our ways of knowing. People must devise effective means for not just appreciating but protecting cultural elements (and people). The process of preservation is ongoing constantly, an evolving process of responsibility that often challenges conventional thinking.

Tradition must be differentiated from "customs" that dominate alleged "traditional societies." The purpose and character of a "tradition" is consistency. The culture to which a tradition refers has established practices that may be repeated. Traditions embody both stability and reliability in each activity. Stability is acknowledged by the repetition of identifiable elements cultivated within the tradition. Reliability is a part of each endeavor, wherein actions may stray from accepted tradition, the enactment remains within normative standards. For example, the Lakalaka of Tonga is a standardized practice. In the performance the Lakalaka group of performers stand still and make gestures with their arms only. It is considered the national dance of Tonga.[7]

Sustaining Cultural Ways

People have an assortment of beliefs that are formed at an early age, and those feelings and emotions promote related assumptions and expectations, prejudices, and beliefs. Focus has shifted from the viewing of the specialness of an object as an objective value to an appraisal of subjective experience. Personal gratification as a factor of human judgment is influencing cultural values and organizational vision. Cultural personnel seek to understand the provisions of "leisure value" and why some things appeal emotionally and intellectually and some do not; consequently, why they influence appreciation of some objects, presentations, and location.

The visitors to cultural spaces are the least comprehended and often the most problematic of all the factors affecting the spaces' efforts to serve. This difficulty arises because people are intricate and unpredictable. In addition, much of the obtainable information on human behavior comes from the discipline of psychology. Often such data aid in clarifying observed but perplexing human activities such as the need to touch, the tendency to avoid some locations and to be drawn to others, and the apparently positive response to some stimuli and the relative indifference toward others.

Numerous studies have been made to ascertain what people assume to obtain from their cultural space visit, why they favor one location and not another, and what is not at the location that they would like or expect to find there. The studies analyze the pre- and post-visit knowledge of people about various activities. When the information gained from such studies is integrated into the space's public agenda, the benefits are generally meaningful for both the culture space and the visitor. When this type of information is put into practice, it usually adds value to the cultural space within the resident community, but is not pertinent in general.

Such studies have a short effective life because visitor needs change. Considerable information is needed about how people behave and what they learn to ensure a positive experience. There are no absolute controls or reasons for people to learn, enjoy, or have a meaningful experience except for the information and the stimulation provided. This means that visitors may not learn that their misunderstandings are wrong, that learning can be exciting, or that things can be not what they seem.

The diversity of visitors makes promoting cultural use and literacy difficult. Literacy is a part of cultural spaces, and that aspect of the cultural activities is a social as well as cultural responsibility. Cultural literacy is more than presentations and educational programs. The material item does not represent the true meaning of culture for most communities although culture is often focused on the object or event. Cultural literacy has both internal and external obligations for traditional locations. Internally it is more than a description of past events augmented by related objects, and externally it requires a commitment to sharing information in a value-motivating manner that involves every aspect of the institution.

For many communities, the intention is to elevate their cultural space into accordance with a preconceived ideal. The object or events may not be necessary on their own, but because they relate to an image the community has of itself. Accordingly, the importance of an object or event is determined less by the pleasure resulting from having it, than the self-satisfaction that goes with possession. Examples may include developing a practice like the Ijele Masquerade ceremonial activity of south-eastern Nigeria or the ritual dance Huaconada from the central Peruvian Andes. Social values are often of this nature. In this case, the desire is not of cognizant reasoning, but of a self-conscious ideal. The value is in the desire itself rather than in any conscious gratification. In these cases, the object (or element) as well as desire are based on an ideal of what the community wants itself to be.

There was probably never a time when local culture was not subject to intervention or adaptation to meet the social, political, or economic requirements of the community. The creation of local culture includes a process of "formalization and ritualization, characterized by reference to the past, if only by imposing repetition."[8] The extant community may have no recollection of the cultural resource being endorsed, and often there is no sense of *déjà vu*. The group that experienced the event no longer exists and there are little or no empirical data to identify them or to verify their existence. Yet, the feeling of myths and quasi-tradition persists.

One is unlikely to find a community that uniformly and completely shares beliefs, values, and ideals in contemporary society, because people have varied life ways based on ambition, personality, and ego, therefore minimal common history. Most societies are pluralistic in the sense of containing differing backgrounds, interests, and motivations; consequently, defining local culture based on common cognition in a diverse community is difficult. Much of the local culture is rediscovered in every generation because of the difficult of describing, and therefore communicating. Anthony Wallace (American philosopher) believes that "The best a culture can do is communicate the general framework of 'its' plan and ensure that the new generation is placed in situations in which they will have to reinvent the details...."[9] The local cultural belief of contemporary society evolves to accommodate different ideas and beliefs.

People have different ideas about what is important for a community. The changes "unfold" across the community in layers, building until a noticeable change occurs. The culture community as well as the social community is subject to this type of evolvement. "Change" is most obvious with technology. Examples of technological changes are numerous and almost all have influenced culture in some direct or indirect way. Cultural patterns change at different times in different locations, and this diversity offers the opportunity to assess human developments. Culture as a social reference is valid regardless of the environment in which it exists or the source of its origination. Concerns about social issues require sustainable values instead of formalized theories.

Changing cultural life may revise itself by reducing the emphasis it formerly placed upon one or more existing elements, or by inventing or assimilating new elements that previously were not considered. These changes may be received with a degree of resistance, but the cultural and social life of contemporary society is in constant flux and the values of one person or group are not those of another. (A changing emphasis and belief, or a change of emphasis within the same belief, may be viewed as inclusive but not acceptable by the community.) The vast amount of information that assails the human thought process may suggest that the differences between the cultural elements of one people and those of another are so mingled that there is no reason to believe there is but one essential human nature.

It is human nature to be attracted to the unusual and one of the conditions inherent in such encounters is the urge to relate to the unique. There is a need to evaluate the unknown in the terms of the known. The outcome of this process may be misunderstanding but confusing whether considering objects, customs, or practices. The seemingly comic or bizarre images, activities, or customs may be more freely understood when considered from a culturally cognizant point of view. One of the reasons people find early (past) locations fascinating is the unusual elements related to the human environment. An example of this phenomenon is the Cossack songs sung by communities of the Dnipropetrovsk region in Ukraine which tell stories about the tragedy of war but also the personal relationships of Cossack soldiers.[10]

Another example, in the Eastern Buddhist life, is believed to be a revolving cycle from "birth to birth, life to life, with no permanent joy obtainable while each life is burdened with all kinds of suffering,"[11] and the Taoists "draw upon any combination of traditional and contemporary cultural elements to facilitate their effort to live the Taoist life as fully as possible."[12] This same attitude was prevalent in both practice and belief. The Taoist tradition gathered examples of the spiritual life practices and in this way met the needs of a broad fellowship. The situation has changed from the traditions of previous practices. It is not the belief that has changed. It is people that have changed.

A comparative assessment that considers a particular culture in universal terms is required to define the cultural identity or practices of a group. This review of social activity is a primary element in defining culture. Verification of cultural values also requires communication and the diffusion of belief. The identity of each culture activity must be recognized as containing a meaningful value.

All people have the right to benefit from and transmit the culture of their progenitors as they determine. It is then imperative that the culture tradition must not reduce the value or importance of the human spirit and diminish the significance of culture regardless of its form, function, monetary value, universality, or belief. Ultimately it is only when culture enriches the humanity in each human being, preserves individual dignity, and equips humanity to meet the challenges of existence that a claim of social responsibility can be justified. The meaning and importance of culture as a necessary resource must not be underestimated.

However, socially endowed culture loses much of its meaning when it is not genuine but only a means for achieving a previously defined goal. Societal integrity implies a public perspective involving the esteem and fair repute that follows upon the correct fulfillment of a public role. That role is one of responsibility and honesty. A person and the cultural life in which the individual lives are the same. They are restrained by time and place. Obligated by the assortment of actions available, cultural life is simply adept at reflecting the history from which it develops. As the world becomes more complex and culture and the margins between cultures become more unstable, humanities lose their interconnection and self-reliance.

Human life is a tradition-directed metaphor that cannot be viewed through the rose-glass. Every feature proposes a discrete symbolic allusion that can be communicated past the sociological horizon. Countless dreams are beyond the sphere of explanation even for those persons installed in generating culture. It is as if humans secrete themselves in immortality to recapture their own morality.

Things to think about:

    1. Why are cultural spaces considered both guardians and interpreters of patrimony?

    2. How does culture provide people with a sense of identity and continuity?

    3. Why are cultural spaces unlimited?

    4. Explain why visitors to cultural spaces are the least understood and usually the most difficult of all the factors influencing the center.

    5. How do cultural spaces benefit the community in which they are located?

    6. Is it possible for cultural traditions to displace recollections that impede the activities of a community and permit its members to be a part of the society?

7. Why are people a mixture of ideas and emotions?

8. Explain why there never been a time when local culture was not subject to intervention.

9. Do people have different ideas about what is important to a community?

10. Why is the meaning of "cultural" important?

TEN

The Idea
of Cultural Identity

PEOPLE REFLECT THEIR HISTORY. They are a product of the society from which they emanated, and they have a natural sympathy for the stories, rituals, and expressions of their predecessors. People have "...an inner guiding factor that is different from the conscious personality."[1] This sentiment often displaces intellect as it resides in the moral fiber of the person along with a variety of other practices that determine the culture of the community, group, or person. Such thinking goes beyond ordinary beliefs to reaffirm group and individual identity. The idea of "identity" relates to the behavioral or personal attributes by which an individual or community is known. It is a psychological arrangement pertaining to perception, definition, and projection of self or group in relation to others. Identity increases self-esteem and recognition for an individual or group and gives a sense of importance, but at the same time, may be at odds with the resident community.

Circumstantial conditions in an evolving cultural context may stimulate identity criteria, including the relationship between objects or situations that acknowledge or verify the difference between groups of seemingly similar cultures. Random diffusion of an idea may instill derivative values by embedding one condition or phenomenon in place of another. It is, therefore, possible to view society as a world-making activity—self-perpetuation—in the sense that it (society) creates or recreates and communicates values within the limits imposed by the group—a circumstantial reality. The human environment is that peculiar set of realities that distinguish one culture, one people, and in some instances, one individual from others. "All the words we use, in any language, spoken, written, or appreciated by touch, as in Braille, are made of mental images."[2]

For example, the Busó festivity at Mohács in southern Hungary is a six-day carnival in late February to mark the end of winter, named for the *busós*, frightening-looking costumed people (traditionally men) wearing wooden masks and big, woolly cloaks.[3] This event addresses how the people relate to their environment and how they relate to each other. The winter is symbolically overcome, and a coffin (of winter) is burned on a bonfire in the central square. This relational activity celebrates human survival and reinforces local belief as well as reinforcing communal values.

The idea of cultural identity is a reference to tradition, and in some sense reflects upon itself in the privileged dimension of time. With or without explicit reference to the pertinence of this notion in the context of historical temporality, and with an association with the historicity of the culture, it is possible to identify certain cultural attributes. Cultural identity and the associated changes are transformed into a requirement of "culture."

Cultural identity is the distinguishing characters of an object, event, or person. It is essentially a psychological phenomenon involving the opinion, definition, and ideals of "self" in relation to others. The conception of identity is a primary concern for human beings. Cultural identity may be defined as whatever makes a person definable and recognizable, but even this approach is often relative.

People require identity, and in search of a cultural identity, people act or react according to the examples defined by their past and the characteristics of their social order. The act of preserving these resources (identity and association) is an expression of resilience of a people or a community. This effort is to serve humanity and its allied history, natural surroundings, and cultural endeavors. The concept of true patrimony accumulation and preservation relates to humans in all locations. The history of a community has an incisive role in the formation of a communal consciousness and unity, as well as economic and social development.

The law of identity states that "Each thing is the same with itself and different from another."[4] Accordingly, things with the same essence are the same thing (theoretically), and things with different essences are different things. Cultural identity relates to the sameness of characteristics including belief, preference, and capacity for rational thought. Thoughts about historical elements generate impressions, and since no object or event can be present in the mind, it is only a perception. This concept calls upon the basic principle of human imagination, that is, that the essential elements of the human thinking process are derived from prior perceptions or impressions. When forming an idea of the object, the image is defined to resemble an incumbent perception prompted by the individual imagination. There is no assumption the two impressions are identical; instead, the cultural element is often considered the same type as the perception.

Cultural identity may be viewed as special and difficult to explain without moving into fields of philosophy and perhaps sociology, behavioral science, and psychology. There are, however, certain considerations to be addressed, particularly the apparent contradiction between the (so-called) formal or abstract character of information associated with cultural resources. The explanatory value of social customs as they are often conceived and promoted is low when it comes to investigating the conditions of social stability or identity validation. It is necessary to examine how resources of signification are used to legitimatize the special interests of a group to analyze the societal implications of any cultural identity.

Cultural identity helps define the distinction that makes each person unique, whereas role confirms the sameness of an individual with society. Social or personal patrimony (life history) serves as an agent that can enhance a sense of identity, pride, and social connectedness. The identity of social patrimony may be the same for the individual just as individuals are a construction of role identities. For example, membership in the Nyau Society is limited to initiated members of the Chewa and Nyanja people. The Nyau is a secret society of the Chewa and a form of relation. Only initiates are considered part of nature. The emotional values associated with this cultural element defines an independent existence unlike that of other values. It is not possible to separate the emotion from the activity as an element of personal patrimony.

Group identity is being interfused due to the blending action of cross-cultural exchange and a variety of other cultural activities. Many persons are completely blank of all positive aspect of awareness of the commonly shared values of people. For them, the negative impact of loss of culture, and the worst situation, the pride of a people, is of marginal importance. The identification of patrimony is a method for giving humanity a valid presence in society, whether it is real culture or manufactured. All people are the same, but different. Just as with thinking, people's differences are due to ego and desire.

The quest for group identity is the natural result of social homogenization. The result of this socially leveling program is commonality—meaning a loss of individual identity. The result is often an artificial construction of a personality built around ideological, historical, or physiological suppositions that attempt to be made real by imagination.

Social customs are more than simply a mind-residing thought. It reflects the pride of identity for a society by defining the intellectual and emotional essence of the cultural and natural systems. The emotions inherent in this instance may also be a part of the human continuum that is passed onward from preceding generations (patrimony as life history). Social custom activities can facilitate the understanding and perpetuation of social values, and reflect the interests, traditions, and beliefs of the people, but it may or may not be real.

Social expectation influences identity. Social expectation, as a custom, is not unique to one land or one people. In the West jobs, marriage, and having a new car or trophy wife or husband are established social expectations. In the East there are arranged marriage, expected male children, filial piety, and many others. Social expectations are the factors that influence people's identity without thinking. (Forced marriages are a form of bondage or slavery. Forced marriage are practiced in some regions of the world.) Social expectations effect every part of society in every land. People call them by different names: "keeping-up-with-the-Jones," "face," "macho," "ego" and "self-importance," to name a few. Social expectation may lack verifiable form as a theoretical concept and rely on emotions, beliefs, and a related number of idealistic factors that promote connections between dissimilar concepts and elements.

The idea of cultural identification is elemental, but after interpretation and politicization, the original simplicity is lost. Nation-states have revised and expanded their heredity in consideration of politics and economics but seldom for revitalizing their patrimony. People enjoy conjecture about things that have little importance, while avoiding responsibility for the culture of communities. It is possible the human capacity for indifference, instead of for social or cultural responsibility, is the foundation of humanity's cultural regression.

The Perceived Transformation

A judgment (opinion) of culture is human generated. Immediate reaction (not thinking) is often a perception with good intention, but without meaningful consideration. Perceptive judgments should remain within the thinking process of the individual, awaiting acknowledgment and verification granting validation. The subjective nature of perceptive judgments, which advocate as good merely that towards which the person has one kind of feeling. What is unacceptable is that towards which the person has a different kind of feeling. When people must exercise choice and prefer this or that of two options, it is necessary to have a distinction of authentic and unauthentic. This difference is not arbitrary, and only concerned with time (the present without equal regard for the past) thereby influencing both the concept and elements of culture.

"The object and its perception are mutually dependent. One does not exist before the other, nor does one enjoy greater ontological status than the other. Objects exist in relation to perceptions, while cognitions exist in relation to their objects."[5] Perception as sensory information, is the result of memory, and the mental processing of elements conveyed from the physical world to the mind as stimulated by recall. The metaphysical nature of the current thinking of much of humanity seeks a reality beyond that perceptible to the senses. The lessening of acquired knowledge and understanding decreases a person's capability to join unique perceptions into a meaningful whole.

Perceptions are usually not intellectually directed but emotionally influenced, and when that happens, it is uncertain whether the mind is truly able to recognize "reality." Emotion and passion (among other feelings) obscure reality by projecting circumstances in an imaginary form. Perceived elements are located within a system of expectations relating to preconceptions. "The world of the percipient defined in terms of temporal experience, is an organized body of expectations based on recollection."[6] Perceptions may be more real than reality, but memory produced imagery is not real.

Philosophers, including Descartes, Bergson, and Dewey, devoted a great deal of time in investigating the idea of perception, and each followed his research to determine what the phenomenon involved. Each philosopher's conclusion was different, but all agreed on the importance of this form of understanding. Perception relates to knowledge and is an expanding process, that is, the longer the mind focuses on an "image" of the perceived element, the more expansive the image becomes. These expansions are thought (intellectually) to be attachments to the basic element (perception).

Immanuel Kant (German philosopher) wrote in *Prolegomena to Any Future Metaphysics*, "All our judgments are at first merely judgments of perception; they hold good only for us (that is, for our subject), and we do not till afterward give them a new reference (to the object)...."[7] Kant states the reason for giving a new reference to the objects is so "they [the judgments] shall always hold good for us and in the same way for everyone else, and thus the objective validity of the judgment of experience signifies nothing else than its necessary universal validity."[8]

A perceptual judgment has no inclusive value. It cannot be universalized. The perception (subjective) is a personal idea, or a determination based on personal insight. It is not objective. The observation is defined by an individual value system and contrasted with judgments based upon forethought (prudence), assessment (evaluation), and confirmation (proof) as Kant describes "*judgments of experience.*" Value judgments may also be based on a predetermined code of values (ethics) such as those relating to professional activities. The judgments, in this latter case, are confirmed by established principles, and therefore, are not arbitrary.

Friedrich Nietzsche (1844–1900) wrote in 1873: "The past is principally used as a model for imitation"[9] A memory passes from a thought to a perception once the appropriate attitude is adopted, but it (the memory) remains attached to the past (nostalgia). The perception must retain the value associated with the original object or it cannot be identified with the present. It is often forgotten that the traditional element is a remembered impression, and it assumes greater value the more it is defined and given reference within the present. The memory of a remembered element enhances a feeling that has cultural value, otherwise the element is disregarded.

Old objects may promote a feeling of similarity or nostalgia; that is, they cause the memory to recall similar objects, shapes or perceptions, and that recollection encourages a sense of familiarity. History pieced together with images of the past are fragments of the present. There may be only "traces" of historical references to verify personal culture such as stories that outline social activity. Stories and practices may represent tradition, or they may be "invented traditions" that have gained a level of popularity for reasons other than faith or belief.

Regardless of perception, the past is an indistinct "time" that is often viewed as being better than the present because it engenders a sense of continuity. "The past we depend on to make sense of the present is, however, mostly recent...." David Lowenthal (American historian and geographer) observed, "It [the past] stems mainly from our own few years of experience. The further back in time, the fewer the traces that survive, the more they have altered, and the less they anchor us to contemporary reality."[10]

The use of objects, whether cultural or scientific, to validate events is often complicated in that events do not always define themselves in terms of equal proportion to the importance assigned to them. "The presentation and interpretation of objects play a large part in shaping our perception of ordinary living conditions as well as important events of the part."[11] The world is often a little-known place, and the transmission of culture has a special measure of relevance that should be thoughtfully considered.

J. Rošker (contemporary Slovenian sinologist) contends that "instead of establishing a clear demarcation line between the subject and the object of comprehension, human perception and recognition of reality were mostly seen as a product of a coherent, structurally ordered and complementary interaction between the heart-mind and the things-events."[12] The thinking of a people includes knowledge as an approach to existence that combined the ideas and values that define perceptions of the world and ways of life. "These elements of personal object experiences ultimately shape people's meaning-making in patrimonial repositories and other informal learning environments."[13]

The culture as patrimony is old in years, but new because of its reintroduction as representatives of another time. It has advanced hypothetically from an objective existence to a subjective identity that replaces the original character. That this change is positive or negative is not the issue, instead it is the ideological influence on identity, and whether that ideology is or should be a factor in determining its value.

Tradition may be a practice that promotes self-esteem and group cohesion with group investment by interpreting related activities in a way that maintains or reinforces group values. Tradition is necessary as a source of examples when needed examples do not exist in contemporary life. This action gives community members (as individuals) a sense of security and a feeling of social value. People are eager to see and to touch those things and places identified as special and that curiosity can be difficult (the touching) for elements humans admire.

Communal beliefs, as convictions of truth, often have a dual quality, that is, they are traditions or remembrances as well as ideas or viewpoints based on current information and imagination. People gave little thought to the distinction between past and present up to the nineteenth century. Until that time, people often referred to past events as though they were occurring in the present. Even today most people who consider the past assume it is much like the present. Although there are obvious changes in life and the environment, people do not believe there is a change in human nature, and the behavior is much like in the past. People change as the world changes. "Venerated as a fount of communal identity, cherished as a precious and endangered resource, yesterday became less and less like today."[14] Knowledge is a part of the decision-making process to achieve clarity of thinking however subtle the possible difference between thoughts may be.

Change (transformation) has a direct influence on culture because much of the world is subject to cultural values and change. Change is inevitable. Buildings, monuments, and locations change or are transformed due to external and internal conditions. Deterioration, restoration, and the natural environment make changes that cause the element to be "different." For example, the Sistine Chapel ceiling was transformed. It is the same painting after cleaning as it was before the smoke, dirt, and candle wax was removed, but it is different. (Again, it is the same but different.) People were told it is the same, the colors have not been changed, the figures are not repainted, and it is not a digital replication. It is the Sistine Chapel ceiling painted in 1512, and most of the public accepts that identity. (Some people remain skeptical.)

This approach allows the concepts of history to change and to become different without eliminating previous representations. History is identified with various forms reflecting its relationship to human activities. "Tradition is one form of shared memory, one in which the line transmitting a version from the past is sanctified, authorized, or even canonized in such a way that it is immune to challenges based on alternative historical lines."[15] Tradition may complicate the past but does not necessarily validate it.

Probably the capacity to make cultural identity more meaningful is in the concept of tradition, and the actual value of patrimony may be not so much in its merging with individual or group identity, as in the immeasurable differences that separate one individual or group from others. The past can only be represented if it is established in the group imagination as an object or place with identifiable features.

Lost Identity

A broad expression of culture as a way of life conveys the essence of humanity. The idea is to combine the thinking connected with tradition and to pull consideration away from efforts that are harmful to people and cultural honesty. People have always tried to acknowledge themselves through their past. This process is frustrated by political unrest, misunderstanding, and fictional representations. These concessions have facilitated the externalization of culture in inappropriate and often calamitous ways.

For example, in about the year 221 BCE the Emperor of the Qin Dynasty burned books and killed scholars. He wanted to change the traditional way of Confucian learning. Another example: in 1933 CE schools, universities, the press, theater, and the arts in Germany were forced to abide by Nazi control. Jewish maltreatment climaxed on *Kristallnacht* (November 9–10, 1938). After *Kristallnacht* Jews were effectively erased from public life in Germany. A third example: in the United States, Sen. Joseph McCarthy conducted a series of investigations and hearings during the 1950s to reveal presumed communist intrusion into various divisions of the U.S. government. The hearings included widely publicized, indiscriminate allegations based on unsubstantiated charges. The accusations greatly defamed the character or reputation of many people. A fourth example: in China, early in 1966, the Cultural Revolution reportedly buried alive 46,000 scholars and burned tens of thousands of books (possibly but not confirmed). People were encouraged to divest themselves of the "Four Olds"—old customs, old culture, old habits, and old ideas. Between these events and continuing today there are ongoing efforts to change the history of a people and the world. Books are revised or destroyed, and people are silenced or in denial.

These are true examples of what can happen when people allow the unusual—the abysmal, the horrible—to happen: the dereliction of thinking. These abhorrent acts were intended to deny people their fundamental rights, and to cancel the cultural and historical significance of society because people did not think and act. This is not "abandoned" history; this is intentional elimination of people and human values. Unlike Suakin, which was an important community on the Red Sea coast at one time and abandoned during the time of British rule to be replaced by Port Sudan. Or, Port Chatham, Alaska, that by 1950 everyone had left, leaving it abandoned. These places and others were abandoned by people either intentionally or for cause.

The removal of symbols and statements of the negative part of history does not change the past. Joseph McCarthy's blacklisting was eventually ignored by many, but caused great upheaval and destroyed people's lives. The symbols are gone like the Cultural Revolution in China but the history remains. They become more important when they are hidden or ignored. Patrimony is important to people and knowing that something happened is not the same as knowing how it happened. Knowledge of events is often an accrual of details devoid of knowing how or why. The truth is that knowing how or why something happened is founded on thinking and knowledge. Facts often tell little about a situation.

Moral thinking advocates the idea of respect and social accountability, and that persons and communities should support cultural and natural patrimony as essential components of life. This thinking supports the right of all people to share in the pleasure and knowledge of their patrimony in an inclusive setting. The contemporary community is a place where the talents of the time and the spirit of the people can find expression. However, human communication, despite its importance, may be altered to the degree that traditions are changed. These alterations may indicate a redefining of what people are culturally and emotionally, as well as of renewing importance on what they have always been. This circumstance is represented by the demolition of monuments, statues, and related images following a catastrophic social events or a change of political system. These elements may be viewed as negative remembrances of an abysmal past, but are nevertheless a part of the history of a nation and should be conserved.

Much of the world has experienced the phenomenon of disposable history, that is, destruction of the symbolic aspects of social life. Most societies and individuals have a short cultural memory, and what remains is often modified by subjective and selective recollection. Individuals can argue that the environment is not human "made"; therefore, people and emotions are not a factor in "natural" issues. It was, however, human intelligence and effort that identifies, names, and classifies flora, fauna and people. Nature went about its business of environmental change for centuries without the benefit of human intervention, but unpardonably, humanity altered the natural process. The endangered elements of the world are the result of human interaction with nature.

The concept of abandoned history includes the idea of rediscovered or redefined cultural tradition. The unpredictable difficulty with rediscovered culture is that it has no referential place in the past and no evidentiary essence. Often the "official" account is a mixture of fact and fiction formulated to validate a general idea. Not only is the concept of rediscovered tradition often not logical and the resources not permanent, but also the conception and association of the approach is subject to historical mutability. Although the idea of rediscovered "cultural tradition" is vague and inconsistent with historic precedent, "people tend to act or react according to the examples given to them by their own history and the characteristics of their social order."

Different from abandoned culture, the "throwaway culture" was created on the ideal of making the world better. For instance, it endorses the practice of producing items that need to be replaced regularly. It also advocates making products that are altered annually to persuade people to buy the latest style. The items made are throwaway instead of long-lasting so people will rebuy the product (new car, new clothing, new telephone). Commodities that were once considered resilient are virtually all disposables. The shift to throwaway culture was supposedly for accessibility and cleanliness, even if the use of utilizing non-durable products is not especially convenient, and there is no verified improvement in sanitation.

The need to protect and preserve (true) culture was eventually realized as a human right as well as for its economic and symbolic values. Consequently, great deal of attention was given to the significance of culture (patrimony) and what it means within the context of social identification and pride. Concerns about cultural patrimony caused governments to enact protective legislation, courts to impose penalties, and organizations to conduct awareness campaigns.

Many of the laws and conventions address the protection of "cultural patrimony" because, for a number of years, countries used the word "culture" as an inclusive term intending to identify anything and everything that humans made, gathered, or recognized, and in most instances, the concern was for tangible (objects or buildings) patrimony only. This confusion of terms led to the destruction of many important lands and objects particular to patrimony. That viewpoint caused culture to be redefined as, "the way of life of a group of people."[16] This perspective has been revised to consider both cultural and natural patrimony as separate but conjoined aspects of human existence, and to give equal attention to intangible elements such as song, dance, languages, and culinary practices.

The safeguarding of cultural patrimony includes maintaining the cultural memory, as well as the cultural diversity of a nation/state, a community, or a group of people. These objects and events are a part of human history. They are a source for ideas about the past that can validate their meaning. Preservation of objects and ideas is an acknowledgment of the importance of the past and of the things that communicate its story. Preserved objects are a part of humanities' memory. It is the real (actual) item that provides information. A replica does not contribute meaningful information to tradition or patrimony. Replicas are surface and not content.

Some people have the mistaken belief that making a replica is the method most practical for reproducing a cultural patrimony object or location that is damaged. They believe a replica is less expensive and more durable than restoring the original. With the replica there is no difficulty about touching or using and when damaged the copy is easily repaired and more cheaply. However, it is not possible to produce a meaningful replica of an object by using "typical" reformation or duplication methods, nor is it possible to resurrect a cultural object to its original form and purpose once the meaning is lost. The time, place, and people are gone. Cultural elements have certain functions for which they are made (not reproduced). Although the element is recognizable, it is not always possible to comprehend the function based on the shape of the object. The meaning of the object is integral to its time and place, but not always so explicit that it transcends time, place, and culture, and an object without meaning (identity) is not taken seriously.

A replica as a reproduction of an original may be utilized for various reasons in a cultural space. Replicas can connect to any figure or image that denotes the prototype. Replicas are made to maintain a supposed connection with previous times. They can be associated with history or to remember an occasion. Replicas often aid in giving a tangible depiction of the bygone era. Many cultural space dinosaurs on exhibition are replicas because the actual bones are too fragile and the Chinese terra-cotta figures (warriors) seen in various locations are replicas. Copies can give a realistic idea of the original location of events and present what people want to see, but they are replicas and not the real object. They should be identified as replicas whenever used.

Instead of advocating the use of replicas, people should recognize their responsibility for maintenance of culture as a meaningful part of an inclusive social environment. Cultural patrimony has value, as a positive aspect of daily existence, and because this approach gives added meaning to humanism. Humanity places responsibility for activities on people as a belief scheme for maintaining harmony. Cultural patrimony expresses the overlapping aspect of time because the present is an ambiguous mixture of the past and future. The present has no true identity because the concept of patrimony as obvious by cultural elements identified with the past.

People often direct their attention toward destruction instead of preservation of culture. The destruction of early sites, for example, is an everyday occurrence and much of it goes unnoticed. This devastation is symptomatic of people's expectations to have access to progress in various ways, and at the same time requiring the protection of culture. Materialism, selfishness, ambivalence, fear of responsibility, and pursuit of the easy way dominate contemporary society. It is dominated by egotism, expediency, and lack of personal value.

The public is only partly to blame for the destruction of cultural elements. Governments and big business encourage site development for construction and for tourism, but operational funding is the responsibility of the site or location causing excessive use and vague rules. Governments are unwilling or unable to provide continuing financial support for cultural site operations and protection, and often the initial funding is not adequate to meet the needs of the site or element. Funding agencies (public or private) are pleased to be associated with the celebration relating to the opening of a site or event, but indifferent to continued funding.

The future of humanity relies not only on preservation of culture, but the preservation of the true meaning of a cultural element. Concerns regarding the preservation of meaning happens when measures taken to preserve the object negate the transcendental or cultural truth of an object. The material evidence of humanity is aligned with social and cultural responsibilities; however, the cultural tradition, like humanity, has a historical and communal condition from which it is derived. The culture of humanity originates in the way the environment is occupied and used. (This use and thinking relates to attitude.)

People have a responsibility for preserving the meaning of the object or event of culture although the preservation process may extend over many years. Change is a constant factor for culture. The meaning of elements changes, elements are damaged, destroyed, or simply fall apart due to a variety of causes; nevertheless, a significant part of the damage to an object is that to its connection to humanity. An extensive reconstruction process may change parts of the cultural element and alter it, as in the case of the traditional dance-drama Mak Yong from the state of Kelantan in northern Malaysia. It was banned by the Pan-Malaysian Islamic Party because of its animist and Hindu-Buddhist roots.[17] Although it was banned, it is still active. The meaning of the idea (belief) is often given greater consideration than its identity.

The intention of cultural preservation is not to integrate what is different into contemporary society while preserving it, but to separate it into a category of "patrimony." The world has changed, and ideology has assumed a universal plane, although perhaps a false plane. Humanism is at the same time relegated to a second (or third) level of importance where appearance is substituted for truth that is only an abstract determination. According to Immanuel Kant, "appearances constitute the matter only, not the form."[18] The images alone offer only a symbolic representation for current and future generations. "For it all depends," Carl G. Jung wrote, "on how we look at things, and not on how they are in themselves. The least of things with a meaning is worth more in life than the greatest of things without it."[19]

Protecting and maintaining culture are parts of an ideology based on value (intellectual or aesthetic and moral). The mechanism of modern humanity needs to be enthusiastic about culture and there is no reason it should not be. The practical elements of the past both monumental and movable elements (of all types) are manifestations of "what came before." Friedrich Nietzsche wrote in 1873, "Whoever has learned to recognize this meaning of history must hate to see curious tourists and laborious beetle-hunters climbing up the great pyramids of antiquity."[20] Although called cultural tourism today and an economic windfall for some locations, concerns about patrimonial exploitation remain. A surplus of history seekers has infected the flexible part of life that does not recognize how to use the past as a way of influence.

Culture has meaning that is both good and bad. Many objects and activities survive because of the cultural affiliation with associated ideas. Cultural activities endure because they are meaningful, but unless people adopt a responsible attitude, that ideal will not withstand materialism. Instead of studying that part of culture nothing will remain except dubious recollections of that facet of life. The issue of "life" adds importance because culture in various forms attracts neglect. Some cultural elements are known as having unique value, thereby attracting added attention. Tourism includes a range of people from the interested person to the pleasure seeker. There are many examples of thoughtless, destructive tourism such as the damage to the Djinguereber Mosque of Timbuktu, Mali, and the vandalization of artworks at Museum Island in Berlin. Although the latter is not the work of tourists, this type of destruction is unacceptable.

Other examples are Enkipaata, Eunoto and Olng'esherr, three related male rituals of the Maasai community (Kenya). Enkipaata is the introduction of boys before initiation; Eunoto is the shaving of the heads as a presentation of adulthood; and Olng'esherr is the meat-eating ceremony that marks the end of youthfulness and the beginning of eldership. Veneration and conscientiousness safeguard the ancestry, the assigning of rights from one group to the next and the diffusion of indigenous knowledge.[21] A tourist audience cannot be a part of this event. It would damage the importance of the activity and give it a trivial atmosphere.

Society is aggressively working to change the cultural tradition in many ways. Technology offers methods and humanity provides the willingness to destroy culture in the disguise of progress. The old can be made new and better with technology so preservation is an irrelevant concept. Advances in printing techniques can print all the important flat material of the past that will not fade or discolor, and will withstand the rough handling of people. For example, a high-value painting can be stored in a vault while the public looks in wonder at a reproduction on display in a gallery. The badly damaged fifteen-hundred-year-old bronze sculpture can be scanned and reproduced in fiberglass with a metallic coating that is not influenced by temperature, humidity, or the touch of human hands. The "new" statue is made at half the cost of repairing the old one, and it is "just as good or better than the original. No one will know the difference."

The preservation of the original forms require not only knowledge and skill, but sensitivity. The human activities cannot be duplicated by technology. For example, the Pueblo de Taos in the Southwestern United States is regularly repaired and maintained. The adobe (the mud-brick material of which the Pueblo is constructed) requires regular repair that is carried out by tribal members using traditional materials and processes. The Pueblo represents the cultural tradition of the Puebloan people of the states of Arizona, New Mexico, and the world. It is invaluable. Determining the provenience of this location and placing it within the social and cultural context is important to humanity.

Documentation is cultural preservation in its earliest form. The earliest historical record of China was written in 1500 BCE in the Shang dynasty (c. 1600–1046 BCE) and in the third-century BCE the library at Alexandria, Egypt was a resource for information gathered from the known world. The library at Alexandria, a part of the Mouseion, was charged with collecting "all the world's knowledge." It is believed more than 1,000 scholars lived and worked in the Mouseion at one time. The scholars conducted research, published, lectured, and collected as much literature as possible from the known world. It is most likely that it was destroyed by fire during the purge of Emperor Aurelian in 272. The damage to the library and the destruction of thousands of scrolls was a catastrophic loss for cultural research of the world.

People normally agree that preservation is an important factor for maintaining the products of culture. That said, preservation on a world level has not greatly influenced the protection of cultural material on a local level. Historically significant structures are destroyed (regularly), roads pass over burial grounds, and underground construction destroys countless archaeological sites, all in the name of progress. Economic growth has escalated far beyond cultural preservation. It is right to wonder whether the preservation of cultural is simply an opportunistic practice or a comprehensive vision that requires public commitment and moral investment. Responsibility for care and preservation of culture cannot be assigned to laws and conventions—that duty is for all humanity. Protection is often the best form of preservation for cultural elements, and preservation requires attention to all aspects of the environment in which the materials are maintained.

David Lowenthal addressed the issue of human responsibility for cultural patrimony three decades ago: "Only in this generation has saving the tangible past become a major global enterprise. Vestiges of the past, whole, dismembered, or discernable only in traces, lie everywhere around us, yet throughout history men [people] have mainly overlooked most of these remnants."[22] Lowenthal admonishes humanity for its apathy regarding cultural patrimony. "Taking their collective material inheritance much for granted, they [people] have allowed antiquity to survive, to decay, or to disappear as the laws of nature and the whims of their fellow men dictated."[23] Again, the question of preservation.

Contrary to the stated objective to protect the culture of humanity, the reality is different. The purpose of preservation should be to preserve the cultural patrimony; otherwise, future generations will have no memory on which to build a humanitarian society. Unfortunately, the patrimonial world is not well preserved nor is it always authentic. Consequently, society often exists out of time, has no contents or meaning, and the ideals of humanity are often meaningless. The search for cultural traditions may be a call for understanding in a world that has a fixation on the present and no concept of the past or future. There is only the present, real or not, but to apply perspective to communal and environmental conditions is an endorsement of disorder. Society is so obsessed with material gains that it ignores saving culture in its preference for profits.

A negative aspect of culture is objectified by commercializing human achievements, and that objectification has communized "objects or events." Culture is consequently identified with the object or events, thereby marginalizing the cultural and philosophical importance of culture and patrimony. Culture has lost its human merit to become a sightseeing tour, a one-hour guided visit to a cultural place, or a curio for the what-not shelf. Culture should be reinstated as human value at the center of being as a democratic process of inclusion irrespective of politics, religion, or economics.

Marilyn Phelan (professor of law) wrote, "The theory [of universal] heritage [patrimony] recognition and preservation maintains that a society learns of itself by studying its artistic treasures and that a nation's artistic treasures can be better investigated and understood in their original setting; thus, the principle demands the protection of international sites and artefacts."[24] Culture, in philosophical terms, is associated with the specialness of humanity and is manifest in products that place the producing society within the world and humanity. These elements are the symbols by which a people are known. The cultural products of a people are meaningful not only because of their special merit, but because they represent the identity and character of their creators. They must be preserved for the people to be understood and appreciated.

Culture is a valued instrument for projecting national identity as well as social importance. Fluctuating socio-political values as the world changes with the movement toward greater interdependence challenges the understanding of humanity as well as the responsibility of cultural institutions to acknowledge community needs without disregarding ethical and social responsibilities. This acknowledged condition exists in many locations as nation/states expand and contract in response to demographics, economic and environmental conditions, and political variances. Adherence to identified objectives reinforced by the institutional values defines the work of a particular location, and reflects differences in methods among similar efforts.

Elements of the material world to which cultural and social value are attributed, include the movable objects, aspects, and events of the physical world that have unique meaning and are often lost to the urges of humanity. The preservation of objects and events is normally associated with culture, but other important and valued elements recognized for their social and spiritual significance as well as their material substance merit safeguarding. For example, the ruins of Copán in Guatemala are one of the most important sites of the Mayan civilization, and it was not excavated until the nineteenth century.[25] When a cultural element is damaged, altered, or destroyed, the cultural integrity of the element is compromised or permanently lost. A record may remain, but the true meaning is gone. That these objects and events are important is a reason for cultural preservation. It is an undeniable fact that people do not safeguard what it does not respect.

The elements of culture are in many forms East and West, North and South, and the locations (cultural spaces) for gathering and preserving cultural elements are equally diverse. It is erroneous to assume all culture is sheltered against the destructive energies of humans and nature. Exposure to weather conditions is a continuing threat to cultural elements whether art, objects, or events located in the open or placed in a protective facility. Many cultural elements are self-destructive in that they decompose, deteriorate, and decay. (For example, the Rangda masks made in Bali.)

The identification of cultural elements is required to determine "that" something happened as opposed to "why it happened." There is a need to differentiate between appearance, story, and reality. Governments, societies, clubs, and special interest groups publish listings of protected patrimonial items that range from the inclusive to the exclusive, and they address these questions. These patrimony lists are intended to inform people about the "things" that are protected or restricted from change, destruction, or removal. The lists define patrimony according to socio-political determinations and establish patrimonial identification by disseminating the relevant information.

Every year (or more often) the world attempts to rewrite history. The bad (unpopular) things are removed, and the good things (popular with the powers that initiate the rewriting) are emphasized, causing some issues to be abandoned (for example, slavery and sex education). This process seems simple and perhaps well intended, but usually it is incorrect and the loss of historical reference is significant. All acts of change may be valid, but they eliminate a part of the culture and history of a country and people. It becomes an act of cancelling culture. The elimination of culture is critical. Gradually, when there is no past of a country to recount, the past disappears and so does the present. The world is presented as it is viewed by the authority that last reprinted the books. The idea of truth is bypassed for political expediency. The truth belongs to those in power.

Human intolerance, hostility, and greed are enemies of cultural elements—they cause its displacement or destruction. Laws, rules, conventions, and appeals do not overcome ignorance and greed. Much of the world is affected by the illicit trafficking of cultural materials. Both developing and developed countries are targets of illicit traffic, contrary to conventional thinking. The attitude is important because culture in various forms attract vandalism and theft. Illegal trafficking and looting not only involves the illegal appropriation of world culture; it often includes the destruction of related materials and documentation. Looters are not interested in the original information relating to the objects or the context in which they were found. Even when an illegally excavated or stolen object is recovered, the contextual data are lost.

Cultural elements are part of the shared patrimony of humankind. They are such an important verification of the development and uniqueness of humanity that their protection has been advocated in numerous locations. Trading in cultural material is a resource for funding of criminal groups and has been linked to the financing of radical extremists. Illegal trade in cultural material occurs in every country, depriving people of their culture, identity, and history.

The criminal trade in cultural objects is recognized as one of the most prevalent categories of international crime and intentional destruction of culture. "There exists a multi-billion-dollar industry in the illicit trading in stolen and illegally exported cultural objects, and most of these cultural treasures are intertwined with cultures as well as the sovereignty of exploited countries and tribal nations."[26] The threats of deterioration, theft, and destruction (human and natural) of cultural elements has never been greater. The attention given to culture during the last years have made protection and preservation more challenging. The inflated valuation of the culture market, and the continuing instability in the international community has increased the illicit trafficking of cultural property. The extent of this activity is unprecedented.

For example, the theft from archaeological sites makes interpretation of the objects impossible. Once removed from their context, the objects cannot provide the information whereby their historical significance can be determined. This situation is dramatic for many countries and is even more so in the case of many nation/states with limited written records. The information of history is lost and it may no longer be possible to reconstitute that history without the information revealed by archaeological excavations.

Because social life takes place through time, the inevitability of continual change causes society to endorse self-defining signs to represent patrimony. Although these objects or events may be randomly selected, they often are qualified by time. Often, the meaning and purpose are defined by the power of the governing authority. Patrimony is the essence of the contemporary debate about identity, social cohesion, and the development of a knowledge-based economy.

The spiritual paintings and sculpture produced in different areas of the world offer links to earlier cultures and traditions that attract the imagination and admiration of people. "The art of a people tells a great deal about their character, worldview, attitudes, hopes and aspirations."[27] It, the art, may not be considered "creative" in the Western sense; however, it offers insight into the beliefs that constitutes the foundation of a people.

The culture of a people develops in relationship to a particular background. The accumulated elements generate an environment in which people gain an awareness of the continuity that exists in human culture, glimpse a past that they can revere, and project a future to which they will transmit the results of their own endeavors. Cultural patrimony is one of the most important factors that allow humankind as a species, to transcend individual destiny to achieve continuity.

Unfortunately, the destruction of patrimonial objects is occurring at a monumental rate. "Cultural tradition has been destroyed, looted and trafficked throughout history, particularly during conflict and post-conflict situations. Today, these phenomena are increasingly linked to international criminal activity including the financing of terrorist groups."[28] The unauthorized removal of cultural material, by any means, from the producing nation/state, territory, or people is deplorable and detrimental.

There is little reason to believe that past inhabitants of this planet did not raid each other to gain possession of objects representing social status or sacred value. It is reasonable, however, to assume the amount of material being removed was small in proportion to modern-day trafficking from African, Latin American, and the Middle Eastern countries where the loss of materials from cultural locations, museums, galleries, and archaeological sites has increased to astronomical proportions.

Although many objects have been identified as illegal in consumer nations and returned to their country of origin, many more are sold. Repatriated or sold, the objects have lost much of their research value (their history is lost, and that history must have provenance). The repatriated pieces continue to have a value but the specific nature of their discovery and relative data is gone, depriving the object of meaningful research and interpretative reference. Restitution of stolen or misappropriated patrimony is a curative process when what is needed is prevention. "...[C]ultural nationalism embraces the theory that all cultural objects belong primarily to or should remain in the country of origin or with the affected tribe."[29]

The meaningfulness of culture can have both a positive and negative effect on human nature. No country and no people are exempt from pointless acts of destruction. This kind of vengeful obliteration of valid and valued culture is repeated daily on a previously unimagined scale. In Afghanistan the large Buddha figures in the Bamiyan Valley were severely damaged for reasons relating to religious intolerance and hostility. The Temple of Baalshamin in Syria, the Great Synagogue of Vilna in Lithuania, the Tuvkhun Monastery in Mongolia, and a mosque in Central African Republic are locations of cultural destruction, and another place (or two or more) will emerge tomorrow or the week after. The reasons for the destruction are always the same—ignorance and intolerance. The attitude of an individual (or group) incorporates fundamental ideals about good and bad and those beliefs are the foundation of value judgments (both good and bad).

Culture should have special value for people even though they do not always understand that importance. Many objects, locations, and activities survive because of the cultural affiliation and the associated agencies. Cultural activities endure because they have meaning, but unless people adopted a more responsible attitude, that protection will not withstand contemporary demands. Instead of studying our culture as it now exists, nothing will remain except memory. The issue of attitude adds importance because culture in various forms does attract negative thinking. Some cultural elements are known as having unique value thereby attracting added attention. There are many examples of cultural destruction. (Tourism is a major challenge for Angkor Wat, and it damaged a 3,000-year-old site in Luxor, damaged the Shwe Nan Daw Kyaung Monastery showing Buddhist myths, and damaged the Machu Picchu Temple. These are examples of tourist damage to cultural patrimony.)

One of the difficulties in implementing laws and practices curtailing trafficking in cultural materials is defining exactly which objects constitute culture. A definition of "culture" usually includes words such as "materials reflecting the customs, beliefs, and symbolic practices by which men and women live," or "all socially significant property."

Materials can include tangible and intangible elements that have religious or secular meaning. With this "general" definition it is difficult to limit the import and export or trafficking of cultural materials. The immediate category of illicitly trafficked cultural materials is usually art, and painting and sculpture are the primary focus.

Most definitions of culture are extensive, inclusive, and formulated to appeal to everyone or anyone, thereby indicating a role and responsibility. However, it is possible, or probable, that people simply believe in certain activities because they want to and what they believe in has minimal value to socio-political or cultural pertinence. Cultural tradition causes people to realize who they are and gives a stable form to their view of themselves that otherwise would fade in the fluctuation of life. This assumption identifies the importance of specific elements and suggests a different reason for defining culture and cultural assignments. It also indicates that the culture of individuals and groups may be dissociated with history but assigned importance by means of social interchange and assumed need.

Many people understand that they must take responsibility for the identification and protection of culture. Human action is not only of universal importance it is a necessity of personal intellectual. The ever-increasing population—coupled with the rapidity of communication by which entire populations can be quickly and radically changed—adds instability at all levels of the human temporal spectrum. Culture in all its manifestations is a stabilizing factor that adds meaning to existence and explains the present. The unity of a cultural element includes the meaning as well as the substance.

Culture should have special meaning for people. Cultural activities endure because they have meaning, but unless people adopt a more responsible attitude, that protection will not remain. Instead of studying our culture as it now exists, nothing will remain except dubious recollections of that part of life that "came before," and cute and meaningless objects that supposedly represent cultural ideas.

Safeguarding cultural traditions is a responsibility of all humanity. The methods of maintaining the current form, integrity, and materials of a cultural asset vary but the responsibility exists. Culture is represented by both comparatively long-lasting and changing elements, which may not be required for identity. Culture supports the creation of information through traditions that are the result of historic processes. The concept of tradition as the notion of holding on to a previous time promotes allegiance to recollections of the past.

If culture is to be valuable, it must be independent from financial and political manipulation. The cultural and intellectual influences of patrimonial elements should extend beyond geographic limitations to where it is possible to comprehend whether the elements constitute meaningful value and where the social and cultural significance (of the elements) is fully understood. Culture is important.

Things to think about:

1. What is the logic of protecting and maintaining culture as parts of an ideology based on value?

2. Why does the future of humanity really rely on preservation of culture?

3. Why is it that the threat of deterioration, theft, destruction of cultural elements has never been greater?

4. Is there a reason why preservation of the meaning of cultural objects and events is important?

5. What is meant by cultural elements that are self-destructive?

6. What is the difficulty in implementing laws curtailing trafficking in cultural materials?

7. How is the meaningfulness of culture a positive and negative influence on human nature?

8. Why does an object lose much of its research value if sold or repatriated?

9. Why is it that humanity does not understand the value of culture?

10. How does culture support the creation of information through traditions?

11. How is it possible that people believe in certain activities because they want to and what they believe in has minimal value to socio-political or cultural pertinence?

12. How does culture support the creation of information through traditions that are the result of historic processes.

13. What was Kristallnacht?

14. Why is culture important?

Chapter Notes

Preface

1. Chuang-Tzu (1997 [1931]). *A Taoist Classic Chuang-Tzu*. Translated by Fung Yu-Lan. Beijing: Foreign Languages Press, p. 44.

Introduction

1. "Art of Crafting and Playing." Accessed March 2021. https://ich.unesco.org/en/RL/art-of-crafting-and-playing.
2. "Secret Society." Accessed March 2021. https://ich.unesco.org/en/USL/secret-society.
3. "False Face Society." Accessed March 2021. https://en.wikipedia.org/wiki/False_Face_Society.
4. Eagleton, Terry (2016). *Culture*, New Haven: Yale University Press, p. 1.
5. Lowenthal, D. (1985). *The Past Is a Foreign Country*, Cambridge: Cambridge University Press, p. 39.
6. UNESCO "Timbuktu." Accessed March 2017. http://whc.unesco.org/en/list/119.
7. "Ak-kalpak." Accessed October 2021), https://en.wikipedia.org/wiki/Ak-kalpak.
8. Wallace, A.F.C. (1970). *Culture and Personality*, 2d. ed. New York: Random House, p. 109.
9. https://whc.unesco.org/en/list/321/documents/. Accessed October 2021.
10. Ricoeur, P. (2007). *History and Truth*, translated with an introduction by Charles A. Kelbley. Evanston, IL: Northwestern University Press, p. 28.
11. Agamben, Giorgio (1999). *The Man Without Content*, translated by Georgia Albert. Stanford: Stanford University Press, p. 107.
12. *Ibid.*

Chapter One

1. Gauvain, M. (2001). *The Social Context of Cognitive Development*. New York: Guilford Press, p. 5.
2. Runes, Dagobert D. (1961) *The Art of Thinking*. New York: The Wisdom Library, p. 1.
3. *Ibid.*, p. 3.
4. *Ibid.*, p. 14.
5. Ricoeur, P. (2007). *History and Truth*. translated by Charles A. Kelbley. Evanston, IL: Northwestern University Press, p. 41.
6. Connerton, P. (1989). *How Societies Remember*. Cambridge: Cambridge University Press p. 6.
7. Holford, Sir W. (1965). "The Shells of Society," pp. 199–208, in Sir Julian Huxley, ed. *The Humanist Frame*. London: George Allen & Unwin Ltd., p. 199.
8. Mason, R. (2002). "Assessing Values in Conservation Planning: Methodological Issues and Choices," pp. 5–33, in Marta de la Torre, ed. *Assessing the Values of Cultural Heritage* (Research Report). Los Angeles: Getty Conservation Institute, p. 11.
9. Jung, C.G. (1970 [1953]). *Psychological Reflections: A New Anthology of His Writings 1905–1961*, 2nd Edition, Selected and Edited by Jolande Jocobi. Bollingen Series XXXI, Princeton: Princeton University Press, re: 47:10, p. 25.
10. Tuan Yi-Fu (1977). *Space and Place: The Perspective of Experience*, Minne-

apolis and London: University of Minnesota Press, p. 86.

11. *Ibid.*

12. https://ich.unesco.org/en/USL/suri-jagek-observing-the-sun-traditional-meteorological-and-astronomical-practice-based-on-the-observation-of-the-sun-moon-and-stars-in-reference-to-the-local-topography-01381 (accessed October 2021).

13. "Angkor." Accessed May 2021. https://whc.unesco.org/en/list/668/.

14. "Petäjävesi Old Church." Accessed May 2021. https://whc.unesco.org/en/list/584/.

15. "Human Nature." Accessed August 2016. https://en.wikipedia.org/wiki/Human_nature.

16. "Annual Pilgrimage to the Mausoleum of Sidi 'Abd El-Qader Ben Mohammed (Sidi Cheikh)." Accessed November 2020. https://ich.unesco.org/en/RL/annual-pilgrimage-to-the-mausoleum-of-sidi-abd-el-qader-ben-mohammed-sidi-cheikh-00660.

17. Hobsbawm, E., and T. Ranger, eds. (1983). *The Invention of Tradition.* Cambridge University Press, p. 10.

18. Connerton, P. (1989). *How Societies Remember.* Cambridge: Cambridge University Press, p.78.

19. Wood, E., and K. F. Latham. (2014). *The Objects of Experience: Transforming Visitor-object Encounters in Museums.* Walnut Creek, CA: West Coast Press, p. 59.

20. "Festival of Folklore in Koprivshtitsa: A System of Practices for Heritage Presentation and Transmission." Acccessed July 2021. https://ich.unesco.org/en/BSP/festival-of-folklore-in-koprivshtitsa-a-system-of-practices-for-heritage-presentation-and-transmission-00970.

21. Lowenthal, D. (1985). *The Past Is a Foreign Country.* Cambridge University Press, p. 39.

22. Csikszentmihalyi, M., and E. Rochberg-Halton. (1981). *The Meaning of Things: Domestic Symbols and the Self.* Cambridge University Press, p. 173.

23. Van Nordon, B.W. (2011). *Introduction to Classical Chinese Philosophy.* Indianapolis: Hackett, p. 27.

24. "Izanami and Izanagi." World History Encyclopedia, accessed March 2021. https://www.ancient.eu/Izanami_and_Izanagi/.

25. "Ramman, Religious Festival and Ritual Theatre of the Garhwal Himalayas, India." Accessed October 2021. https://ich.unesco.org/en/RL/ramman-religious-festival-and-ritual-theatre-of-the-garhwal-himalayas-india-00281.

26. "Gióng Festival of Phù Đông and Sóc Temples." Accessed September 2020. https://ich.unesco.org/en/RL/giong-festival-of-phu-ong-and-soc-temples-00443.

Chapter Two

1. Damasio, Antonio. (2018). *The Strange Order of Things: Life, Feeling, and the Making of Cultures.* New York: Pantheon Books, p. 165.

2. May, Rollo. (1975). *The Courage to Create.* New York: Norton, p. 134.

3. Bain, Read. (1937). "Technology and State Government." *American Sociological Review* 2 (6): 860–874. doi:10.2307/2084365.

4. Bergson, H. (1907). *An Introduction to Metaphysics*, with an Introduction by John Mullarkey and translated by T. E. Hulme. New York: Macmillan, p. 1.

5. Adajian, Thomas. "The Definition of Art" in *The Stanford Encyclopedia of Philosophy* (Fall 2018 Edition), Edward N. Zalta (ed.), https://plato.stanford.edu/archives/fall2018/entries/art-definition/.

6. Schiller, F. (2006). *Aesthetical and Philosophical Essays.* Fairford, UK: Echo Press, p. 8.

7. Lubar, Steven, and W. David Kingery, ed. (1993). *History from Things: Essays on Material Culture.* Washington, DC: Smithsonian Institution Press, p. 5.

8. Shramko, Yaroslav, and Heinrich Wansing, "Truth Values" in *The Stanford Encyclopedia of Philosophy* (Winter 2020 Edition), Edward N. Zalta (ed.), accessed April 2021. https://plato.stanford.edu/archives/win2020/entries/truth-values/.

9. Jackson, P.W. (1998). *John Dewey and the Lessons of Art.* Yale University Press, p. xiv.

10. "Chinese Calligraphy." Accessed April 2021. https://ich.unesco.org/en/RL/chinese-calligraphy-00216.

11. "Mongolian Calligraphy." Accessed April 2021. https://ich.unesco.org/en/USL/mongolian-calligraphy-00873.

12. "Oldest Cave Art Found in Sulawesi." Accessed May 2021. https://advances.sciencemag.org/content/7/3/eabd4648.

13. "Living Culture of Three Writing Systems of the Georgian Alphabet." Accessed October 2021. https://ich.unesco.org/en/RL/living-culture-of-three-writing-systems-of-the-georgian-alphabet-01205.

14. Cirlot, J.E. (1962). *A Dictionary of Symbols*, translated by Jack Sage. London: Routledge, p. lii.

15. Csikszentmihalyi, M., and E. Rochberg-Halton. (1981). *The Meaning of Things: Domestic Symbols and the Self.* Cambridge University Press, p. 21.

16. Kihlstrom, J.F., J.S. Beer, and S.B. Klein. (2003). "Self and Identity as Memory," in Mark R. Leary and June Price Tangney, eds., *Handbook of Self and Identity*, New York: Guilford Press, pp. 68–90.

17. *Ibid.*

18. Eliade, M. (1991). *Images and Symbols: Studies in Religious Symbolism*, translated by Philip Maier. Princeton University Press, p. 12.

19. Campbell, H.Z. (1969). *Philosophies of India*, edited by Joseph Campbell. Princeton University Press. pp. 1–2.

20. Edson, G. (2009). *Shamanism: A Cross-Cultural Study of Beliefs and Practices.* Jefferson, NC: McFarland, p. 68.

21. Cirlot, J. E. (1962) *A Dictionary of Symbols*, translated by Jack Sage. London: Routledge, p. xiv.

Chapter Three

1. "Property." Accessed August 2020. https://en.wikipedia.org/wiki/Property.

2. Lamont, C. (1949). *Humanism as a Philosophy.* New York: Philosophical Library, p. 19.

3. Ricoeur, P. (2007). *History and Truth*, translated by Charles A. Kelbley. Evanston, IL: Northwestern University Press, p. 271.

4. "Humanism." Accessed September 2016. https://en.wikipedia.org/wiki/Humanism.

5. James, W. (1997 [1911]). *The Meaning of Truth.* New York: Prometheus, p. 124.

6. Kant, I. (1959 [1785]). *Foundations of the Metaphysics of Morals*, Translated with an Introduction by Lewis White Beck. Indianapolis: Bobbs-Merrill, p. 3.

7. Dolák, J. (1994). "Some Remarks on Museum Terminology," ICOFOM Study Series Issue 38, *Museology: Back to Basics.* Morlanwelz (Belgique): Musée royal de Mariemont, p. 202.

8. Lowenthal, D. (1985). *The Past Is a Foreign Country.* Cambridge University Press, p. 197.

9. Huxley, Sir J. ed. (1965). *The Humanist Frame.* London: George Allen & Unwin, p. 14.

10. Csikszentmihalyi, M. (1993) "Why We Need Things" in Lubar, Steven, and W. David Kingery (1993) *History from Things: Essays on Material Culture.* Washington: Smithsonian Institution Press, p. 23.

11. *Ibid.*

12. Gauvain, M. (2001). *The Social Context of Cognitive Development.* New York: Guilford, p. 103.

13. Connerton, Paul. (1989). *How Societies Remember.* Cambridge University Press, p. 4.

14. Weiming, Tu, and Ikeda Daisaku. (2011). *New Horizons in Eastern Humanism.* New York: Macmillan, p. 115.

15. Kihlstrom, J.F., J.S. Beer, and S.B. Klein. (2003). "Self and Identity as Memory," in Mark R. Leary and June Price Tangney. ed. *Handbook of Self and Identity.* New York: Guilford, p. 69.

16. Dewey, J., and A.F. Bentley. (1949). *Knowing and the Known.* Boston: Beacon, p. 147.

17. *Ibid.*

18. Grassi, E. (1983). *Heidegger and the Question of Renaissance Humanism: Four Studies*, Binghamton, NY: Center for Medieval and Early Renaissance Studies, p. 20.

19. Rošker, J. "Epistemology in Chinese Philosophy," in *Stanford Encyclopedia of Philosophy* (Winter 2015 Edition), Edward N. Zalta (ed.), accessed January 2017. https://plato.stanford.edu/archives/win2015/entries/chinese-epistemology/.

20. "Remembrance Hall Yad Vashem."

Accessed April 2017. http://www.yadvashem.org/yv/en/remembrance/hall_of_names.asp.

21. Jinpa, T. (2002). *Self, Reality and Reason in Tibetan Philosophy: Tsongkhapa's Quest for the Middle Way*. London: Routledge Curzon, pp. 160–161.

22. Brennan, A. (1988). *Conditions of Identity: A Study of Identity and Survival*. Oxford: Clarendon, p. 7.

23. Wang, Youfen. (2008). *Chinese Calligraphy*. Beijing: Foreign Languages Press, p. 52.

Chapter Four

1. Freud, S. (1991). *On Metaphsychology—The Theory of Psychoanalysis*. London: Penguin Freud Library, p. 36.

2. Eagleton, Terry. (2016). *Culture*. Yale University Press, p. 1.

3. Lewis, G. (1992). "Museums and Their Precursors: A Brief World Survey," in John Thompson, ed. *Manual of Curatorship: A Guide to Museum Practices* 2nd edition. Oxford: Butterworth Heinemann, p. 7.

4. Lowenthal, D. (1985). *The Past Is a Foreign Country*. Cambridge University Press, p. 369.

5. James, W. (2003 [1907]). *Pragmatism*. New York: Barnes and Noble Books, p. 87.

6. Blackburn, S. (2005). *Truth: A Guide*. Oxford University Press, p. 188.

7. Koller, J.M. (1985.) *Oriental Philosophies* 2nd edition. New York: Charles Scribner, p. 87.

8. Firth, R. (1985). "Degrees of Intelligibility" in Overling, Joanna, ed. *Reason and Morality*. New York: Tavistock Publications, p. 31.

9. "Temple of Philae." Accessed March 2021. https://www.introducingegypt.com/philae-temple.

10. "Risco Caido and the Sacred Mountains of Gran Canaria Cultural Landscape." Accessed January 2021. https://whc.unesco.org/en/list/1578.

11. Fardon, R., ed. (1985). *Power and Knowledge: Anthropological and Sociological Approaches*. Edinburgh: Scottish Academic Press, p. 157.

12. Thomas, J. (1996). *Time, Culture and Identity: An Interpretive Archaeology*. London: Routledge, p. 90.

13. Saint Augustine (2002 [AD 401]). *The Confessions of Saint Augustine*, translated and introduced by R. S. Pine-Coffin (1961). New York: Penguin, pp. 265–266.

14. Lowenthal, D. (1985). *The Past Is a Foreign Country*. Cambridge University Press, p. 63.

15. Cassirer, E. (1955). *The Philosophy of Symbolic Forms Vol. 1: Language*, translated by Ralph Manheim. Yale University Press, p. 215.

16. Smythies, J. (2003). "Space, Time and Consciousness," quoting Immanuel Kant, *Journal of Consciousness Studies* 10 (3), pp. 47–56.

17. *Ibid*.

18. Sartre, J-P. (1964). *Nausea*, translated by Lloyd Alexander. New York: New Directions, pp. 95–96.

19. Robert-Hauglustaine, A–C. (2016). "The Role of Museums in the Twenty-first Century," pp. 9–13, in Bernice Murphy, ed., *Museums, Ethics, and Cultural Heritage*. New York: Routledge, p. 10.

20. Janiak, A. "Kant's Views on Space and Time," in *The Stanford Encyclopedia of Philosophy* (Winter 2016 Edition), Edward N. Zalta (ed.), accessed November 2016. http://plato.stanford.edu/archives/win2016/entries/kant-space-time/.

21. Thomas, J. (1996). *Time, Culture and Identity*. London and New York: Routledge, p. 31.

22. *Ibid*., p. 32.

23. *Ibid*.

24. Smythies, J. (2003). "Space, Time and Consciousness," quoting Lord Brain (1955), *Journal of Consciousness Studies*, 10 (3), p. 50.

25. James, W. (1977). *The Meaning of Truth*. Amherst, NY: Prometheus, p. 130.

26. Potter, K.H. (1964). *The Naturalistic Principle of Karma*, Philosophy East and West, 14 (1), pp. 39–49.

Chapter Five

1. Ricoeur, P. (2007). *History and Truth*, translated by Charles A. Kelbley. Evanston, IL: Northwestern University Press, p. 42.

2. Deutsch, E. (1979). *On Truth: An Ontological Theory*. University Press of Hawaii, p. 1.

3. "The Correspondence Theory of Truth." *Stanford Encyclopedia of Philosophy.* Accessed September 2015. http://plato.stanford.edu/entries/truth-correspondence/#8.3.

4. Wood, E. and K.F. Latham. (2014). *The Objects of Experience: Transforming Visitor-object Encounters in Museums.* Walnut Creek, CA: West Coast Press, p. 58.

5. James, W. (1977). *The Meaning of Truth,* Amherst, NY: Prometheus, p. 156.

6. Ricoeur, P. (2007). *History and Truth,* translated by Charles A. Kelbley. Evanston, IL: Northwestern University Press, p. 165.

7. Edson, G. (2017). *Museum Ethics in Practice.* New York: Routledge, p. 173.

8. "Rituals and Practices Associated with Kit Mikayi Shrine." Accessed September 2021. https://ich.unesco.org/en/USL/rituals-and-practices-associated-with-kit-mikayi-shrine-01489.

9. Ricoeur, P. (2007). *History and Truth,* translated by Charles A. Kelbley. Evanston, IL: Northwestern University Press, p. 166.

10. Edson, G. (2017). *Museum Ethics in Practice.* New York: Routledge, pp. 175–176.

11. Ellis, B.D. (1990). *Truth and Objectivity.* Cambridge: Basil Blackwell, p. 11.

12. Agamben, Giorgio. (1999). *The Man Without Content.* Stanford University Press, p. 10.

13. "Festival of Saint Francis of Assisi, Quibdó." Accessed May 2021. https://ich.unesco.org/en/RL/festival-of-saint-francis-of-assisi-quibdo-00640.

14. "Škofja Loka Passion Play." Accessed September 2021. https://ich.unesco.org/en/RL/kofja-loka-passion-play-01203.

15. "Saman (dance)." Accessed October 2021. https://en.wikipedia.org/wiki/Saman_(dance).

16. "Khon, Masked Dance Drama in Thailand." Accessed September 2021. https://ich.unesco.org/en/RL/khon-masked-dance-drama-in-thailand-01385.

17. "Alasitas." Accessed September 2021. https://en.wikipedia.org/wiki/Alasitas.

18. Bruner, J.S. (1960). "Myth and Identity," pp. 176–187, in Murray, Henry A., ed. *Myth and Mythmaking.* New York: George Braziller, p. 176.

19. *Effortless Being: The Yoga Sutras of Patanjali* (1982). Translated by Alistair Shearer. London: Mandala, Unwin Paperbacks, p. 10.

20. Edson, G. (2012). *Mysticism and Alchemy Through the Ages.* Jefferson, NC: McFarland, p. 95.

Chapter Six

1. Gauvain, M. (2001). *The Social Context of Cognitive Development.* New York: Guilford, p. 104.

2. Sutton, J. "Memory," *The Stanford Encyclopedia of Philosophy* (Summer 2016 Edition), Edward N. Zalta (ed.), https://plato.stanford.edu/archives/sum2016/entries/memory/.

3. Margalit, A. (2002). *The Ethics of Memory.* Harvard University Press, p. 99.

4. Hume, D. (1963). *The Philosophy of David Hume,* edited with an Introduction by V. C. Chappell. New York: The Modern Library, p. 32.

5. Shweder, R.A. (1996). *Thinking Through Cultures: Expeditions in Cultural Psychology.* Harvard University Press, p. 245.

6. Nietzsche, F. (2005 [1873]). *The Use and Abuse of History.* New York: Cosimo Classics, p.19.

7. Margalit, A. (2002). *The Ethics of Memory.* Harvard University Press, p. 59.

8. *Ibid.*

9. *Ibid.,* p. 14.

10. Gauvain, M. (2001). *The Social Context of Cognitive Development.* New York: Guilford, p. 104.

11. Ackermann, R.J. (1965). *Theories of Knowledge: A Critical Introduction.* New York: McGraw-Hill Book Company, p. 178.

12. "Byzantine Chant." Accessed May 2021. https://ich.unesco.org/en/RL/byzantine-chant-01508.

13. "Radif of Iranian Music." Accessed May 2021. https://ich.unesco.org/en/RL/radif-of-iranian-music-00279.

14. Lao Tzu (1979) *The Complete Works of Lao Tzu,* translated and elucidated by Hua-Ching Ni. Los Angeles: Tao of Wellness, p. 127.

15. Edson, Gary. (2009). *Shamanism:*

A Cross-Cultural Study of Beliefs and Practices. Jefferson, NC: McFarland, p. 6.

16. James, W. (1907). *Pragmatism*, New York: Barnes and Noble, pp. 20–21.

17. Gauvain, M. (2001). *The Social Context of Cognitive Development.* New York: Guilford, p. 103.

18. Cohen, G. (2005). *The Mature Mind: The Positive Power of the Aging Brain.* New York: Basic, pp. 105–106.

19. Thomas, J. (1996). *Time, Culture and Identity: An Interpretive Archaeology.* New York: Routledge, p. 89.

20. Kihlstrom, J.F., J.S. Beer, and S.B. Klein. (2003). "Self and Identity as Memory," pp. 68–90, in Mark R. Leary and June Price Tangney, eds., *Handbook of Self and Identity.* New York: Guilford, p. 68.

21. Sartre, J-P. (2007). *Existentialism Is a Humanism*, translated by Carol Macomber. Yale University Press, p. 29.

22. Sartre, J-P. (1956) *Being and Nothingness*, translated with introduction by Hazel E. Barnes. New York: Philosophical Library, p. 108.

23. Lowenthal, D. (1985). *The Past Is a Foreign Country.* Cambridge University Press, p. 214.

24. Nehamas, A. (1985). *Nietzsche: Life as Literature.* Harvard University Press, p. 7.

25. "Mapoyo Oral Tradition and Its Symbolic Reference Points Within Their Ancestral Territory." Accessed July 2021. https://ich.unesco.org/en/USL/mapoyo-oral-tradition-and-its-symbolic-reference-points-within-their-ancestral-territory-00983.

26. Deutsch, E. (1979). *On Truth: An Ontological Theory.* University Press of Hawaii, p. 1.

27. Margalit, A. (2002). *The Ethics of Memory.* Harvard University Press, p. 66.

28. James, W. (1977). *The Meaning of Truth.* Amherst, NY: Prometheus, p. 133.

29. Hume, D. (1963). *The Philosophy of David Hume*, edited with an Introduction by V.C. Chappell. New York: Modern Library, p. 32.

30. Margalit, A. (2002). *The Ethics of Memory.* Harvard University Press, p. 62.

31. *Ibid.*, p. 58.

32. Jordanova, L. "Objects of Knowledge: A Historical Perspective on Museums," pp. 22–40, in P. Vergo, ed. (1991).
The New Museology. London: Reaktion, p. 25.

33. *Ibid.*

Chapter Seven

1. UNESCO, "Joya De Cerén Archaeological Site." Accessed September 2017. http://whc.unesco.org/en/list/675.

2. "Moussem of Tan-Tan." Accessed November 2021. https://ich.unesco.org/en/RL/moussem-of-tan-tan-00168.

3. James, W. (1997). *The Meaning of Truth.* New York: Prometheus, p. x.

4. Sorokin, P. (1970.) *Social and Cultural Dynamics*, 2nd edition. Boston: Extending Horizons, p. 20.

5. Clifford, T. (1984). *Tibetan Buddhist Medicine and Psychiatry.* Delhi: Motilal Banarsidass, p.17.

6. Layton, R., ed. (1989). *Who Needs the Past?* New York: Routledge, p. 5.

7. "Early Christian Necropolis of Pécs (Sopianae)." Accessed December 2020. https://whc.unesco.org/en/list/853/.

8. Bowne, B.P. (1892). *The Principles of Ethics.* New York: American Book Company, p. 11.

9. *Ibid.*

10. "Serer Religion." Accessed September 2021. https://en.wikipedia.org/wiki/Serer_religion.

11. Wood, E. and K.F. Latham. (2014). *The Objects of Experience: Transforming Visitor-object Encounters in Museums.* Walnut Creek, CA: West Coast Press, p. 9.

Chapter Eight

1. Confucius. (1992). *The Analects*, Translated by Lau, D.C. The Chinese University of Hong Kong, II-15.

2. Csikszentmihalyi, M., and E. Rochberg-Halton. (1981). *The Meaning of Things: Domestic Symbols and the Self.* Cambridge University Press, p. 1.

3. "Cultural Complex of Bumba-meu-boi from Maranhão." Accessed October 2021. https://ich.unesco.org/en/RL/cultural-complex-of-bumba-meu-boi-from-maranho-01510.

4. Geshe, Sonam Richen. (2003). *The Heart Sutra*, Translated by Ruth Sona. New York: Snow Lion, p. 1.

5. Van Wyk, R.N. (1990). *Introduction to Ethics.* New York: St. Martin's, p. 122.

6. "Knowledge." Accessed September 2016. https://en.wikipedia.org/wiki/Knowledge.

7. Coleburt, R. (1960). *The Search for Values.* New York: Sheed and Ward, p. 81.

8. Lowenthal, D. (1985). *The Past Is a Foreign Country.* Cambridge University Press, p. 214.

9. Leone, M., and B. Little in Lubar, S. and W.D. Kingery, eds. (1993). *History from Things.* Washington, DC: Smithsonian Institution Press, p. 162.

10. Rošker, J. "Epistemology in Chinese Philosophy," *The Stanford Encyclopedia of Philosophy* (Winter 2015 Edition), Edward N. Zalta (ed.), accessed January 2017. https://plato.stanford.edu/archives/win2015/entries/chinese-epistemology/.

11. Ackermann, R.J. (1965). *Theories of Knowledge: A Critical Introduction.* New York: McGraw-Hill, p.15.

12. Meredith, P. (1965). "The Frame of Humanist Communication," pp. 251–265, in Huxley, Sir Julian, ed. *The Humanist Frame.* London: George Allen & Unwin, p. 257.

13. Ackermann, R.J. (1965). *Theories of Knowledge: A Critical Introduction.* New York: McGraw-Hill, p. 16.

14. Connerton, P. (1989). *How Societies Remember.* Cambridge University Press, p. 2.

15. James, W. (1977). *The Meaning of Truth.* Amherst, NY: Prometheus, p. 140.

16. Coleburt, R. (1960). *The Search for Values.* New York: Sheed and Ward, p. 80.

17. Brennan, A. (1988). *Conditions of Identity: A Study in Identity and Survival.* Oxford: Clarendon, p. 6.

18. Russell, B. (1929) *Mysticism and Logic.* New York: Norton, p. 14.

19. *Ibid.*

Chapter Nine

1. Eagleton, T. (2016). *Culture.* Yale University Press, p. 10.

2. Morris, Jerry W. and Michael H. Stuckhardt, "Art Attitude: Conceptualization and Implication," *Studies in Art Education*, 19 (1), 1977, 21–28.

3. "Cultural Heritage." Accessed September 2016. https://en.wikipedia.org/wiki/Cultural_heritage.

4. Morris, Jerry W. and Michael H. Stuckhardt, "Art Attitude: Conceptualization and Implication," *Studies in Art Education*, 19 (1), 1977, 21–28:23.

5. Borgström, B-M. (2013). "Museums and Memories—Stimulating the Memory and Estimating the Quality of Life," pp. 102–113, in Hansen, Anna, Sofia Kling, Jakoba Sraml González, eds. *Creative, Lifelong Learning and the Ageing Population.* Östersund, Sweden: Jamtli Förleg, p. 103.

6. "WHO's Definition of Health." Accessed September 2018. http://www.who.int/mediacentre/factsheets/fs220/en/.

7. "Lakalaka." Accessed September 2021. https://en.wikipedia.org/wiki/Lakalaka.

8. Liu, J-L. (2006). *An Introduction to Chinese Philosophy from Ancient Philosophy to Chinese Buddhism.* Oxford: Blackwell, p. 190.

9. Kirkland, R. (2004). *Taoism and Enduring Tradition.* New York and London: Routledge, p. 190.

10. Liu, J-L. (2006). *An Introduction to Chinese Philosophy from Ancient Philosophy to Chinese Buddhism.* Oxford: Blackwell, p. 212.

11. *Ibid.*, p. 215.

12. "Cossack's Songs of Dnipropetrovsk Region." Accessed September 2021. https://ich.unesco.org/en/USL/cossacks-songs-of-dnipropetrovsk-region-01194.

Chapter Ten

1. Jung, Carl G. (1968). *Man and His Symbols.* New York: Dell, p. 163.

2. Damasio, Antonio. (2018). *The Strange Order of Things.* New York: Pantheon, p. 89.

3. "Busó Festivities at Mohács: Masked End-of-winter Carnival Custom." Accessed June 2021. https://ich.unesco.org/en/RL/buso-festivities-at-mohacs-masked-end-of-winter-carnival-custom-00252.

4. "Law of Identity." Accessed February 2017. https://en.wikipedia.org/wiki/Law_of_identity.

5. Jinpa, T. (2002). *Self, Reality, and*

Reason in Tibetan Philosophy: Tsongkhapa's Quest for the Middle Way. New York: Routledge, p. 160.

6. Connerton, P. (1989). *How Societies Remember.* Cambridge University Press, p. 6.

7. Kant, I. (1950). *Prolegomena to Any Future Metaphysics,* with introduction by Lewis White Beck. Indianapolis: Bobbs-Merrill, p. 46 [K. 298–299].

8. *Ibid.*

9. Nietzsche, F. (2005 [1873]). *The Use and Abuse of History.* New York: Cosimo Classics, p. 15.

10. Lowenthal, D. (1985). *The Past Is a Foreign Country.* Cambridge University Press, p. 40.

11. Hein, H.S. (2000). *The Museum in Transition: A Philosophical Perspective.* Washington: Smithsonian Institution Press, p. 30.

12. Rošker, J. "Epistemology in Chinese Philosophy," *The Stanford Encyclopedia of Philosophy* (Spring 2017), Edward N. Zalta (ed.), accessed June 2017. https://plato.stanford.edu/archives/spr2017/entries/chinese-epistemology/.

13. Wood, E. and K.F. Latham. (2014). *The Objects of Experience: Transforming Visitor-object Encounters in Museums.* Walnut Creek, CA: West Coast Press. p. 9.

14. Lowenthal, D. (1985). *The Past Is a Foreign Country.* Cambridge University Press, p. xvii.

15. Margalit, A. (2002). *The Ethics of Memory.* Harvard University Press, p. 61.

16. Ladkin, N. (1998). "Laws in the United Kingdom Protecting Its Cultural Heritage," pp. 21.01–21.56, in M. Phelan, ed. *The Law of Cultural Property and Natural Heritage.* Ewvanston, IL: Kalos Kapp, pp. 21.01–21.56.

17. Lowenthal, D. (1985). *The Past Is a Foreign Country.* Cambridge University Press, p. 385.

18. "Mak Yong." Accessed September 2021. https://en,wikipedia.org/Makyong.

19. Kant, I. (1950). *Prolegomena to Any Future Metaphysics,* with an introduction by Lewis White Beck. Indianapolis: Bobbs-Merrill.

20. Jung, C.G. (1968). *Modern Man in Search of a Soul.* London: Kegan Paul, Trench, Teubner & Co. p. 75.

21. Nietzsche, F. (2005 [1873]). *The Use and Abuse of History.* New York: Cosimo Classics, pp. 12–13.

22. "Enkipaata, Eunoto and Olng'esherr, Three Male Rites of Passage of the Maasai Community." Accessed November 2021. https://ich.unesco.org/en/USL/enkipaata-eunoto-and-olng-esherr-three-male-rites-of-passage-of-the-maasai-community-01390.

23. Conversation at conservation meeting at Foguangshan in Fall 2017.

24. Lowenthal, D. (1985). *The Past Is a Foreign Country.* Cambridge University Press, p. 385.

25. *Ibid.*

26. Phelan, M. (2016). "Stolen and Illegally Exported Artefacts in Collections," pp. 113–120, in Murphy, Bernice L. *Museums, Ethics, And Cultural Heritage.* New York: Routledge, p. 114.

27. "Protecting Cultural Heritage." Accessed May 2017. https://www.interpol.int/Crime-areas/Works-of-art/Protecting-Cultural-Heritage.

28. Phelan, M. (2016). "Stolen and Illegally Exported Artefacts in Collections," pp. 113–120, in Murphy, Bernice L. *Museums, Ethics, and Cultural Heritage,* New York: Routledge, p. 115.

29. *Ibid.*, p. 117.

Bibliography

Ackermann, Robert. (1965) *Theories of Knowledge: A Critical Introduction.* New York: McGraw-Hill.

Adajian, Thomas. (2018) "The Definition of Art," in: *The Stanford Encyclopedia of Philosophy* (Fall Edition). Edward N. Zalta, ed. https://plato.stanford. edu/archives/fall2018/entries/art-definition/.

Agamben, Giorgio. (1999) *The Man Without Content.* Translated by Georgia Albert. Stanford University Press.

Barnouw, Victor. (1973) *Culture and Personality.* Homewood, IL: Dorsey.

Bergson, Henri. (1911) *Matter and Memory.* Translated by Nancy M. Paul and W. Scott Palmer. New York: Macmillan.

Blackburn, Simon. (2005) *Truth: A Guide.* Oxford University Press.

Bowne, Borden Parker. (1892) *The Principles of Ethics.* New York: American Book Company.

Brennan, Andrew. (1988) *Conditions of Identity: A Study in Identity and Survival.* Oxford: Clarendon.

Brodie, Neil. (2005) "Illicit Antiquities: The Theft of Culture," pp. 122–140, in: Gerald Corsane, ed. *Heritage, Museums, and Galleries: An Introductory Reader.* London and New York: Routledge.

Bruner, Jerome S. (1960) "Myth and Identity," pp. 176–187, in: Henry A. Murray, ed. *Myth and Mythmaking.* New York: George Braziller.

Buber, Martin. (1953) *Good and Evil: Two Interpretations.* New York: Charles Scribner's Sons.

Campbell, Heinrich Zimmer. (1969) *Philosophies of India.* Joseph Campbell, ed. Princeton University Press.

Campbell, Mei Wan. (1998) "Laws in the Republic of China Protecting Its Cultural and Intellectual Properties," pp. §10–01–10–60, in Marilyn Phelan, ed. *The Law of Cultural Property and Natural Heritage.* Evanston, IL: Kalos Kapp.

Cassirer, Ernst. (1955) *The Philosophy of Symbolic Forms, Vol. 1: Language.* Translated by Ralph Manheim. Yale University Press.

Cirlot, Juan Eduardo. (1962) *A Dictionary of Symbols.* Translated by Jack Sage. London: Routledge.

Clifford, Terry. (1984) *Tibetan Buddhist Medicine and Psychiatry.* Delhi: Motilal Banarsidass.

Cohen, Gene. (2005) *The Mature Mind: The Positive Power of the Aging Brain.* New York: Basic.

Coleburt, Russell. (1960) *The Search for Values.* New York: Sheed and Ward.

Connerton, Paul. (1989) *How Societies Remember.* Cambridge University Press.

Csikszentmihalyi, Mihaly. (1993) "Why We Need Things," pp. 20–30, in: Steve Lubar and W. David Kingery, eds. *History from Things: Essays on Material Culture.* Washington, DC: Smithsonian Institution Press.

Csikszentmihalyi, Mihaly, and Eugene Rochberg-Halton. (1999) *The Meaning of Things: Domestic Symbols and the Self.* Cambridge University Press.

Damasio, Antonio. (2018) *The Strange Order of Things: Life, Feeling, and the Making of Cultures.* New York: Pantheon.

Deutsch, Eliot. (1979) *On Truth: An Ontological Theory.* University Press of Hawaii.

Dewey, John. (1971) *The Philosophy of John Dewey*. Paul Arthur Schilpp, ed. La Salle, IL: Northwestern University and Southern Illinois University.

Dewey, John, and Arthur F. Bentley. (1949) *Knowing and the Known*. Boston: Beacon.

Dolák, Jan. (1994) "Some Remarks on Museum Terminology," *ICOFOM Study Series* Issue 38. "Museology: Back to Basics," Morlanwelz (Belgique): Musée royal de Mariemont.

Eagleton, Terry. (2016) *Culture*. Yale University Press.

Edson, Gary. (2009) *Shamanism: A Cross-Cultural Study of Beliefs and Practices*. Jefferson, NC: McFarland.

Edson, Gary. (2017) *Museum Ethics in Practice*. New York: Routledge.

Eliade, Mircea. (1960) *Myths, Dreams, and Mysteries*. Translated by Philip Mairet. New York: Harper & Row Publishers.

Eliade, Mircea. (1963) *Myth and Reality*. New York: Harper & Row.

Ellis, Brian David. (1990) *Truth and Objectivity*. Cambridge: Basil Blackwell.

Ethics Committee. (2006) *ICOM Code of Ethics for Museums*. Paris: International Council of Museums.

Fardon, Richard, ed. (1985) *Power and Knowledge: Anthropological and Sociological Approaches*. Edinburgh: Scottish Academic Press.

Firth, Raymond. (1985) "Degrees of Intelligibility," pp. 29–47, in: Joanna Overling, ed. *Reason and Morality*. New York: Tavistock.

Freud, Sigmund. (1991) *On Metapsychology—The Theory of Psychoanalysis*. London: Penguin Freud Library.

Gauvain, Mary. (2001) *The Social Context of Cognitive Development*. New York: Guilford.

Grassi, Ernesto. (1983) *Heidegger and the Question of Renaissance Humanism*. Binghamton, NY: Center for Medieval and Early Renaissance Studies.

Grut, Sara. (2013) "The Challenge of Ageing Populations—Assessing the Contribution of Heritage and Creative Learning," pp. 23–34 in: Anna Hansen, Sofia Kling, and Jakoba Sraml González, eds. *Creative, Lifelong Learning and the Ageing Population*. Östersund, Sweden: Jamtli Förleg.

Habermas, Jürgen. (2003) *Truth and Justification*. Edited and translated by Barbara Fultner. Cambridge: Massachusetts Institute of Technology.

Halbwachs, Maurice. (1992) *On Collective Memory*. Edited, translated and introduced by Lewis A. Coser. University of Chicago Press.

Hansen, Anna. (2013) "Older People as a Developing Market for Cultural Heritage Sites," pp. 35–42, in: Anna Hansen, Sofia Kling, and Jakoba Sraml González, eds. *Creative, Lifelong Learning and the Ageing Population*. Östersund, Sweden: Jamtli Förleg.

Hansen, Anna, Sofia Kling, and Jakoba Sraml González, eds. (2013) *Creative, Lifelong Learning and the Ageing Population*. Östersund, Sweden: Jamtli Förleg.

Heidegger, Martin. (2002) *Identity and Difference*. Translated and introduction by Joan Stambaugh. University of Chicago Press.

Heidegger, Martin. (2002) *Time and Being*. Translated with introduction by Joan Stambaugh, University of Chicago Press.

Hein, Hilde S. (2000) *The Museum in Transition: A Philosophical Perspective*. Washington, DC: Smithsonian Institution Press.

Hobsbawm, Eric, and Terence Ranger. (1983) *The Invention of Tradition*. Cambridge University Press.

Holden, John. (2006) *Cultural Value and the Crisis of Legitimacy: Why Culture Needs a Democratic Mandate*. London: DEMOS.

Holford, Sir William. (1965) "The Shells of Society," pp. 199–208, in Sir Julian Huxley, ed. *The Humanist Frame*. London: George Allen & Unwin.

Hume, David. (1963) *The Philosophy of David Hume*. Edited with an introduction by V.C. Chappell. New York: Modern Library.

Huxley, Aldous. (1946) *The Perennial Philosophy*. London: Chatto and Windus.

Jackson, P.W. (1998) *John Dewey and the Lessons of Art*. Yale University Press.

James, William. (1977) *The Meaning of Truth*. Amherst, NY: Prometheus.

James, William. (2003 [1907]) *Pragmatism*. New York: Barnes and Noble.

Janiak, Andrew. (2016) "Kant's Views on Space and Time," in: *The Stanford Encyclopedia of Philosophy* (Winter Edition). Edward N. Zalta, ed. http://plato.stanford.edu/archives/win2016/entries/kant-spacetime/.

Jinpa, Thupten. (2002) *Self, Reality, and Reason in Tibetan Philosophy: Tsongkhapa's Quest for the Middle Way.* New York: Routledge Curzon.

Jordanova, Ludmilla. (1991) "Objects of Knowledge: A Historical Perspective on Museums," pp. 22–40, in: Peter Vergo, ed. *The New Museology.* London: Reaktion.

Jung, Carl G. (1933) *Modern Man in Search of a Soul.* London: Kegan Paul, Trench, Trubner & Co.

Jung, Carl G. (1965) *Memories, Dreams, Reflections.* Edited by Aniela Jaffe, translated by Richard and Clara Winston. New York: Vintage Books.

Jung, Carl G. (1968) *Man and His Symbols.* New York: Dell.

Kant, Immanuel. (1950) *Prolegomena to Any Future Metaphysics*, with an introduction by Lewis White Beck. New York: The Library of Liberal Arts.

Kant, Immanuel. (1959 [1785]) *Foundations of the Metaphysics of Morals.* Translated with an introduction by Lewis White Beck. Indianapolis: Bobbs-Merrill.

Kihlstrom, John F., Jennifer S. Beer, and Stanley B. Klein. (2003) "Self and Identity as Memory," pp. 68–90, in: Mark R. Leary and June Price Tangney, eds. *Handbook of Self and Identity.* New York: Guilford.

Kirkland, Russell. (2005) *Taoism: The Enduring Tradition.* New York: Routledge.

Kjeldbaek, Esben, ed. (2009) *The Power of the Object: Museums and World War II.* Edinburgh: MuseumsEtc.

Koller, John M. (1985) *Oriental Philosophies*, 2nd edition. New York: Charles Scribner's Sons.

Ladkin, Nicola. (1998) "Laws in the United Kingdom Protecting Its Cultural Heritage," pp. §21–01–21–56, in: Marilyn Phelan, ed. *The Law of Cultural Property and Natural Heritage.* Evanston, IL: Kalos Kapp.

Lao Tzu. (1963) *The Way of Lao Tzu* (Tao-te Ching), translated with introduction by Wing-Tsit Chan. Upper Saddle River, NJ: Prentice-Hill.

Layton, Robert, ed. (1989) *Who Needs the Past?* New York: Routledge.

Lewis, Geoffrey. (1992) "Museums and Their Precursors: A Brief World Survey," pp. 5–21, in: John Thompson, ed. *Manual of Curatorship: A Guide to Museum Practices* 2nd edition. Oxford: Butterworth Heinemann.

Liu, Jee-Loo. (2006) *An Introduction to Chinese Philosophy: From Ancient Philosophy to Chinese Buddhism.* Malden, MA: Blackwell Publishing.

Lowenthal, David. (1985) *The Past Is a Foreign Country.* Cambridge University Press.

Lubar, Steve. (1993) "Machine Politics: The Political Construction of Technological Artifacts," pp. 197–214, in Steve Lubar and W. David Kingery, eds. *History of Things: Essays on Material Culture.* Washington, DC: Smithsonian Institution Press.

Lubar, Steve, and W. David Kingery, eds. (1993) *History from Things: Essays on Material Culture.* Washington, DC: Smithsonian Institution Press.

Mann, Nicholas. (1996) *The Origins of Humanism.* Cambridge University Press.

Margalit, Avishai. (2002) *The Ethics of Memory.* Harvard University Press.

Mason, Randall. (2002) "Assessing Values in Conservation Planning: Methodological Issues and Choices," pp. 5–33, in: Marta de la Torre, ed. *Assessing the Values of Cultural Heritage.* Los Angeles: The Getty Conservation Institute.

Maynell, Hugo. (1986) *The Nature of Aesthetic Value.* State University of New York Press.

McNeill, William. (2006) *The Time of Life: Heidegger and Ethos.* State University of New York.

Morris, Jerry W., and Michael H. Stuckhardt. (1977) "Art Attitude: Conceptualization and Implication," *Studies in Art Education* 19(1), pp. 21–28.

Murphy, Bernice, ed. (2016) *Museums, Ethics and Cultural Heritage.* New York: Routledge.

Nauert, Charles G. (2006) *Humanism and the Culture of Renaissance Europe.* 2nd edition. Cambridge University Press.

Nehamas, Alexander. (1985) *Nietzsche: Life as Literature*. Harvard University Press.

Nietzsche, F. (2005 [1873]) *The Use and Abuse of History*. New York: Cosimo Classics.

Oderberg, David S. (1993) *The Metaphysics of Identity Over Time*. New York: St. Martin's.

Overing, Joanna, ed. (1985) *Reason and Morality*. New York: Tavistock.

Phelan, Marilyn, ed. (1998) *The Law of Cultural Property and Natural Heritage: Protection, Transfer and Access*. Evanston, IL: Kalos Kapp.

Potter, Karl H. (1964) *The Naturalistic Principle of Karma, Philosophy East and West* 14(1), pp. 39–49.

Pritchard, Duncan, and John Turri. (2014) "The Value of Knowledge," in: *The Stanford Encyclopedia of Philosophy* (Spring Edition). Edward N. Zalta, ed. https://stanford.edu/archives/spr2014/entries/knowledge-value/.

Protecting Cultural Heritage. https://www.interpol.int/Crime-areas/Works-of-art/Protecting-Cultural-Heritage.

Rajchman, John, ed. (1995) *The Identity in Question*. New York and London: Routledge.

"Reality in Buddhism." Wikipedia. https://en.wikipedia.org/wiki/Reality_in_Buddhism.

"Remembrance Hall Yad Vashem." http://www.yadvashem.org/yv/en/remembrance/hall_of_names.asp.

Ricoeur, Paul. (2007) *History and Truth*. Translated by Charles A. Kelbley. Evanston, IL: Northwestern University Press.

Robert-Hauglustaine, Anne-Catherine. (2016) "The Role of Museums in the Twenty-first Century," pp. 9–13, in: Bernice Murphy, ed. *Museums, Ethics, and Cultural Heritage*. New York: Routledge.

Rošker, Jana. (2015) "Epistemology in Chinese Philosophy," in: *The Stanford Encyclopedia of Philosophy* (Winter Edition). Edward N. Zalta, ed. https://plato.stanford.edu/archives/win2015/entries/chinese-epistemology/.

Runes, Dagobert D. (1961) *The Art of Thinking*. New York: The Wisdom Library.

Russell, Bertrand. (1929) *Mysticism and Logic*. New York: W.W. Norton.

Saint Augustine. (2002 [AD 401]) *The Confessions of Saint Augustine*. Translated by Edward B. Pusey. Project Gutenberg EBook, http://www.gutenberg.org/files/3296/3296-h/3296-h.htm.

Sartre, Jean-Paul. (1956) *Being and Nothingness: An Essay on Phenomenological Ontology*. Translated with an introduction by Hazel E. Barnes. New York: Philosophical Library.

Sartre, Jean-Paul. (1964) *Nausea*. Translated by Lloyd Alexander. New York: New Directions.

Sartre, Jean-Paul. (2007) *Existentialism Is a Humanism*. Translated by Carol Macomber. Yale University Press.

Shramko, Yaroslav, and Heinrich Wansing. (2020) "Truth Values," in: *The Stanford Encyclopedia of Philosophy* (Winter Edition). Edward N. Zalta, ed. https://plato.stanford.edu/archives/win2020/entries/truth-values/.

Shweder, Richard A. (1991) *Thinking Through Cultures: Expeditions in Cultural Psychology*. Cambridge University Press.

Smythies, John. (2003) "Space, Time and Consciousness," in: *Journal of Consciousness Studies* 10(3), pp. 47–56.

Sorokin, Pitirim. (1970) *Social and Cultural Dynamics* 2nd edition, Boston: Extending Horizons Books—Porter Sargent Publishing.

Sutton, John. (2016) "Memory," in: *The Stanford Encyclopedia of Philosophy* (Summer Edition). Edward N. Zalta, ed. https://plato.stanford.edu/archives/sum2016/entries/memory/.

Thayer, Lee. (1987) *On Communication*. Norwood, NJ: Ablex.

Thomas, Julian. (1996) *Time, Culture and Identity: An Interpretive Archaeology*. New York: Routledge.

Tu, Weiming, and Daisaku Ikeda. (2011) *New Horizons in Eastern Humanism*. New York: I.B. Tauris.

Tuan Yi-Fu. (1977) *Space and Place: The Perspective of Experience*. Minneapolis: University of Minnesota Press.

UNESCO. (1972) "Conservation Concerning the Protection of the World Culture and Natural Heritage," Article 2. Paris: United Nations Educational, Scientific and Cultural Organization.

UNESCO. (2001) *Declaration on Cultural Diversity*. Paris: United Nations Educational, Scientific and Cultural Organization.

UNESCO. (2003) "Convention for the Safeguarding of the Intangible Cultural Heritage," Article 2, Definitions. Paris: United Nations Educational, Scientific and Cultural Organization.

UNESCO. (2005) "Protecting Our Heritage and Fostering Creativity." http://en.unesco.org/themes/protecting-our-heritage-and-fostering-creativity.

UNESCO. "Archaeological Site of Delphi." http://whc.unesco.org/en/list/393.

UNESCO. "Intangible World Heritage List." Paris: United Nations Educational, Scientific, and Cultural Organization. http://www.unesco.org/culture/ich/en/lists.

UNESCO. "World Heritage List." Paris: United Nations Educational, Scientific, and Cultural Organization. http://whc.unesco.org/en/list.

UNESCO. "World Heritage Sites." https://en.wikipedia.org/wiki/World_Heritage_Site.

Unidroit Convention on Stolen or Illegally Exported Cultural Objects. http://www.unidroit.org/instruments/cultural-property/1995-convention.

Van Wyk, Robert N. (1990) *Introduction to Ethics*. New York: St. Martin's Press.

Wallace, Anthony F.C. (1970) *Culture and Personality* 2nd edition. New York: Random House.

Walsh, Kevin. (1992) *The Representation of the Past*. New York: Routledge.

Wood, Elizabeth, and Kiersten F. Latham. (2014) *The Objects of Experience: Transforming Visitor-object Encounters in Museums*. Walnut Creek: West Coast Press.

Zhongshi, Ouyang, and Wen C. Fong. (2002) *Chinese Calligraphy*. Translated and edited by Youfen Wang. Beijing: Foreign Language Press.

Index